ANTIDUMPING EXPOSED

ANTIDUMPING
EXPOSED

THE DEVILISH DETAILS
OF UNFAIR TRADE LAW

BRINK LINDSEY AND DANIEL J. IKENSON

CATO
INSTITUTE
Washington, D.C.

Library of Congress Cataloging-in-Publication Data

Lindsey, Brink.
    Antidumping exposed : the devilish details of unfair trade law /
    Brink Lindsey and Daniel J. Ikenson.
      p. cm.
    Includes bibliographical references and index.
    ISBN 1-930865-48-1 (cloth : alk. paper)
     1. Antidumping duties--Law and legislation--United States.
2. Antidumping duties--United States.   3. Competition, Unfair--
United States.   4. Dumping (International trade)   5. Competition,
Unfair.   I. Ikenson, Daniel J.   II. Title.

KF6708.D8L56 2003
343.73'087--dc22

                                           2003055528

Cover design by Elise Rivera.
Printed in the United States of America.

CATO INSTITUTE
1000 Massachusetts Ave., N.W.
Washington, D.C. 20001

Contents

Introduction

Antidumping laws allow national governments to impose special duties on "unfairly traded" imports. Before duties are imposed, the authorities that administer the law must make two findings: (1) that imported goods are being "dumped," or sold at prices less than "normal value," and (2) that the dumped imports are causing or threatening material injury to the domestic import-competing industry. Under the U.S. system, the Department of Commerce determines whether dumping is occurring, while the International Trade Commission examines whether dumped imports are injuring the domestic industry. When both the DOC and the ITC make affirmative findings, the goods under investigation are subject to duties equal to the margin of dumping—that is, the difference between the U.S. prices of the imports and their "normal value."

Supporters of antidumping laws argue that they are needed to create a "level playing field" for domestic industries that face unfair import competition. Specifically, they contend that various distortions in foreign markets—trade barriers, monopoly or collusion, government subsidies, and "barriers to exit" (e.g., poor bankruptcy laws, ineffective protection of creditors' rights) that prevent loss-making businesses from reducing capacity or going out of business—allow foreign producers to charge lower prices in export markets than would otherwise be possible. In one scenario, firms may enjoy supernormal profits at home (in a protected or cartelized "sanctuary market") and then use those profits to cross-subsidize the low-price export sales. Alternatively, subsidies or barriers to exit may allow firms to sell abroad (and at home as well) at below-cost prices without suffering the normal marketplace consequences.

According to supporters, antidumping laws ensure a level playing field by offsetting artificial sources of competitive advantage. Dumping, it is alleged, demonstrates the existence of one or more of the market distortions discussed above; antidumping duties, by making up the difference between dumped prices and "normal value," extinguish the foreign producer's artificial advantage and put the domestic industry back on an equal footing. At least that is the theory.

There is, however, a yawning gap between theory and practice. Antidumping laws, contrary to the claims of their supporters, do not ensure a level playing field. Instead, they penalize foreign producers for engaging in commercial practices that are perfectly legal and unexceptionable when engaged in by domestic companies. Such discrimination against foreign firms creates an unlevel playing field for imports. In other words, antidumping laws discriminate against imports, and that is the essence of protectionism.

Unfortunately, this particular form of protectionism enjoys the sanction of multilateral trading rules. Article VI of the original General Agreement on Tariffs and Trade authorizes national governments to impose duties on dumped imports. Today, the authority to engage in antidumping protectionism is recognized by the World Trade Organization. The WTO Antidumping Agreement, finalized in 1994 during the Uruguay Round of trade talks, specifies the standards and procedures that national antidumping regulations must follow. Although the requirements of this agreement do impose modest restraint on what WTO members can do in the name of antidumping, the sad fact is that the agreement allows wide scope for protectionist abuses. Under the present rules, antidumping is a major loophole in the free-trade disciplines of the world trading system.

For many decades, antidumping protectionism was a vice exclusive to rich industrialized nations—specifically, the United States, Canada, members of what is now the European Union, Australia, and New Zealand. In recent years, however, dozens of less-developed countries have followed the U.S. example and adopted antidumping laws. Antidumping actions worldwide have increased dramatically over levels in previous decades; in particular, American exports are increasingly encountering the same unpredictable, arbitrary, and disruptive obstacles that have long been inflicted on other countries' exports in the United States. Indeed, from 1995 to 2000, the United States was the third most frequent target of world antidumping measures.

Market access for U.S. exports is one important component of a much broader national interest in an open and prosperous international economy. That larger interest is also menaced by the recent proliferation of antidumping measures. The rapid spread of anti-dumping protectionism throughout the developing world threatens to undo many of the liberalizing gains made possible by the elimination of quotas and import licenses and the slashing of tariff rates. The integrity of the world trading system is being undermined by the increasing frequency and virulence of antidumping activity.

In the U.S. trade policy debate, antidumping policy has become a hot-button issue. The U.S. antidumping law has long been unpopular with countries whose exports suffer from its operation. In recent years, many of those countries have been urging the U.S. government to agree to new international rules at the World Trade Organization that would tighten the requirements that must be met before antidumping protection can be granted.

Powerful U.S. lobbying interests, and their supporters in Congress, have vehemently opposed such changes in antidumping rules. American industries that frequently seek antidumping protection—in particular, steel producers—argue that a "strong" law is needed to ensure a level playing field and to maintain public support for generally open markets. They insist that any effort to "weaken" current law through trade negotiations must be rejected out of hand.

Up to this point, antidumping supporters have had the upper hand in the U.S. policy debate. Despite the harm caused to downstream import-using industries and consumers by U.S. antidumping measures, the increasing disruption of U.S. exports by foreign measures, and the larger threat to the U.S. interest in a healthy world trading system posed by the global spread of antidumping protectionism, the U.S. antidumping law has enjoyed strong political support from Republicans and Democrats alike.

What accounts for this enduring, bipartisan popularity? In the first place, the law's rhetoric is compelling. After all, which members of Congress would like to stand up and say they favor illegal and unfair dumped imports? Who could be opposed to a level playing field? Meanwhile, the reality behind the rhetoric is obscure. The antidumping law is notoriously complicated, and its inner workings are known only to a select handful of users, targets, bureaucrats, and lawyers. As a result, most supporters of the law simply take its appealing rhetoric at face value. If it sounds good, it must be good.

In this book we attempt to cut through the fog of technical complexity that surrounds antidumping laws—to show how they really operate and to show in particular that their actual operation all too often has nothing to do with their fine-sounding rhetoric.

This task absorbs the first three chapters of the book. In them we focus exclusively on the specific rules and methodologies of the U.S. antidumping law. We do this, not because the U.S. law is uniquely abusive, but simply because data on U.S. antidumping practice are much more accessible than equivalent data from other countries. Furthermore, the United States is among the most active users of antidumping remedies worldwide, and its law has served as a model for new users as they have adopted and begun to enforce their own laws. Accordingly, the U.S. law is a good proxy for antidumping practice globally.

In these initial chapters we do not pretend to offer a comprehensive analysis or critique of the U.S. law. In particular, we do not address the ITC's analysis of whether dumped imports are causing or threatening injury to a domestic industry. Neither do we address various procedural aspects of antidumping investigations—including standing requirements, initiation standards, use of "facts available," or the distribution of duties to domestic producers under the so-called Byrd amendment.

Although much in these other elements of antidumping practice is ripe for criticism, we choose to home in on the central question of antidumping policy: What constitutes dumping? How that question is answered determines the fundamental character of antidumping practice. If it can be shown that normal, healthy competition is regularly stigmatized as dumping because of methodological flaws and biases, then the law itself is fundamentally flawed—not just according to the ivory-tower standards of economists and policy wonks, but according to the very standards upheld by the law's supporters.

This last point deserves some elaboration, since it highlights the distinctiveness of our approach. Economic analysis judges antidumping policy according to the criterion of consumer welfare. Since consumer welfare is normally served by the lowest possible prices, economists tend to regard antidumping laws—which, after all, seek to raise the prices of imported goods above "unfairly" low levels—with immediate suspicion. According to standard economic analysis, low prices are a problem in need of a remedy only if they tend to lead to higher prices in the long term. Consequently, economists generally consider antidumping remedies justified only to the extent that they combat predatory pricing—that is, pricing designed to monopolize a market by knocking competitors out of business. The consensus among economists is that antidumping laws have virtually nothing to do with addressing predatory pricing—and therefore their existence lacks any economic justification.[1]

We have no quarrel with the economists' verdict on antidumping laws—indeed, we heartily endorse it. The problem is that it is all but irrelevant to the antidumping policy debate. The leading supporters of antidumping laws freely admit that they are not designed to combat predatory pricing—or to serve consumer welfare in the economists' definition of that term. They defend antidumping, not on the grounds of efficiency, but rather on the grounds of fairness. Antidumping remedies, they claim, address pricing practices that reflect artificial competitive advantages created by market-distorting government policies abroad. Even if dumping may benefit consumers in the short term, they argue, it is unfair for producers to have to compete under such conditions.

Accordingly, the supporters and critics of antidumping laws have often talked past each other because they define the proper objectives of antidumping policy altogether differently. We seek to resolve this impasse and join the debate squarely by evaluating antidumping laws according the the standards established by their supporters. We leave aside the question of whether antidumping laws promote economic efficiency, and look instead at the more basic question of whether these laws do what their supporters say they do. In other words, do antidumping laws really uphold fair trade under any plausible definition of that term?

We tackle that question as follows. The first chapter offers a detailed overview of the complicated procedures and methodologies whereby dumping is determined and measured. The second chapter proceeds to evaluate the extent to which antidumping remedies target the effects of various market-distorting government policies. In the third chapter, we focus on what is touted by antidumping supporters as the paradigmatic scenario that gives rise to dumping: a closed or "sanctuary" home market enables foreign producers to engage in international price discrimination. The conclusion drawn in these first three chapters is that antidumping laws, as currently written and enforced, do not reliably target unfair trade as antidumping supporters typically define that term. Consequently, antidumping remedies routinely punish normal, healthy competition.

Having established the fundamentally protectionist nature of contemporary antidumping practice, we turn in the fourth chapter to documenting and analyzing the rapid proliferation of antidumping laws in recent years. In particular, we detail the effect of antidumping's global spread on U.S. exports.

Finally, the fifth chapter addresses what is to be done. Negotiations are now under way at the World Trade Organization to improve existing WTO antidumping rules and thereby limit the scope for protectionist abuses afforded by national antidumping laws. These negotiations, part of the larger "Doha Round" of global trade talks, offer promising opportunities for antidumping reform here and abroad. We suggest a general framework for how negotiations should proceed to make the most of those opportunities, and then follow up with detailed proposals for changes to the WTO Antidumping Agreement. Those proposals address not only the determination and calculation of dumping, but also the determination of injury as well as antidumping procedures and remedies.

The antidumping policy debate in the United States has long suffered from serious misunderstandings about how antidumping laws actually work. We hope that by exposing antidumping's devilish details, we can make some contribution toward nudging the policy debate in a more constructive direction.

1. How Dumping Is (Mis)calculated

There is no way around it: antidumping is complicated. The jargon alone—EP, CEP, POI, POR, CONNUM, FUPDOL, TOTPUDD, model match, cost test, arm's-length test, CV, facts available, DIFMER, and on and on—is enough to make a nonspecialist's eyes glaze over.

Nevertheless, it is impossible to understand how antidumping laws really operate—and thus to evaluate whether they actually do what their supporters say they do—without diving into their technical intricacies. In this chapter we introduce the intrepid reader to the basic procedures and methodologies for determining and calculating dumping under U.S. law. If it is any consolation, we have left out great reams of additional, complicating detail.

Investigations and Reviews

Dumping is defined as the sale of a commodity in an export market (i.e., the United States under U.S. law) at a price less than "normal value."[1] Normal value is based either on the price of the same or a similar product in a comparison market (normally the foreign producer's home market) or on "constructed value," the cost to produce the product plus some amount for profit.[2] The extent of dumping is called the "dumping margin," which is calculated by subtracting the export price from normal value and dividing the difference (assuming it is positive) by the export price. In other words, if a foreign producer sells widgets for 10 at home and for 8 in the United States, its dumping margin is $(10 - 8)/8$, or 25 percent.

For antidumping duties to be imposed, it is not enough that dumping be found to exist. In addition, the authorities must determine that the domestic industry is materially injured or threatened with material injury, or else that the development of an industry is materially retarded, by reason of dumped imports.

1

In the United States, an industry can seek relief under the antidumping law by filing a petition with the International Trade Commission and the Department of Commerce. Domestic producers joining the petition are thus called "petitioners." Producers accounting for at least 25 percent of domestic production (by volume) must support the petition, and opposition by other producers must constitute less than 50 percent of the total output of all producers expressing an opinion one way or the other. Petitions are required to contain some evidence of dumping and injury in order to initiate an investigation. However, the evidentiary requirements are quite modest.

Figure 1.1 outlines the timetable for a typical antidumping investigation. Once an investigation is initiated, the ITC has 45 days after the filing of the petition to determine whether there is reason to believe that dumped imports are causing or threatening injury to a domestic industry. Affirmative preliminary findings are rendered in about 79 percent of cases.[3]

Following an affirmative preliminary finding by the ITC, the DOC issues questionnaires to "mandatory respondents"—the largest known foreign producers and exporters of subject merchandise from the countries in question.[4] Failure to respond to the DOC's questionnaire or failure to cooperate fully in the proceeding typically results in the assignment of an adverse rate of duty, which is usually based on allegations in the domestic industry's petition. If a foreign producer has any hope of maintaining access to the U.S. market, it is forced to respond to the DOC's voluminous requests for information. Responding to an antidumping questionnaire usually requires the diversion of significant company resources and retaining legal, accounting, and economic expertise.

The DOC normally makes its preliminary determination (prelim) within 160 days of the petition's filing (although the deadline can be extended by 50 days). If the DOC prelim is affirmative, liquidation (i.e., final determination of duties owed to the Customs Service) is suspended for all future subject imports, and a bond must be posted to cover possible antidumping duties at the rate announced in the prelim. The DOC then makes its final determination (final) within 75 days of the prelim (although, here again, the deadline can be extended—this time by up to 60 days). Between the prelim and the final, the DOC conducts an on-site verification of the respondents' questionnaire data and considers factual and legal arguments submitted by petitioners and respondents. After the final, assuming it

2

Figure 1.1
TIMING OF EVENTS IN ANTIDUMPING PROCEEDINGS

Investigation

	Jan	Feb	Mar	Apr	May	Jun	Jul	Aug	Sep	Oct	Nov	Dec
2002												
2003							a	b				c
2004		d		e f								
2005												

■ Period Investigated   ▨ Preliminary Rate   ▨ Final Rate

Symbol	Date	Action	Comment
a	7/1/03	Petition Filed with ITC and DOC	
b	8/15/03	ITC Preliminary Determination	Day 45
c	12/8/03	DOC Preliminary Determination	Day 160-Deposits due on entries
d	2/21/04	DOC Final Determination	Day 235 -Revised deposit rate
e	4/7/04	ITC Final Determination	Day 280
f	4/14/04	AD Duty Order Issued	Within one week of ITC final

Administrative Review

	Jan	Feb	Mar	Apr	May	Jun	Jul	Aug	Sep	Oct	Nov	Dec
2002												
2003							a	b				c
2004		d		e f								
2005				g								

■ Period of 1st Administrative Review

Symbol	Date	Action	Comment
g	4/1/05	Request for Admin. Review	Still paying investigation rate until preliminary review rate established

is affirmative (an outcome that occurs about 94 percent of the time),[5] respondents must pay cash deposits on possible antidumping duties at the rate announced in the final.

Once the DOC issues its final determination, the ITC normally has 45 days to make its final injury finding. If that determination is affirmative (an outcome that occurs about 83 percent of the time),[6]

3

an antidumping order is issued, which subjects prospective imports to antidumping duty deposits equal to the calculated rate of dumping.

The antidumping deposit rate is only an estimate of dumping liability. The rate is based on dumping margins calculated for the period of investigation, normally the four most recently completed calendar quarters before initiation—that is, a period that concludes months before duty liability generally begins (Figure 1.1).

Final liability is determined by administrative reviews conducted later by the DOC. As shown in Figure 1.1, the first period of review (POR) covers imports from the beginning of duty liability to the first anniversary of the antidumping duty order. Subsequent PORs cover imports from one anniversary date to the next. The DOC's final determination in a review settles final dumping liability for imports during the POR. If the amount of dumping found is more than the amount of cash deposits, the respondent owes the difference with interest. If, on the other hand, the amount of dumping is less, the respondent gets a refund with interest. In addition to settling final liability for past imports, the final determination in a review also establishes a new deposit rate for future imports.

Dumping margins can thus be recalculated annually through administrative reviews. The continued existence of injury, on the other hand, is revisited only once every five years in so-called sunset reviews. Under the sunset review provision, an antidumping duty order is terminated automatically after five years unless a sunset review is requested. In this review, the DOC and the ITC determine whether termination of the order would be likely to lead to the continuation or resumption of dumping and injury, respectively. If both make affirmative determinations, the order continues for another five years. Between July 1998 and August 2002, 354 sunset reviews were initiated, of which 265 were contested by petitioners. The outcomes in 2 of these 265 contested cases were still pending. The DOC made affirmative sunset determinations to continue the order in all but 4 of the 263 decided cases, while the ITC voted affirmative 72 percent of the time.[7]

The DOC Questionnaire

To conduct its dumping investigation, the DOC issues detailed questionnaires to the primary foreign producers of the "subject merchandise," as the investigated imports are known. The questionnaire has four and sometimes five distinct parts—Sections A, B, C, D, and sometimes E. Section A seeks information on the company's corporate structure and affiliations, distribution process, sales process, accounting and financial practices, and the products under investigation generally.

Section B concerns the company's sales of "such or similar" merchandise (i.e., products that are identical or similar to the subject merchandise under investigation) in the comparison market. The comparison market is normally the foreign producer's home market, but a third-country export market may be used instead if the home market is deemed not "viable."[8] The DOC seeks information on products sold, selling prices, quantities sold, customer relationships, customer class (i.e., distributor, wholesaler, retailer), transportation and warehousing expenses, insurance costs, selling expenses, discounts and rebates, warranties, commissions, packing costs, and anything else related to home-market sales. This portion of the response is supplemented by a separate computer data file containing detailed information for each sales transaction made during the period of investigation and is used to calculate the "foreign market value" or normal value—in other words, the benchmark against which U.S. prices are compared.

Section C is analogous to Section B but covers sales made in the United States. Typically, more information is sought with respect to U.S. sales because the process of selling in an export market involves additional transportation and selling processes. Also, in many cases, the U.S. importer is related to the foreign respondent and therefore the prices to the importer are not used as the basis for the dumping calculation. In such cases—known as constructed export price transactions—the U.S. price is based on the price of the resale by the related importer to the first unaffiliated customer. When U.S. sales involve importation by a related company, expenses incurred by that related importer are required to be reported in Section C.

Section D covers the cost of producing the subject merchandise and the foreign such or similar merchandise. This portion of the questionnaire seeks to obtain data on production quantities, labor costs, materials costs, overhead, and general and administrative expenses associated with production. The computer data files supplementing the narrative response to Section D must contain detailed unit cost elements for every product subject to the investigation that was sold in both markets.

In cases where there is further processing of subject merchandise after importation by a related company and before sale to an unaffiliated customer, the DOC issues a Section E, which seeks information on the additional manufacturing processes and costs.

CONNUMs and Product Definition

The first step in comparing U.S. and foreign-market prices consists of determining which prices to compare to each other. If products identical to those sold in the United States are not sold in the home market—which is the case in most antidumping investigations—the DOC compares the average U.S. price to the average home-market price of the "next most similar" product. Among the most important aspects of antidumping calculation methodology, therefore, are product definition and determination of the next most similar products.

The product as defined by the DOC will almost always be different from the product as defined by the respondent. That is, the DOC compares prices (and calculates costs) at the DOC-defined product level, not at the company-specific product code level. This departure from a respondent's record-keeping protocol can add significant complications to the preparation of sales and cost records in response to the DOC's questionnaire.

Products are defined for antidumping purposes by the specific product characteristics that the DOC determines are necessary for "model matching"—that is, the characteristics that determine which products are more or less similar to each other and thus which products are compared with each other. For some products, the relevant characteristics are few and the options within each characteristic are limited. For example, widgets may be classified by size (large or small) and material (rubber or plastic). Using these classifications, there are only four possible models (large rubber, large plastic, small rubber, small plastic). And since there are only two possibilities within each characteristic, it is necessary only to determine "rank between" the characteristics, not "rank within" each characteristic. If size is considered a more important matching characteristic than material, then the best match for a large rubber widget in the absence of an identical product in the home market is a large

6

plastic widget. Alternatively, if material is more significant than size, the best match for a large rubber widget would be a small rubber widget.

The DOC creates its own product code, known as the CONNUM, or control number, which reflects the relevant characteristics of the product. The CONNUM is constructed as a series of the relevant product characteristics. So, for example, a small, rubber widget might be assigned a CONNUM of 11, where the first digit corresponds to "size" (small = "1"; large = "2") and the second digit corresponds to "material" (rubber = "1"; plastic = "2"). This construction would reflect the decision that size is more important than material for this particular product because the "next most similar product" to an 11 is a 12, not a 21. Matching across sizes would occur only if there were no match across materials in the same size.

If there were a third type of material (say vinyl) and a third size (say medium), then there would be nine possible products, and it would be necessary to rank the order of similarity "within" each characteristic, as well as "between." Here things can get tricky. Which is more similar to medium—large or small? Is rubber more similar to plastic or to vinyl?

In some cases there are only a few characteristics and a few alternatives within each characteristic. But for others, particularly those involving steel, there are 10 to 20 characteristics, each with several or dozens of alternative values. For example, in the 2002 investigation of cold-rolled carbon steel from Germany, there were 14 relevant product characteristics, including carbon content, tensile strength, thickness, tolerance, surface quality, and hardening process. In this and other steel cases there can be literally hundreds of thousands of actual products.[9]

Price Adjustments

Dumping calculations are never made on the basis of comparing actual sales prices. Instead, the DOC subjects actual sales prices to a dizzying variety of adjustments. Dumping margins are then determined by comparing adjusted U.S. to adjusted home-market prices.

Selling and delivering products to different markets entail incurring certain expenses that are unique to each market. The DOC addresses these issues by attempting to quantify all expenses incurred after production and through the sale of the product in each market. These expenses are then deducted from the gross selling prices, yielding ex-factory prices (the prices the products would have fetched at the factory door), which presumably permit apples-to-apples comparisons. For example, it may be necessary to advertise in one market, where the product is less known or where greater competition prevails, while it is unnecessary to advertise in another market. The sales operation in one market might involve selling agents, who receive commissions on sales, whereas in another market, customers purchase directly from a catalogue without any sales intermediary.

Selling in different markets, particularly markets at different distances from the point of production, involves differences in transportation costs. Selling in one's home market might involve some trucking fees and other local expenses, but selling in an export market usually entails additional transportation costs such as outbound freight to the port of exit, warehousing fees, ocean shipping, insurance, brokerage and handling fees, customs duties, and inland freight costs.

Some of these expenses are precisely quantifiable; others can be estimated only roughly. The DOC seeks to obtain information on all sorts of expenses, direct and indirect, realized and imputed. Many of the expenses are deducted from gross selling prices, while others are used to offset or limit deductions made from gross prices in a particular market.

Discounts and Rebates

Discounts and rebates are the first class of expenses deducted from gross selling prices. Companies often provide incentives for customers in particular markets to entice early payment or large-volume purchases, or to pass along savings afforded them by their own suppliers. All discounts and rebates are deducted from gross selling prices in both markets.

Movement Expenses

Movement expenses comprise all of the costs incurred by the seller to transport merchandise from the factory to the customer. Depending on the sales and delivery terms specified on the invoice, these expenses could include freight from the factory to a warehouse, warehousing costs, freight from the warehouse to the customer,

8

freight to the port of exit, marine shipping and insurance, brokerage and handling fees, customs duties, and inland freight in the export market. All movement expenses are deducted from gross selling prices in both markets.

Direct Selling Expenses

Direct selling expenses are characterized generally as expenses incurred to facilitate specific sales. These expenses include advertising costs involved in promoting the subject or such or similar merchandise, warranty expenses associated with materials and labor to service defective merchandise, and commissions paid on particular sales. Adjustments to gross selling prices are made for all direct selling expenses in both markets.

Indirect Selling Expenses

Indirect selling expenses are costs incurred on behalf of a company's sales operation that are not directly attributable to particular sales. These expenses include sales department overhead such as rent, salaries, and supplies. They can also include advertising of a general nature, used to promote the company name or brand but not specific products. The overhead expenses of a technical service department devoted to honoring warranties and to providing customer support may also be considered indirect selling expenses. Unlike each of the previous expense groups described, indirect selling expenses are not given similar treatment in both markets. They are deducted from U.S. prices under certain situations—so-called constructed export price transactions—but are not always deducted, at least not entirely, from the prices of the home-market products.

Imputed Expenses

Imputed expenses are implicit costs that do not accrue in an actual accounting sense but are presumed to affect prices. An imputed expense is not actually incurred; it is instead an opportunity cost. In antidumping cases, the DOC calculates imputed credit expenses and inventory carrying costs. Together, these expense adjustments reflect the opportunity cost of not receiving payment immediately after a product is produced. Inventory carrying costs impute the costs associated with the period between production and sale; credit expenses impute the costs associated with the period between sale and receipt of payment. Each is calculated typically by multiplying the number of days in the respective period, divided by 365, times the prevailing local short-term interest rate, times the gross price (in the case of credit) or the cost of production (in the case of inventory carrying costs). Imputed credit expenses are treated as direct selling expenses; inventory carrying costs are treated as indirect expenses.

Level-of-Trade Adjustments

Often, customers in the home market are of a different "class" than those in the U.S. market. For example, U.S. customers may be large wholesalers, while home-market customers are small retailers or even end users. The common commercial practice in many industries is to offer different prices to different classes of customers because their size or function may affect the volume or variety of purchases. Sellers may offer different services or incentives to different classes of customers to attract their business or cement their loyalty. When sales are made to disparate customer classes, any price differences may simply reflect the different nature of the customers' businesses. The DOC addresses this issue by attempting to match prices of U.S. and home-market sales at the same "level of trade." When there are no home-market sales at the same level of trade, and comparisons must be made across such levels, the DOC will consider making a level-of-trade adjustment to account for the difference. If it can be demonstrated that a consistent pattern of price differences prevails between the levels of trade, and that the seller performs distinctly different functions on behalf of the customers in the different levels, and that the home-market level is more remote from the factory, an adjustment will be made to normal value.

Difference-in-Merchandise Adjustments

As the DOC attempts to account for inevitable disparities in prices asked at different levels of trade, it also makes price adjustments when nonidentical products are compared. When products identical to the U.S. product are not sold in the home market, or are sold but deemed ineligible for price comparisons through the various tests and procedures described below, the prices of similar, but not identical, products are compared. An elaborate imagination is not required to appreciate that different products sold in different markets might have different prices.

The DOC makes a difference-in-merchandise (DIFMER) adjustment when prices of nonidentical products are compared. A

DIFMER adjustment is calculated as the difference between the variable costs of manufacturing the two distinct products. So, instead of directly comparing the net U.S. price and the net home-market price of different products, the home-market price is adjusted by the difference in variable production costs first, presumably to countervail the price difference arising from the product difference.

CEP Profit and CEP Offset

Sales in the United States fall into one of two classifications. Export price sales are transactions between the exporter and an unaffiliated importer; constructed export price (CEP) sales are transactions in which the importer is affiliated in some manner with the exporter, and thus the transaction is deemed unreliable for purposes of dumping calculations. Rather than use the information in this primary transaction, the DOC uses the U.S. prices of the resales by that affiliated importer to the first unaffiliated customer.

In CEP transactions, the DOC deducts from U.S. prices not only the U.S. indirect selling expenses but also the estimated profit on U.S. operations. The CEP profit is determined by calculating total revenues (quantity times price) in both the U.S. and home markets and subtracting from that figure the total cost of producing, selling, and transporting (quantity times [cost plus selling expenses plus movement expenses]) the merchandise in both markets. This aggregate figure is allocated to each CEP transaction on the basis of the ratio of the sales-specific CEP expenses to the total costs.

When indirect selling expenses are deducted from U.S. prices, the DOC calculates a CEP offset that is deducted from the foreign-market price before the unit margins are calculated. The value of the offset is determined by following a complicated set of computer instructions to ultimately evaluate various expenses in both markets. If certain conditions are met (e.g., commissions are paid in the home market but not in the U.S. market), the offset takes on a certain value. If the conditions are not met but others are, the offset takes on a different value. Although the offset can have a smaller value than the U.S. indirect selling expenses, it can never exceed the amount of U.S. indirect selling expenses. Finally, if the DOC is able to calculate a level-of-trade adjustment, it does not calculate the CEP offset.

Arm's-Length and Cost Tests

After defining the products in both markets, but before matching home-market sales to U.S. sales, the DOC filters out some (or maybe even all) home-market sales with two separate tests: the arm's-length test and the cost test. These filters are used, ostensibly, to eliminate from consideration all home-market sales that may be aberrational, or outside "the ordinary course of trade."

The purpose of the arm's-length test is to determine whether sales to affiliated[10] customers in the home market have been made at prices and on terms comparable with those granted to unaffiliated customers. The test involves comparisons of the average net selling prices per product for each affiliated customer to the average net selling prices per product to all unaffiliated customers.

A ratio is calculated in which the numerator is the average net price per product per affiliate and the denominator is the average net price of that same product to all unaffiliated customers. A similar ratio is calculated for each unique combination of affiliated customer and product.[11] Finally, a weighted-average ratio is calculated for each affiliate. If that ratio is no less than 98 percent and no greater than 102 percent, then all sales to the affiliate are accepted as having been made at arm's length. Otherwise, all sales to that affiliate are excluded from the calculation of average home-market prices.[12] When sales are excluded, the DOC can require the foreign producer to report resales by the affiliated customer.

The purpose of the cost test is to eliminate from consideration sales made in the home market at prices lower than the full cost of production. Like the arm's-length test, the cost test (and the whole antidumping analysis, for that matter) is conducted at the CONNUM level. The selling price of each home-market transaction, net of all nonimputed expenses, is compared with the full cost of producing the CONNUM sold in the respective transaction. After each transaction is evaluated in this manner, a summary for each CONNUM is generated.

If 80 percent or more, by volume, of the sales of a specific CONNUM are made at net prices at or above the full cost of production, then all sales of that CONNUM are considered to have passed the cost test. Subsequently, all of those sales enter into the pool of potential matches for U.S. sales. If less than 80 percent of the sales of a specific CONNUM are made at net prices at or above the cost of production, then all sales at below-cost prices are considered to have failed the cost test and are excluded from that pool.

Conceivably, exercise of the arm's-length and cost tests could cause all home-market sales to become ineligible as matches for U.S. sales. If no comparable sales are found in what is deemed to be the ordinary course of trade, an alternative basis for normal value, known as constructed value, is used.

CV is a cost-based approximation for home-market selling prices. When there are no eligible home-market sales comparisons, the DOC resorts to CV, which is calculated as the cost of producing the particular U.S. CONNUM, plus an average amount for home-market expenses, plus an amount for profit.[13] The value is "constructed" as an estimation of what the product would have sold for if it had been sold in the home market.

Ineligibility of all home-market sales is not the only basis for resorting to constructed value. CV can be used in situations where home-market sales still remain, but none of the eligible home-market CONNUMs are considered appropriate matches for specific U.S. products. Following is a discussion of when and whether a match is appropriate.

Model Matching

After net prices in both markets have been calculated, and the home-market database has been purged to exclude all sales that fail the arm's-length and cost tests, the DOC determines which products to compare. The preference is to compare the prices of identical products. But given the differences in tastes and customer requirements that often exist between markets, identical merchandise is not always sold in each. This problem is compounded by the fact that the pool of eligible matches is only a subset of the merchandise actually sold in the home market, since the arm's-length and cost tests tend to reduce the number of available sales.

In the absence of an identical product match, the next most similar product is sought for comparing prices. That home-market product is the one most similar to the U.S. product according to the relevant product characteristics (as discussed earlier). In some cases, the ultimate match may have characteristics quite different from those of the U.S. CONNUM. As long as that product is the most similar available, and the difference in variable costs of manufacturing between the two does not exceed 20 percent of the total cost of manufacturing the U.S. product (the DIFMER test), it will be the selected match.

It is possible that the most similar match can fail the DIFMER test. When this is the case, the next most similar match is sought, and also subjected to the DIFMER test. If this match fails, the search continues. Ultimately, each U.S. product is compared with the most similar home-market product that passes the DIFMER test. If no matches satisfy the DIFMER test, then the U.S. product is compared with constructed value.

Dumping Calculation

In an antidumping investigation, the dumping margin is based on a comparison of the average net U.S. price for each CONNUM[14] during the period of investigation with its normal value. Normal value is either the average net price of the most similar home-market product during that same period or, in the absence of such or similar merchandise, constructed value. In either case, normal value is converted to U.S. dollars by multiplying its foreign-currency-denominated average by the average exchange rate in place on the dates of all U.S. sales comprising the average U.S. price.

Normal value expressed in dollar terms is known as FUPDOL (foreign unit price in dollars) in the DOC's dumping calculation computer program. FUPDOL minus the average U.S. price (USPR) equals the unit margin of dumping (UMARGIN). The full impact of the unit margin is determined by the volume of sales of the U.S. product in question (QTYU). The "extended" margin or full-dollar value of the incidence of dumping of that specific U.S. CONNUM, or EMARGIN, is the product of UMARGIN times QTYU.

The calculations just described are undertaken for each unique combination of U.S. CONNUM and sales type. If there are 50 such unique combinations, then 50 unique EMARGINs are calculated. The total amount of dumping, which is also known as the total potentially uncollected dumping duties (TOTPUDD), is the sum of all positive EMARGINs. All price comparisons that generate negative dumping margins because FUPDOL was less than USPR are effectively set equal to zero, regardless of the amount of "negative" dumping. In other words, if 25 of the 50 unique combinations generated positive dumping margins of an aggregate of, say, $10,000, and the other 25 generated negative dumping margins of the same aggregate amount, $10,000, the total amount of dumping would be $10,000, not $0. The practice of disregarding negative dumping margins is known as zeroing because the negative dumping amounts are treated as equivalent to zero.

Ultimately, the level of dumping is expressed on an ad valorem basis to determine an antidumping duty rate. This percentage margin, which is identified in the DOC's computer program as PCTMARG, equals the sum of the positive TOTPUDDs divided by the total net value of all U.S. sales (USPR times QTYU). For example, if TOTPUDD equals $10,000, and the total net U.S. sales value is $100,000, then the percentage margin is 10 percent.

2. Rhetoric versus Reality

Advocates of the U.S. antidumping law claim that dumping is an unfair trade practice that takes two different forms: price discrimination and below-cost sales. Both types of dumping allegedly reflect underlying market distortions caused by foreign government policies. Those distortions confer an artificial advantage on foreign producers when they are selling in the United States—they can sell at lower prices than would otherwise be possible.

Thus, price discrimination (i.e., selling at lower prices in the export market than at home) supposedly signals the existence of a protected "sanctuary" home market. According to Greg Mastel, one of the few economists who firmly supports the use of antidumping laws:

> If a company engages in dumping in foreign markets and its home market is open, the price differential will induce the company's competitors or other resellers to re-export dumped products to the dumper's home market. These re-exports would quickly pull the home market price down to the dumped price and erase home market profits. Thus, a closed or restricted home market is also a virtual precondition to a successful dumping strategy.[1]

This situation gives the foreign producer an arguably unfair competitive advantage over U.S. rivals. "A closed home market allows companies to charge high prices at home because they face no foreign competition," Mastel explains. "Foreign companies can then use the profits from these domestic sales to cross-subsidize export sales at dumped prices."[2]

As to sales below cost, the contention is that the foreign producer could not sustain its losses in the absence of market-distorting government policies back home. Here again, a domestic sanctuary market could be the culprit: profits at home could allow a company to take losses abroad. Alternatively, government subsidies could prop up a company in spite of its losses. The subsidies might take the form of explicit grants or soft loans, or they might be considerably more subtle. Under "crony capitalism," for example, a politicized banking system can allow a well-connected but money-losing company to receive financing without any regard to the commercial considerations.

Another possibility is that loss-making export sales reflect basic structural flaws in a foreign country's economic policies. For example, the absence of functional bankruptcy laws could allow money-losing companies to continue in existence simply because their creditors have no better remedy than to keep them afloat and hope for a turnaround. In another possible scenario, hyperinflation or other severe monetary disorder may reduce companies to barter operations in which concepts of profit and loss no longer obtain.

Note that dumping as described above is not anticompetitive in the sense that economists use the term. Although politicians and protectionist business leaders may rail against "predatory dumping," the more sophisticated supporters of antidumping shy away from such rhetoric. They recognize that true predatory pricing—aggressive underselling of rivals in the hope of driving them out of business and eventually establishing a monopoly—is rarely attempted and even more rarely succeeds. "There are only a handful of cases in recent history," Mastel concedes, "in which it reasonably can be argued that such a systematic predatory strategy was being followed."[3]

The primary justification for the antidumping law is really more political than economic. The guiding precept is *legitimacy* rather than *efficiency*. Specifically, the argument is that international competition should be subject to certain agreed-upon "rules of the game" according to which some sources of competitive advantage—trade barriers, subsidies, and other market-distorting government policies—are condemned as unfair. In this conception, the legitimacy of international trade flows—and ultimately, political support for maintaining those flows—is contingent upon denying competitors the benefits of any unfair advantage and thereby ensuring the much-invoked level playing field.

We choose not to explore here whether such rhetoric makes sense—whether the distinction between "natural" and "artificial" competitive advantages is intellectually coherent, and whether erecting trade barriers against imports that enjoy those advantages characterized as artificial constitutes sound trade policy or indeed promotes fairness in any meaningful sense of that term.[4] Our aim is narrower: it is simply to examine whether the reality of antidumping practice matches its rhetoric. Are antidumping duties, for better or worse, really offsetting the effects of market-distorting government policies?

This question needs to be answered in two stages. First, it is necessary to determine the effectiveness of current antidumping methodologies at targeting the supposedly unfair pricing practices of price discrimination and selling below cost. Second, to the extent that the antidumping law does indeed find its targets, it must be ascertained whether those pricing practices are reliable indicators of underlying market distortions.

Missing the Target

The first step in this inquiry is to review in broad brush how dumping is actually calculated under U.S. law. In general, the DOC compares the prices of imported merchandise sold in the United States to some measure of "normal value." There are, however, a number of different ways to perform such comparisons—and in particular, a number of different benchmarks for determining normal value.

In the most familiar method, the DOC compares "net" U.S. prices to "net" home-market prices. To arrive at net values, the DOC subtracts freight charges, brokerage and handling fees, commissions, and various other selling expenses; the idea here is to compare prices on an "ex-factory" basis.

The antidumping statute indicates that comparing U.S. and home-market prices is the preferred method of calculating dumping margins. If specified conditions exist, though, the DOC will employ alternative methodologies. Thus, if the foreign producer does not sell the subject merchandise in the domestic market, or its total domestic sales are less than 5 percent of its U.S. sales, the home market is considered not viable. In that case the DOC will select another export market to serve as the comparison market; U.S. prices are then compared to prices in some third-country market. If there are no viable third-country markets, the DOC will compare U.S. prices to "constructed value"—which is equal to the company's total cost of production plus some amount for profit.

The DOC can deviate from normal price-to-price comparisons even when there is a viable domestic or third-country market. Within

19

the broad category of merchandise under investigation, there may be many different specific product types or models. For each model sold in the United States, the DOC tries to identify sales of identical or similar products in the comparison market; if it cannot find any such sales, the U.S. sales of that model will be compared to constructed value.

More important, the DOC examines comparison-market prices to determine whether they are below the full cost of production. If more than 20 percent of comparison-market prices of a particular model are below cost, the DOC will exclude all the below-cost sales of that model from its calculations on the ground that they are "outside the ordinary course of trade." In that case, U.S. prices are compared to above-cost comparison-market prices only; if there are no above-cost sales of identical or similar merchandise, U.S. prices are compared to constructed value.

The DOC employs another methodology altogether for imports from "nonmarket economies," that is, China and selected members of the former Soviet bloc. In NME cases, DOC rejects prices as unreliable, since they are not the product of genuine market transactions. Constructed value is also rejected on the ground that the company's costs are likewise not market based. Instead, the DOC obtains the company's "factors of production"—the physical quantities of all the inputs used in producing the merchandise—and values those inputs on the basis of prices in a "surrogate country." Surrogate countries are market economies judged to be at a level of economic development similar to that of the NME country in question. The DOC then compares U.S. prices to a cost-based normal value derived from company-specific factors of production and surrogate-country prices of those factors (including surrogate-country averages for selling, general, and administrative expenses and profit).

Finally, the DOC sometimes calculates dumping on the basis of "facts available" rather than actual company data.[5] Determinations are based on facts available when a foreign producer fails to provide all the price and cost information requested by the DOC, or when the information provided is judged to be inaccurate or incomplete (an ever-present possibility given the byzantine complexity of documentation that foreign companies are required to provide). In those situations, the facts available used by the DOC are generally derived from the allegations contained in the domestic industry's antidumping petition.

Table 2.1
ANTIDUMPING'S POOR AIM

Calculation Methodology	Relevance to Price-Discrimination Dumping	Relevance to Below-Cost Dumping
U.S. prices to home-market prices	overinclusive	none
U.S prices to third-country prices	none	none
Constructed value	none	overinclusive
NME surrogate-country-based normal value	none	overinclusive
"Facts available"	none	none

What do the various calculation methodologies have to do with finding either price discrimination or sales below cost? As it turns out, not very much. As to price discrimination, only one methodology even attempts to measure relevant international price differences; and none of the methodologies seeks to determine whether sales below cost are occurring (Table 2.1).

Of all the different ways that the DOC measures dumping, only the straightforward comparison of home-market and U.S. prices is capable of identifying price discrimination that reflects a protected sanctuary market. On the other hand, the apparent price discrimination may be nothing more than an artifact of imperfect price comparisons.

In the typical antidumping investigation, the DOC compares home-market and U.S. prices of physically different goods, in different kinds of packaging, sold at different times, in different and fluctuating currencies, to different customers at different levels of trade, in different quantities, with different freight and other movement costs, different credit terms, and other differences in directly associated selling expenses (e.g., commissions, warranties, royalties, and advertising). Is it any wonder that the prices aren't identical?

Admittedly, the DOC's dumping calculation methodologies try to adjust for some of the differences, but the adjustments are necessarily imprecise. For example, when the DOC compares physically different merchandise, it adjusts for differences in materials, direct labor, and variable overhead costs. While this makes a certain amount of sense, in a real-world commercial context it goes without saying that actual price differences may be more or less than the differences in variable manufacturing costs. And in many cases, the DOC makes no adjustment. Thus, prices of goods sold in the United States may be compared to prices of goods sold many months earlier or later in the home market without any adjustment for market fluctuations over the intervening time. And although unit prices typically decline with larger order quantities, the DOC rarely adjusts for quantity discounts.

Critics of antidumping have focused considerable attention on asymmetries in the DOC's methodologies that produce a bias in favor of finding price differences.[6] Without a doubt, such asymmetries exist. But the more fundamental and too often neglected problem is that the practice of comparing each and every U.S. sale to some sale in the home market will produce spurious price differences that are purely the product of "apples-and-oranges" comparisons.

Whatever the problems associated with comparing home-market and U.S. prices, at least such comparisons bear directly on the question of international price discrimination and possible sanctuary markets. By contrast, the other methodologies have nothing to do with finding relevant international price differences.

Thus, a comparison of U.S. and third-country prices can possibly show international price discrimination, but it cannot reveal a sanctuary market. Any foreign producer under investigation is an "outsider" as far as all third-country markets are concerned; it is hindered, not helped, by any government barriers that block access to its export sales. If for some reason the company is earning higher prices in that third country, the reason clearly is not that government-imposed barriers are shielding it from competition. On the contrary, it had to overcome any barriers that were present in that third-country market to be selling there at all. Meanwhile, prices charged in a third country indicate nothing about whether a firm's *home* market is closed.

Comparison of U.S. prices to a cost-based normal value—whether it is derived from the company's own costs (in constructed-value cases) or from surrogate-country prices (in NME cases)—cannot show price discrimination, for the simple reason that price data are not used for one side of the comparison. Furthermore, a finding of dumping using constructed value offers no evidence of the existence of a sanctuary home market. All such a finding can show is that *U.S. sales* are being made *below* some baseline level of profitability; it cannot show that *home-market sales* are *above* any similar baseline, since home-market sales are excluded from the dumping calculation.

Indeed, when constructed value is used because there are no above-cost sales of identical or similar merchandise in the home market, the available evidence weighs *against* the existence of a sanctuary market. A sanctuary market is one in which a foreign company is making profits due to government intervention; here, though, the company is apparently losing money at home. The supposed source of unfair advantage—namely, the opportunity to cross-subsidize low-price export sales—is missing.

The situation is similar when U.S. sales are compared to above-cost sales only. A dumping finding based on such comparisons tells us nothing about the existence of international price discrimination, since the comparisons are skewed: low-price sales have been excluded from the home-market side, but not the U.S. side. And here again, as in constructed-value cases, the evidence affirmatively rebuts claims of a sanctuary market. Below-cost sales are excluded only when they constitute at least 20 percent of sales; such widespread losses are inconsistent with the supposedly supernormal profits of a sanctuary market.

Finally, a dumping finding based on facts available provides no evidence of either price discrimination or a sanctuary market. The facts available are generally taken from the domestic industry's antidumping petition, hardly a source of objective analysis. Indeed, it is expressly recognized that determinations on the basis of facts available are punitive; it is the threat of such determinations that is used to compel foreign producers' cooperation with the DOC's often onerous information requests.[7] In any event, the dumping allegations in antidumping petitions are often based on estimates of constructed value, and thus are incapable of substantiating the existence of price discrimination or a sanctuary market.

If the antidumping law takes poor aim at price discrimination, it fires completely blindly when it comes to sales below cost. Not one of the methodologies employed by the DOC measures whether imported merchandise is sold at a loss. The DOC does determine whether home-market or third-country sales are below cost in deciding whether to exclude them as "outside the ordinary course of trade." That inquiry, though, is irrelevant to the issue of whether *U.S. sales* are below cost.

The closest the DOC comes to determining whether U.S. sales are made at a loss is in constructed-value and NME cases. In those cases, the DOC does calculate the production costs of the merchandise sold in the United States,[8] but then it adds an amount for profit before the resulting normal value is compared to U.S. sales prices. Thus, the criterion for deciding whether imports are unfairly traded under this methodology is not the existence of losses, but insufficient profitability. Sales at a loss are considered dumped, but so are profitable sales if the profit rate is too low.[9]

That overinclusiveness is exacerbated by the specific way in which dumping margins are calculated in cost-based cases. The DOC compares average U.S. prices of specific models to a single product-wide or industry-wide profitability rate. Sales below the profitability benchmark are considered dumped; sales above the benchmark are deemed to have dumping margins of zero. Consequently, even if U.S. sales average a "normal" profit, dumping will be found simply because profit rates vary by model.

Finally, there is an additional layer of methodological distortion in NME cases. In those cases, the cost data used are not those of the firm under investigation; instead, surrogate values from another country are applied to that firm's factors of production. This methodology is fraught with potential for gross inaccuracy. The extent to which the end result bears any relation to market-based costs is open to serious question.

Examining the Case Record

To evaluate the problems with current antidumping practice in fuller detail, we examined all DOC final determinations through December 31, 1998, in original antidumping investigations initiated since January 1, 1995 (see Appendix 2.1). This sample includes 141 company-specific dumping determinations in 49 different anti-dumping investigations.[10] The DOC made affirmative dumping findings for 107 of the 141 companies investigated and in 48 of the 49 investigations. The average dumping margin in the sample, including all the zero and *de minimis* dumping findings,[11] is 44.68 percent.

The most striking fact that emerges from a review of this case record is how few antidumping determinations have anything to do with targeting—or even attempting to target—price discrimination associated with possible sanctuary markets. Price discrimination bulks very large in antidumping rhetoric but commands much less attention in actual antidumping practice.

Of the 141 total determinations, 36 were based on facts available rather than actual company data.[12] Another 47 of the determinations are from the 14 NME investigations included in the sample. In 16 of the determinations, constructed value was used either because there was no viable comparison market or because there were no identical or similar products sold in the comparison market. For 37 determinations, at least 20 percent of the sales of some or all comparison products were below cost, so the DOC compared U.S. prices to some combination of comparison-market prices, above-cost comparison-market prices only, and constructed value. And one determination was based purely on a comparison of U.S. and third-country prices.

That leaves only 4 determinations in which the DOC calculated dumping strictly on the basis of comparisons of U.S. and home-market prices. Furthermore, in 2 of the 4 determinations in question, the DOC concluded that there was zero or *de minimis* dumping. Thus, in only 2 of the 107 total affirmative determinations (both of which were made in the same investigation) did the DOC find dumping by relying exclusively on the only currently used calculation methodology that bears any *possible* connection to the existence of market–distorted price discrimination (Table 2.2).

Another 31 determinations, encompassing 17 different investigations, relied partially on comparisons of U.S. and home-market prices.[13] In all of those determinations, however, the DOC skewed at least some of the comparisons by using only above-cost home-market sales, or by substituting constructed value for actual price data. In those mixed cases, the DOC found dumping in 25 of the determinations. For those determinations, however, it is impossible to tell from the public record how much of each dumping margin is attributable to normal comparisons of U.S. and home-market prices, how much to comparisons of U.S. prices and above-cost prices only,

Table 2.2
SUMMARY OF ANTIDUMPING INVESTIGATIONS, 1995–98

Calculation Methodology	Determinations (affirmative only)	Average Dumping Margins (affirmative only)
U.S. prices to home-market prices	4 (2)	4.00% (7.36%)
U.S. prices to third-country prices	1 (0)	0% (0%)
U.S. prices to mixture of home-market prices, above-cost home-market prices, and constructed value	31 (25)	14.59% (17.95%)
U.S. prices to mixture of third-country prices, above-cost third-country prices, and constructed value	2 (2)	7.94% (7.94%)
Constructed value	20 (14)	25.07% (35.70%)
Nonmarket economy	47 (28)	40.03% (67.05%)
"Facts available"	36 (36)	95.58% (95.58%)
Total	141 (107)	44.68% (58.79%)

and how much to comparisons of U.S. prices and constructed value. In other words, there is insufficient publicly available information to distinguish between the "signal" of international price differences and the "noise" of dumping margins generated by methodologies that do not detect price differences.

There are good grounds for assuming that the "noise" is considerable. Mixing methodologies tends to increase dumping margins above what would be found if only normal price-to-price comparisons were made. Comparing U.S. sales to only above-cost sales always exaggerates dumping margins, since all the lowest-price sales are excluded from the comparison. And resorting to constructed value often exaggerates dumping margins because of the artificially high profit rates that are frequently used.[14]

To illustrate the kinds of distortions that can be created by mixing methodologies, we gained access to the full confidential record of one of the mixed determinations in the sample. The investigation in question was of static random access memory (SRAM) semiconductors from Taiwan, and the specific company examined was Integrated Silicon Solution, Inc. (ISSI).[15] The actual company data submitted in the investigation and the dumping margin calculation program employed by the DOC in the final determination were used to recalculate ISSI's dumping margin; the computer program was altered so that only normal price-to-price comparisons were made.[16] As a result, the company's dumping margin fell by almost two-thirds, from 7.56 percent to 2.74 percent (Table 2.3).

In sum, a review of the actual case record confirms that the antidumping law as currently written and implemented is miserably ineffective at identifying price discrimination caused by sanctuary markets. In only 27 of the 107 affirmative determinations, or 25.2 percent of the total, did the DOC make at least some use of the only methodology relevant to detecting price discrimination, and all but 2 of those determinations were distorted by resorting to other methodologies. Meanwhile, in the other 80 affirmative determinations, or 74.8 percent of the total, there is absolutely nothing in the DOC's findings that in any way points to the existence of price discrimination.

What about the antidumping law's track record with respect to the other form of dumping—below-cost sales caused by market distortions? In as many as 100 of the 141 determinations in the sample, the DOC relied fully or partially on cost-based analysis. Nearly half of the determinations—67 of 141—depend exclusively on comparisons of U.S. prices to some cost-based benchmark of normal value. In 20 of those cases, the DOC used the foreign producer's own cost information to calculate constructed value,[17] the remaining 47 were NME cases in which the DOC calculated costs using surrogate-country values. In an additional 33 determinations,

Table 2.3

HOW DUMPING MARGINS ARE INFLATED

Company	Investigation	Methodological Distortion	DOC'S Result (%)	Corrected Result (%)
ISSI	SRAMs from Taiwan	Mixing cost-based and price-to-price methodologies	7.56	2.74
Dieng/Surya Jaya	Preserved mushrooms from Indonesia	Inclusion of profit in below-cost investigation	7.94	4.88
		Comparison of model-specific profits to product-wide profit benchmark	7.94	0
		Failure to examine whether sales are above variable costs	7.94	0.04
Liaoning	Cut-to-length steel plate from China	Inclusion of profit in below-cost investigation	17.33	5.43
		Failure to examine whether sales are above variable costs	17.33	0

the DOC made at least some use of constructed value in its calculations, although perhaps not in every determination.[18]

The most obvious problem with all of the cost-based determinations is that they do not attempt to measure whether U.S. sales are below cost. As discussed above, they measure instead whether U.S. sales are below some measure of cost plus profit. Because of the inclusion of profit, sales can be considered dumped even when they are above cost and the dumping margins of below-cost sales are exaggerated.

For specific examples of how this methodological distortion affects dumping margins, access was gained to the confidential case records of two cost-based determinations: PT Dieng Djaya/PT Surya Jaya Abadi Perkasa (Dieng/Surya Jaya), a respondent in the investigation of preserved mushrooms from Indonesia,[19] and China Metallurgical Import & Export Liaoning Company (Liaoning), a respondent in the investigation of cut-to-length steel plate from China. For both determinations, the dumping margin was recalculated by setting profit equal to zero.[20] Dieng/Surya Jaya's dumping margin fell from 7.94 percent to 4.88 percent, and Liaoning's margin plunged from 17.33 percent to 5.43 percent (Table 2.3).

Even if subnormal profitability, rather than sales below cost, is taken to be the appropriate threshold indicator of "unfair" trade, current antidumping practice still exaggerates dumping margins. The DOC's calculation methodologies are biased in favor of finding U.S. sales to be insufficiently profitable.

Most obviously, the profit rates used by the DOC in constructed-value and NME cases are frequently much higher than any conceivable industry norm. Table 2.4 gives a few examples taken from case records. It compares the profit rates actually used by the DOC (but expressed as a percentage of sales)[21] to the average profit rates of the equivalent U.S. industries during the year the respective investigations were initiated.[22] In these cases the profit rates used in the DOC's antidumping investigations were grossly excessive. Inflated profit rates translate directly into inflated dumping margins.

Even when the DOC uses more reasonable profit figures, its practice of comparing model-specific prices to product- or industry-average profit rates is skewed in favor of higher dumping margins. Consider a hypothetical antidumping investigation of widgets, in which the DOC determines the "normal" profit rate to be 5 percent.

Table 2.4
COMPARISON OF PROFIT RATES

Company/Investigation	DOC Rate (%)	U.S Industry Rate (%)
Chen Hao Taiwan/ Dinnerware from Taiwan	25.77	5.23
Brake drums and rotors from China	12.50	5.93
Cut-to-length steel plate from China	10.14	3.43
PT Multi Raya/Dinnerware from Indonesia	22.61	5.23
Collated roofing nails from China	20.50	7.20

The foreign producer in the case had equal sales of three different widget models—Models A, B, and C. The foreign producer averaged a 1 percent profit on U.S. sales of Model A, a 4 percent profit for Model B, and a 10 percent profit for Model C. The average profit margin was thus 5 percent, or equal to the DOC's benchmark. Nevertheless, the DOC determines dumping model by model and treats "negative" dumping margins (i.e., instances in which the U.S. price is higher than normal value) as equal to zero.[23] Accordingly, it concludes that sales of Models A and B are dumped.

The case of Dieng/Surya Jaya, the Indonesian producer of mushrooms discussed above, provides an example of the effect of this distortion in actual practice. To remove the distortion, the company's dumping margin was recalculated by subtracting "negative" dumping margins from the positive margins.[24] The revised dumping calculation makes a proper apples-to-apples comparison of product-wide profitability to a product-wide profit benchmark, as opposed to the normal method of comparing model-specific profitability to a product-wide benchmark. In the revised calculation, Dieng/Surya Jaya's dumping margin completely disappears: it drops from 7.94 percent to zero (Table 2.3).

Market Distortions Assumed, Not Proven

The evidence reviewed thus far shows that the antidumping law is highly prone to finding dumping even when there is no price discrimination or selling below cost. But there is another, deeper problem with the law. Namely, it simply assumes that those pricing practices, when found, indicate the existence of government-caused market distortions. As shown below, this assumption is entirely unwarranted.

It is true that international price differences can reveal a sanctuary home market. Likewise, sales below cost, under certain circumstances, can signal the presence of government-caused market distortions. But just because they *can* does not mean that they usually *do*. There are many other possible explanations—explanations that rest entirely on normal business practices and have nothing to do with any "unfair" competitive advantage. By ignoring alternative causes of the pricing behavior it targets, the antidumping law routinely punishes foreign firms for normal commercial conduct.

Price Differences and Sanctuary Markets

As to the connection between affirmative dumping findings and the existence of sanctuary markets, consider Table 2.5. It identifies, for each of the 18 investigations in the sample in which the DOC relied at least partially on price-to-price comparisons, the primary U.S. Harmonized Tariff System 10-digit number under investigation.[25] It then compares the tariff rates for that product in the United States and the corresponding product in the relevant home market at the time of the investigation.[26]

The upshot of this comparison is that in only 3 of the 18 investigations was the home-market tariff rate more than 10 percentage points higher than the U.S. rate. In only 2 additional cases was the rate more than 5 percentage points higher than the U.S. rate. In short, at least as far as the most obvious form of protectionism is concerned, there is no evidence that the home market is significantly more protected than the U.S. market in the vast majority of relevant cases. Furthermore, there is no correlation between the degree of relative protection in the home market and the range of dumping margins found.[27]

Especially interesting is the case of open-end spun rayon singles yarn from Austria. This was the only investigation in the entire

Table 2.5
COMPARISON OF TARIFF RATES

Case Name	HTS No.	U.S. Rate (%)	Home Rate (%)	Dumping Margins (%)
Polyvinyl alcohol from Taiwan	3905.20.00.00	3.2	5.0	19.21
Certain pasta from Italy	1902.19.20.00	0.0	11.3 + 31 ecu/100 kg	0.00–19.09
Framing stock from the United Kingdom	3924.90.20.00	3.4	6.5	0.00–20.01
Dinnerware products from Indonesia	3924.10.20.00	3.4	30.0	8.95
Dinnerware products from Taiwan	3924.10.20.00	3.4	5.0	0.00–3.25
Reinforcing bars from Turkey	7214.20.00.00	3.9	15.0	9.84–18.68
Rayon singles yarn from Austria	5510.11.00.00	10.6	7.5	2.36–12.36
Steel plate from South Africa	7208.52.00.00	4.8	5.0	26.01–50.87
Steel wire rod from Canada	7213.91.30.00	1.3	0.6	0.91–11.94
SRAM semiconductors from Korea	8542.13.80.49	0.0	8.0	1.00–5.08
SRAM semiconductors from Taiwan	8542.13.80.49	0.0	1.0	7.56–93.71
Steel wire rod from Trinidad and Tobago	7213.91.30.00	1.3	10.0	11.85
Stainless steel wire rod from Italy	7221.00.00.15	3.3	4.2	1.27–12.73
Stainless steel wire rod from Japan	7221.00.00.15	3.3	3.2	21.18–34.21
Stainless steel wire rod from Korea	7221.00.00.15	3.3	7.0	5.19
Stainless steel wire rod from Spain	7221.00.00.15	3.3	4.2	4.73
Stainless steel wire rod from Sweden	7221.00.00.15	3.3	4.2	5.71
Stainless steel wire rod from Taiwan	7221.00.00.15	3.3	7.5	0.02–8.29

NOTES: HTS = U.S. Harmonized Tariff System; SRAM = static random access memory sample of 49 in which the DOC made affirmative dumping determinations strictly on the basis of comparing U.S. and home-market prices. And yet in this case, the U.S. tariff rate at the time of the investigation was actually *higher* than the Austrian rate.

It is possible, of course, that some of these foreign product markets may be shielded from foreign competition by nontariff barriers. If such barriers were significant, however, one would expect that they would merit inclusion in the U.S. Trade Representative's annual compendium of foreign trade barriers, the National Trade Estimates report. A review of the NTE reports for 1995–98 found allegations that might pertain to 2 of the 18 relevant antidumping investigations.[28] With respect to the other 16 cases, though, the NTE reports do not even allege (much less prove) the existence of protectionist policies that would create sanctuary markets.

Even if a foreign producer does enjoy significantly more protection in its home market than U.S. companies do here at home, the case for an "artificial" and "unfair" competitive advantage still has not been established. Although the foreign producer may be able to charge higher prices at home, it may also be burdened by higher costs; accordingly, its profitability may not be superior to that of its U.S. competitors. And even if a company is earning supernormal profits, it does not gain any significant advantage if its domestic market is much smaller than its U.S. market. A high profit rate earned on relatively few sales will not provide a sufficient "war chest" to offer significant opportunities for subsidizing its U.S. sales.

For a concrete illustration of these issues, consider again the case of ISSI, one of the respondents in the investigation of SRAMs from Taiwan. As already discussed, most of its dumping margin was due to deviations from a pure price-to-price comparison. But does its remaining dumping margin of 2.74 percent provide any evidence of government-caused market distortions? As shown in Table 2.5, the Taiwan SRAM market was not overtly protected: the tariff rate at the time of the investigation was only 1 percent. Assuming for the sake of argument that other "hidden" barriers did in fact shield the Taiwan market, the antidumping investigation nonetheless revealed that ISSI was not enjoying supernormal profits in Taiwan. The profit rate on ISSI's *above-cost-only* sales in Taiwan was only 7.61 percent of sales; by comparison, the average profit rate for the U.S. electrical and electronics products industry in 1997 was 10.85

percent.[29] Meanwhile, even if ISSI had been earning inflated profits in Taiwan, the fact is that ISSI's Taiwan sales during the period of investigation were only about 40 percent of its U.S. sales in value terms.[30] Consequently, its Taiwan market was not sufficiently large to serve as a base for subsidizing export sales.

The lack of connection between affirmative dumping determinations and evidence of sanctuary markets is not surprising. As discussed above, the methodological flaws in pure price-to-price comparisons, compounded by the practice of using both price-to-price and cost-based comparisons in a single case, can result in findings of dumping even when there is no real pattern of international price differences. Furthermore, even when antidumping investigations do stumble onto cases of actual price discrimination, they are incapable of distinguishing between those that reflect the existence of a sanctuary market and those that are attributable to normal commercial factors. There are in fact many unexceptionable business reasons for charging more in one market than in another, and the persistence of those price differences over time by no means proves that the high-price market is closed.

International price differences can arise when a firm's status differs between national markets. A consumer goods firm may enjoy brand recognition in its home market that allows it to command a premium price, while abroad its brand name may be less valuable. Similarly, a producer goods firm may have built a reputation at home as a reliable supplier of high-quality products, while remaining a relative unknown in foreign markets. Or it may have carefully cultivated long-term business relationships with its domestic customers while serving export markets on more of a spot-market basis. In all of those situations, the firm is exposed to greater pricing pressure abroad than at home and consequently will be forced to accept a lower price on its export sales.

Business strategists recognize that, whether in domestic or international markets, established "incumbents" enjoy a built-in competitive advantage over new market entrants. As Michael Porter, a leading expert on business strategy, puts it:

> Product differentiation means that established firms have brand identification, and customer loyalties, which stem from past advertising, customer service, product differences, or simply being first into the industry. Differentiation creates a barrier to entry by forcing entrants to spend heavily to overcome existing customer loyalties.[31]

New entrants can offset the incumbent's advantage and wrest away market share by introducing a superior new product, by advertising frequently or especially effectively, *or by offering a lower price*. In the international setting, if a new entrant in an export market enjoys an incumbent position at home, it may well find that the most effective way for it to gain ground abroad is by pricing more aggressively than it does in the domestic market.

Price differences can also result when the market structures or conditions in which a firm must operate vary from country to country. For example, market concentration may be higher in the firm's home market than abroad, and pricing pressures may consequently be less severe. Or numerical market concentration may have nothing to do with it; the vagaries of business culture and market history may combine to render a firm's home market less prone to aggressive price-cutting than a particular export market. The distinction here is not between competitive behavior in one market and anticompetitive behavior in another; rather, it is a matter of competitive rivalry of greater or less intensity.

Variations in competitive intensity among a firm's customers are also capable of producing international price differences. Consider the example of a foreign manufacturer that sells to small, traditional, family-owned distributors in the home market and highly sophisticated, nationwide retail chains in the United States. The manufacturer's bargaining position will be much weaker when facing a Wal-Mart or a Home Depot than when dealing with a mom-and-pop wholesaler back home; as a result, the prices it charges in the United States are likely to be lower than those in the domestic market.[32]

All of the sources of international price differences discussed above boil down to differences in market power. When a company has greater market power in one country than another—whether caused by brand recognition, reputation, the business decisions of its rivals, or the bargaining positions of its customers—it will be able to command a higher price. The resulting price differences across national markets reflect purely commercial factors and have nothing to do with government intervention or sanctuary markets.

Not only differences in market power, but differences in marketing strategy as well, can create price gaps between countries. In Country A a manufacturer may choose to market its products (say, cosmetics) as premium goods: its strategy is to sell limited volumes at high prices through a carefully selected upscale distribution network. Meanwhile, in Country B the same manufacturer may opt to sell the very same products as mass-market items: this time, the strategy is to sell high volumes at low prices through mass-merchandise outlets. Price points in Countries A and B will be very different, but again sanctuary markets will not be to blame.

Antidumping supporters argue that these kinds of commercially caused price differences are unsustainable: without government imposed market barriers, they say, all such price differences will simply be arbitraged away. Savvy entrepreneurs in the low-price markets will buy up goods and sell them in the high-price markets; increased demand in the former and increased supply in the latter will cause prices to converge somewhere in the middle.

Such a scenario makes sense in theory, but in practice things don't work quite so smoothly. It is true that price differences will create incentives for arbitrage, but taking advantage of arbitrage opportunities entails costs. Most obviously, there are the costs of shipping goods to the high-price market. In addition, there are all kinds of hidden transaction costs: the cost of identifying the price differences in the first place, the cost of obtaining supplies in the low-price market, and the cost of finding willing buyers in the high-price market. Those costs may not be significant for fungible commodities with well-established spot markets and public prices, but for other commodities they are capable of overwhelming the price gaps in question. When transportation costs are significant, when prices are negotiated and treated as trade secrets, or when distribution is dominated by established relationships and long-term contracts, price differences across national markets can easily persist in the absence of government-imposed trade barriers. The normal marketplace frictions of relatively illiquid product markets can suffice to prevent the forces that push toward price equalization from reaching their logical, textbook conclusion.

For empirical evidence in support of this proposition, consider the billions of dollars of "gray-market" imports that flow into the United States every year.[33] Gray-market goods, also known as parallel imports, are copyrighted, trademarked, or patented products that enter the country without the intellectual property owner's permission. Often those goods are "reverse imports"—products originally exported to other markets and then imported back through unauthorized channels. Why do the goods boomerang? They come back because prices are higher in the United States. As a legal commentator explains:

> Parallel importations occur because of price differentials in the global marketplace. A publisher of computer software may, for example, have only a small market share in Mexico. As a business strategy, that publisher may legitimately decide to introduce a new product into the Mexican market at a substantial discount compared to the sales price for the same product in the United States. If the discount is large enough, U.S. parties are able to purchase the software in Mexico and import it into the United States for resale at a discount over the same product in authorized channels.
>
> In other cases, a manufacturer may limit its retail distribution to upscale markets. This strategy is common in the cosmetics trade, in which some products are sold only through salons or selected stores. Discount retailers who would like to sell the same product often find it on sale abroad at deeply discounted prices.[34]

The existence of gray-market imports refutes the assumption that international price differences require government intervention in the home market. Reverse imports show that, for some products, prices are higher in the relatively open U.S. market than elsewhere, and thus that price differentials can arise without government-imposed barriers to competition. Furthermore, the fact that gray-market imports of certain products persist year after year proves that price gaps can continue even in the face of arbitrage activity. In other words, arbitrage cannot always be counted on to achieve full price convergence.

Sales below Cost and Market Distortions

Just as price discrimination can reflect the existence of market distortions, so can below-cost pricing be associated with "abnormal" market behavior. First, sales below *marginal* cost generally do not make commercial sense. While sales above marginal cost (but below full unit cost) at least make some contribution to recovering sunk costs, sales below marginal cost only compound total losses and therefore are almost always to be avoided. Likewise, firms cannot normally sell below full unit costs for a protracted period of time. Over the long term, chronic loss-making firms cannot attract the capital needed to stay in business. In these scenarios, firms exhibiting a pattern of making losses—whether of the acute, marginal cost variety or the chronic, below-unit-cost variety—may be benefiting from some form of government intervention that allows them to ignore normal market signals.

The usual reason for sales at a loss is nothing other than a normal, healthy, competitive marketplace. Here in this country, for example, of the 4.47 million U.S. corporations that filed tax returns in 1995, only 2.46 million—or 55 percent—reported any net income.[35] Even the mightiest corporations are not immune from red ink. Looking back a few years, General Motors lost money three years in a row in 1990–92, with accumulated pre-tax losses during that period of $11.4 billion. IBM posted two straight years of negative earnings in 1992 and 1993, racking up a staggering $17.8 billion of pre-tax losses—14 cents in the red for every dollar of sales.[36] Meanwhile, the recent economic downturn has, unfortunately, afforded many additional examples.

Sales at a loss can indicate all kinds of normal market phenomena. Companies that are going out of business generally leave a trail of red ink on the way out. At other times, losses are only temporary, as companies make mistakes or business conditions deteriorate; companies can get back in the black by correcting errors and riding out the storm. During down periods, it may make good business sense to go on producing at a loss instead of cutting back production. For example, there may be long-term strategic benefits that accompany a certain market position (and market share); staying the market leader through a temporary downturn may maximize long-term profitability.

Also, if a downturn is seen as too temporary to justify permanent capacity cutbacks, it may pay to continue producing instead of allowing capacity to go idle. Here the distinction between marginal and sunk costs, or their real-world equivalents of variable and fixed costs, is crucial. If a company can continue to produce and sell goods above variable costs, it can at least make some contribution to fixed costs—costs that would be incurred even if those goods had not been produced. Under these conditions—which are typical for industries that face cyclical peaks and troughs of demand—continuing to produce and sell minimizes total losses during the downturn.

For young companies, losses are not just common; they are the norm. Investment must come first, followed (eventually, if all goes well) by returns on that investment. In these circumstances, even fast-growing companies can generate significant red ink. Meanwhile, for established companies, losses are common on new products. By virtue of the well-known phenomenon of the "learning curve," production costs tend to decline in line with cumulative production volume. Knowing this, businesses often price new goods below full current cost in order to increase sales volumes and accelerate passage down the learning curve. Such a strategy is intended to maximize profitability over the full life cycle of the product. This practice of "forward pricing" is particularly well known in high-tech products like semiconductors, but learning curves have been found in a wide variety of industries.[37]

Eventually, of course, companies must turn a profit on their overall operations if they are to stay in business. Likewise, specific products must generally earn a profit sooner or later or else be dropped from a company's business line. There are, however, important exceptions. On some products, companies can lose money indefinitely; indeed, under certain conditions they may be well advised to do so.

For example, a multiproduct firm may intentionally charge a money-losing price for one good to encourage higher sales of another good. Such a "cross-subsidization" strategy, if successful, can actually maximize overall firm profits. Michael Porter explains:

> When a firm offers products that either are complementary in the strict sense of being used together or are purchased at the same time, pricing can potentially exploit the relatedness among them. The idea is to *deliberately* sell one product (which I term the base good) at a low profit or even a loss in order to sell more profitable items (which I term profitable goods).
>
> The term "loss leadership" is commonly used to describe the application of this concept in retailing. Some products are priced at or below cost in order to attract bargain-conscious buyers to the store. The hope is that these buyers will purchase other more profitable merchandise during their visit. Loss leader pricing is also a way of establishing a low price image for the store.
>
> The same pricing principle is at work in the so-called "razor and blade" strategy, which involves complementary products. The razor is sold at or near cost in order to promote future sales of profitable replacement blades. The same strategy is also common in amateur cameras, aircraft engines, and elevators. . . .

Another variation of cross-subsidization is a trade-up strategy. Here product varieties that are typically first purchases are sold at low prices, in the hopes that the buyer will later purchase other more profitable items in the line as trade-up occurs. This strategy is sometimes employed, for example, in light aircraft, motorcycles, copiers, and computers.[38]

Selling below full unit costs may also make sense in the case of so-called coproducts or joint products—two or more different goods that are produced simultaneously in the same manufacturing process. Examples include different cuts of meat from the same animal, different ores extracted in the same mining operation, different chemicals produced by the same reaction, and products of varying quality produced in the same manufacturing batch. For those types of products, some allocation of shared manufacturing costs among the various joint products is necessary for cost-accounting purposes. Depending on how costs are allocated, a given coproduct may show a profit or a loss.

Accounting results, however, are ultimately irrelevant to proper business decisions. Managers must decide what product mix to target and what further processing to do after "split-off" of the joint products; in doing so, they should focus not on total unit costs but on marginal costs. As a leading cost-accounting textbook explains:

> No technique for allocating joint-product costs should guide management decisions regarding whether a product should be sold at the split-off point or processed beyond split-off. When a product is an inevitable result of a joint process, the decision to further process should not be influenced either by the size of the total joint costs or by the portion of joint costs allocated to particular products. . . .
> The decision to incur additional costs beyond split-off should be based on the incremental operating income attainable beyond the split-off point.[39]

Joint products are manufactured from the same raw materials, but there are many other ways for products to share costs. Sharing of factory overhead costs (e.g., electricity, fuel, maintenance, plant and equipment depreciation, engineering support, research and development) and selling, general, and administrative expenses is the norm in multiproduct firms. Indeed, economists explain the very existence of multiproduct firms in terms of the benefits of cost sharing, also known as economies of scope.[40] As a leading textbook on the economics of business strategy explains, "Economies of scope are usually defined in terms of the relative cost of producing a variety of goods together in one firm versus separately in two or more firms."[41] The same textbook goes on to clarify that "these economies arise because of inputs that can be shared to produce several products."[42]

The ubiquitousness of cost sharing suggests that focusing on product-specific total unit costs (which include overhead and selling, general, and administrative expenses) can be deceptive. A particular product that is never profitable when viewed in isolation may nonetheless contribute to fixed costs that would be incurred anyway on other, profitable products. Paradoxically, then, a perennially money-losing product can help to maximize firmwide profits.

In sum, sales below cost can mean many things other than the presence of government-caused market distortions. The antidumping law, however, completely ignores this possibility. When below-cost sales do end up getting caught in the wide net thrown in constructed-value and NME cases, the DOC's calculation methodologies fail to distinguish between normal commercial losses and those that point to the existence of government interventionism. As a result, antidumping law too often penalizes normal commercial practices having nothing to do with anyone's definition of unfair trade.

For the existence of below-cost sales to raise any serious question of government interventionism, the losses must either be acute (i.e., sales must be below variable costs) or chronic (i.e., losses must persist for a period of years). The current antidumping law makes no attempt to identify either acute or chronic losses.

An examination of specific cases reveals the impact of this omission. With respect to acute losses, the dumping margins of Liaoning (respondent in the NME investigation of cut-to-length steel plate from China) and Dieng/Surya Jaya (respondent in the constructed-value investigation of preserved mushrooms from Indonesia) were recalculated by comparing U.S. prices to an estimate of variable costs (as opposed to full unit costs plus profit).[43] As Table 2.3 shows, dumping margins for both companies disappeared completely: Liaoning's margin fell from 17.33 percent to zero, and Dieng/Surya Jaya's fell from 7.94 percent to 0.04 percent (*de minimis*). These results show that the DOC's affirmative dumping determinations cannot be taken as reliable indicators of acute below-cost sales.

For chronic losses, the period investigated by the DOC in anti-dumping cases is only 12 months. Consequently, the DOC lacks the evidentiary record to determine whether a company's losses are abnormally persistent. Because the DOC does not take a longer view, it cannot determine whether losses reflect a temporary market downturn or business reversal, or whether the losses flow from a conscious growth-oriented strategy for a new company or a new product. The DOC does make some adjustment for losses incurred on new products, but the adjustment is restricted to situations in which technical factors during the start-up phase limit production levels. There is no adjustment for losses incurred to take advantage of learning-curve effects, or for investments in growth at the expense of current earnings.

Likewise, antidumping investigations develop no evidentiary record for determining whether acute or chronic losses, to the extent they exist, have a reasonable commercial explanation. The DOC does not examine combined profitability in joint product situations, or possible reasons for cross-subsidization when goods are complementary or share costs.[44]

Most fundamental, the DOC does not examine whether the supposedly below-cost U.S. sales it identifies are in any way connected with government interventionism in the home market. There is no investigation of whether trade barriers or other restrictions on competition create a domestic sanctuary market that bankrolls losses abroad; nor of whether the foreign producer receives government grants, soft loans, special tax breaks, preferential access to credit on noncommercial terms, or any other form of assistance that supports its loss-making operations; nor of whether there are basic structural flaws in a country's economic policy that impede normal market responses to losses.

On this point, the case record reviewed in this study argues against any reliable connection between constructed-value cases and under-lying market distortions. In as many as 33 of the 53 possible determinations in which the DOC relied fully or partially on constructed value, the DOC resorted to constructed value only because of an absence of above-cost sales. Such an absence is flatly inconsistent with the profits supposedly associated with sanctuary markets.

Meanwhile, in another 13 constructed-value-based determinations, the DOC found that there was no viable home market at all.

In addition, there is reason to doubt that constructed-value cases point with any regularity to the existence of foreign government subsidies. Here it is instructive to examine the interplay between constructed-value-based antidumping actions and investigations under the countervailing duty law. The CVD law directly targets foreign government subsidies, while the antidumping law allegedly does so indirectly by targeting pricing practices (e.g., U.S. sales at prices below constructed value) that supposedly reflect underlying subsidies.[45] Consequently, if indeed constructed-value cases are addressing the effects of foreign government subsidies, one would expect to find affirmative CVD determinations with respect to the same imported products. After all, simultaneous pursuit of antidumping and CVD remedies offers the prospect of double relief for the same underlying market distortions—surely an attractive outcome from the petitioning U.S. industry's perspective.[46]

Yet only 4 of the 26 antidumping investigations in which constructed value was used covered products with respect to which the DOC also made affirmative CVD findings.[47] The absence of any associated affirmative CVD findings with respect to any of the other 22 investigations calls into serious question whether in fact there were any market-distorting government policies in those cases that would have accounted for any below-cost sales.[48]

Conclusion

The antidumping law is defended as a remedy for market distortions caused by foreign government policies. Yet in actual practice, the methods of determining dumping under the law fail, repeatedly and at multiple levels, to distinguish between normal commercial pricing practices and those that reflect market-distorting government policies.

As a result, the antidumping law as it currently exists routinely punishes normal competitive business practices—practices commonly engaged in by American companies at home and abroad. It is therefore not the case that the law guarantees a level playing field for American companies and their foreign competitors. On the contrary, it actively discriminates against foreign goods by subjecting them to requirements not applicable to American products.

An antidumping law that actually did target government-caused market distortions would look very different from the law in its present form. Bringing the reality of antidumping practice into line with the rhetoric of antidumping supporters would require dramatic reforms.

Appendix 2.1

U.S. ANTIDUMPING INVESTIGATIONS, 1995–98

Country	Product	Inv. No.	Initiation Date	Final Date	Respondent	Rate	Methodology
China	Polyvinyl alcohol	A-570-842	4/4/95	3/29/96	Guangxi	116.75%	NME
China	Polyvinyl alcohol	A-570-842	4/4/95	3/29/96	Sichuan	0.00%	NME
Taiwan	Polyvinyl alcohol	A-583-824	4/4/95	3/29/96	Chang Chun	19.21%	HM mixed
Japan	Polyvinyl alcohol	A-588-836	4/4/95	3/29/96	Kuraray	77.49%	FA
Japan	Polyvinyl alcohol	A-588-836	4/4/95	3/29/96	Nippon Goshei	77.49%	FA
Japan	Polyvinyl alcohol	A-588-836	4/4/95	3/29/96	Unitika	77.49%	FA
Japan	Polyvinyl alcohol	A-588-836	4/4/95	3/29/96	Shin-Etsu	77.49%	FA
China	Bicycles	A-570-843	5/1/95	4/30/96	Bo An	0.00%	NME
China	Bicycles	A-570-843	5/1/95	4/30/96	CBC	2.95%	NME
China	Bicycles	A-570-843	5/1/95	4/30/96	CATIC	2.02%	NME
China	Bicycles	A-570-843	5/1/95	4/30/96	Giant	0.67%	NME
China	Bicycles	A-570-843	5/1/95	4/30/96	Hua Chin	0.00%	NME
China	Bicycles	A-570-843	5/1/95	4/30/96	Merida	0.37%	NME
China	Bicycles	A-570-843	5/1/95	4/30/96	Overlord	0.00%	NME
China	Bicycles	A-570-843	5/1/95	4/30/96	Chitech	1.83%	NME
China	Bicycles	A-570-843	5/1/95	4/30/96	Universal	2.27%	NME
Japan	Clad steel plate	A-588-838	10/25/95	5/9/96	Japan Steel Works	118.53%	FA
Romania	Circular welded nonalloy steel pipe	A-485-804	5/22/95	5/14/96	Metagrimex	85.12%	NME
Romania	Circular welded nonalloy steel pipe	A-485-804	5/22/95	5/14/96	Metalexportimport	77.61%	NME
South Africa	Circular welded nonalloy steel pipe	A-791-803	5/22/95	5/14/96	RIH Group	117.66%	FA
Italy	Certain pasta	A-475-818	6/8/95	6/14/96	Arrighi	19.09%	HM mixed
Italy	Certain pasta	A-475-818	6/8/95	6/14/96	De Cecco	46.67%	FA
Italy	Certain pasta	A-475-818	6/8/95	6/14/96	Delverde	1.68%	HM mixed
Italy	Certain pasta	A-475-818	6/8/95	6/14/96	De Matteis	0.00%	HM mixed

(continued next page)

Appendix 2.1
U.S. ANTIDUMPING INVESTIGATIONS, 1995–98 (continued)

Country	Product	Inv. No.	Initiation Date	Final Date	Respondent	Rate	Methodology
Italy	Certain pasta	A-475-818	6/8/95	6/14/96	La Molisana	14.73%	HM mixed
Italy	Certain pasta	A-475-818	6/8/95	6/14/96	Liguori	11.58%	HM mixed
Italy	Certain pasta	A-475-818	6/8/95	6/14/96	Pagani	17.47%	HM mixed
Turkey	Certain pasta	A-489-805	6/8/95	6/14/96	Filiz	63.29%	FA
Turkey	Certain pasta	A-489-805	6/8/95	6/14/96	Maktas	60.87%	FA
Germany	Large newspaper printing presses	A-428-821	7/27/95	7/23/96	MRD	30.72%	CV
Germany	Large newspaper printing presses	A-428-821	7/27/95	7/23/96	KBA	46.40%	FA
Japan	Large newspaper printing presses	A-588-837	7/27/95	7/23/96	Mitsubishi	62.26%	CV
Japan	Large newspaper printing presses	A-588-837	7/27/95	7/23/96	Tokyo Kikai Seisakusho	56.28%	CV
United Kingdom	Foam extruded PVC & polystyrene framing stock	A-412-817	10/6/95	10/2/96	Ecoframe	20.01%	HM mixed
United Kingdom	Foam extruded PVC & polystyrene framing stock	A-412-817	10/6/95	10/2/96	Robobond	0.00%	HM mixed
United Kingdom	Foam extruded PVC & polystyrene framing stock	A-412-817	10/6/95	10/2/96	Magnolia	84.82%	FA
Indonesia	Melamine institutional dinnerware products	A-560-801	3/1/96	1/13/97	Mayer Crocodile	12.90%	FA
Indonesia	Melamine institutional dinnerware products	A-560-801	3/1/96	1/13/97	Multi Raya	8.95%	HM mixed
China	Melamine institutional dinnerware products	A-570-844	3/1/96	1/13/97	Chen Hao Xiamen	0.46%	NME
China	Melamine institutional dinnerware products	A-570-844	3/1/96	1/13/97	Gin Harvest	0.47%	NME

Country	Product	Inv. No.	Initiation Date	Final Date	Respondent	Rate	Methodology
China	Melamine institutional dinnerware products	A-570-844	3/1/96	1/13/97	Sam Choan	0.04%	NME
China	Melamine institutional dinnerware products	A-570-844	3/1/96	1/13/97	Tar Hong Xiamen	2.74%	NME
Taiwan	Melamine institutional dinnerware products	A-583-825	3/1/96	1/13/97	Chen Hao Taiwan	3.25%	HM mixed
Taiwan	Melamine institutional dinnerware products	A-583-825	3/1/96	1/13/97	Yu Cheer	0.00%	HM
Taiwan	Melamine institutional dinnerware products	A-583-825	3/1/96	1/13/97	IKEA	53.13%	FA
Taiwan	Melamine institutional dinnerware products	A-583-825	3/1/96	1/13/97	Gallant	53.13%	FA
Kazakstan	Beryllium metal and high beryllium alloys	A-834-805	4/9/96	1/17/97	Ulba	16.56%	NME
China	Brake drums	A-570-845	4/3/96	2/28/97	CMC	0.00%	NME
China	Brake drums	A-570-845	4/3/96	2/28/97	Qingdao	0.00%	NME
China	Brake drums	A-570-845	4/3/96	2/28/97	Xinchangyuan	0.00%	NME
China	Brake drums	A-570-845	4/3/96	2/28/97	Yantai	0.00%	NME
China	Brake rotors	A-570-846	4/3/96	2/28/97	CAIEC & Laizhou CAPCO	0.00%	NME
China	Brake rotors	A-570-846	4/3/96	2/28/97	Shenyang and Laizhou	0.00%	NME
China	Brake rotors	A-570-846	4/3/96	2/28/97	Xinjiang	0.00%	NME
China	Brake rotors	A-570-846	4/3/96	2/28/97	Yantai	3.56%	NME

(continued next page)

47

Appendix 2.1
U.S. Antidumping Investigations, 1995–98 (continued)

Country	Product	Inv. No.	Initiation Date	Final Date	Respondent	Rate	Methodology
China	Brake rotors	A-570-846	4/3/96	2/28/97	Southwest	16.07%	NME
Turkey	Certain steel concrete reinforcing bars	A-489-807	4/4/96	3/4/97	Colakoglu	9.84%	HM mixed
Turkey	Certain steel concrete reinforcing bars	A-489-807	4/4/96	3/4/97	Ekinciler	18.68%	HM mixed
Turkey	Certain steel concrete reinforcing bars	A-489-807	4/4/96	3/4/97	Habas	18.54%	CV
Turkey	Certain steel concrete reinforcing bars	A-489-807	4/4/96	3/4/97	IDC	41.80%	FA
Turkey	Certain steel concrete reinforcing bars	A-489-807	4/4/96	3/4/97	Metas	30.16%	HM/CV
Austria	Open-end spun rayon singles yarn	A-433-807	9/13/96	3/26/97	Linz	12.36%	HM
Austria	Open-end spun rayon singles yarn	A-433-807	9/13/96	3/26/97	Borckenstein	2.36%	HM
Japan	Engineered process gas turbo-compressor systems	A-588-840	6/4/96	5/5/97	Mitsubishi Heavy	38.32%	CV
China	Persulfates	A-570-847	8/6/96	5/19/97	Wuxi	34.41%	NME
China	Persulfates	A-570-847	8/6/96	5/19/97	AJ	32.22%	NME
China	Persulfates	A-570-847	8/6/96	5/19/97	Guangdong	34.97%	NME
China	Freshwater crawfish tail meat	A-570-848	10/17/96	8/1/97	China Everbright	156.77%	NME
China	Freshwater crawfish tail meat	A-570-848	10/17/96	8/1/97	Binzhou	119.39%	NME
China	Freshwater crawfish tail meat	A-570-848	10/17/96	8/1/97	Huaiyin FTC	91.50%	NME
China	Freshwater crawfish tail meat	A-570-848	10/17/96	8/1/97	Yangchen FTC	108.05%	NME
Japan	Vector supercomputers	A-588-841	8/23/96	8/28/97	Fujitsu	173.08%	FA
Japan	Vector supercomputers	A-588-841	8/23/96	8/28/97	NEC	454.00%	FA
China	Collated roofing nails	A-570-850	12/20/96	10/1/97	Top United	0.00%	NME
China	Collated roofing nails	A-570-850	12/20/96	10/1/97	Qingdao Zongxun	0.00%	NME
Korea	Collated roofing nails	A-580-827	12/20/96	10/1/97	Senco	0.00%	3C
Korea	Collated roofing nails	A-580-827	12/20/96	10/1/97	Kabool	0.00%	CV
Taiwan	Collated roofing nails	A-583-826	12/20/96	10/1/97	Unicatch	0.07%	CV

Country	Product	Inv. No.	Initiation Date	Final Date	Respondent	Rate	Methodology
Taiwan	Collated roofing nails	A-583-826	12/20/96	10/1/97	Lei Chu	0.00%	CV
Taiwan	Collated roofing nails	A-583-826	12/20/96	10/1/97	S&J	2.98%	CV
Taiwan	Collated roofing nails	A-583-826	12/20/96	10/1/97	Romp	40.28%	FA
Taiwan	Collated roofing nails	A-583-826	12/20/96	10/1/97	K.Ticho	40.28%	FA
China	Cut-to-length carbon steel plate	A-570-849	12/3/96	11/20/97	Anshan	30.68%	NME
China	Cut-to-length carbon steel plate	A-570-849	12/3/96	11/20/97	Baoshan	34.44%	NME
China	Cut-to-length carbon steel plate	A-570-849	12/3/96	11/20/97	Liaoning	17.33%	NME
China	Cut-to-length carbon steel plate	A-570-849	12/3/96	11/20/97	Shanghai Pudong	38.16%	NME
China	Cut-to-length carbon steel plate	A-570-849	12/3/96	11/20/97	WISCO	128.59%	NME
South Africa	Cut-to-length carbon steel plate	A-791-804	12/3/96	11/20/97	Highveld	26.01%	HM mixed
South Africa	Cut-to-length carbon steel plate	A-791-804	12/3/96	11/20/97	Iscor	50.87%	HM mixed
Russian Fed.	Cut-to-length carbon steel plate	A-821-808	12/3/96	11/20/97	Severstal	53.81%	NME
Ukraine	Cut-to-length carbon steel plate	A-823-808	12/3/96	11/20/97	Azovstal	81.43%	NME
Ukraine	Cut-to-length carbon steel plate	A-823-808	12/3/96	11/20/97	Ilyich	155.00%	NME
Korea	Static random access memory semiconductors	A-580-828	3/21/97	2/23/98	Samsung	1.00%	HM mixed
Korea	Static random access memory semiconductors	A-580-828	3/21/97	2/23/98	Hyundai	5.08%	HM mixed
Korea	Static random access memory semiconductors	A-580-828	3/21/97	2/23/98	LG Semicon	55.36%	FA
Taiwan	Static random access memory semiconductors	A-583-827	3/21/97	2/23/98	Advanced Microelectronics	113.85%	FA
Taiwan	Static random access memory semiconductors	A-583-827	3/21/97	2/23/98	Alliance	50.15%	HM/CV
Taiwan	Static random access memory semiconductors	A-583-827	3/21/97	2/23/98	BIT	113.85%	FA

(continued next page)

Appendix 2.1
U.S. ANTIDUMPING INVESTIGATIONS, 1995–98 *(continued)*

Country	Product	Inv. No.	Initiation Date	Final Date	Respondent	Rate	Methodology
Taiwan	Static random access memory semiconductors	A-583-827	3/21/97	2/23/98	ISSI	7.56%	HM mixed
Taiwan	Static random access memory semiconductors	A-583-827	3/21/97	2/23/98	TI-Acer	113.85%	FA
Taiwan	Static random access memory semiconductors	A-583-827	3/21/97	2/23/98	UMC	93.71%	HM mixed
Taiwan	Static random access memory semiconductors	A-583-827	3/21/97	2/23/98	Winbond	101.53%	FA
Canada	Steel wire rod	A-122-826	3/24/97	2/24/98	Ispat-Sidbec	11.94%	HM mixed
Canada	Steel wire rod	A-122-826	3/24/97	2/24/98	Ivaco	6.95%	HM mixed
Canada	Steel wire rod	A-122-826	3/24/97	2/24/98	Stelco	0.91%	HM mixed
Germany	Steel wire rod	A-428-822	3/24/97	2/24/98	Brandenburg	153.10%	FA
Germany	Steel wire rod	A-428-822	3/24/97	2/24/98	IHSW	72.51%	FA
Germany	Steel wire rod	A-428-822	3/24/97	2/24/98	Saarstahl	153.10%	FA
Germany	Steel wire rod	A-428-822	3/24/97	2/24/98	Thyssen	153.10%	FA
Trinidad & Tobago	Steel wire rod	A-274-802	3/24/97	2/24/98	CIL	11.85%	HM mixed
Venezuela	Steel wire rod	A-307-813	3/24/97	2/24/98	Sidor	66.75%	FA
Chile	Fresh Atlantic salmon	A-337-803	7/10/97	6/9/98	Aguas Claras	5.44%	CV
Chile	Fresh Atlantic salmon	A-337-803	7/10/97	6/9/98	Camanchaca	0.16%	CV
Chile	Fresh Atlantic salmon	A-337-803	7/10/97	6/9/98	Eicosal	10.69%	CV
Chile	Fresh Atlantic salmon	A-337-803	7/10/97	6/9/98	Mares Australes	2.23%	3C mixed
Chile	Fresh Atlantic salmon	A-337-803	7/10/97	6/9/98	Marine Harvest	1.36%	CV

Country	Product	Inv. No.	Initiation Date	Final Date	Respondent	Rate	Methodology
Germany	Stainless steel wire rod	A-428-824	8/26/97	7/29/98	Krupp	21.28%	FA
Germany	Stainless steel wire rod	A-428-824	8/26/97	7/29/98	BGH Edelstahl	21.28%	FA
Italy	Stainless steel wire rod	A-475-820	8/26/97	7/29/98	Valbruna	1.27%	HM
Italy	Stainless steel wire rod	A-475-820	8/26/97	7/29/98	CAS	12.73%	HM mixed
Japan	Stainless steel wire rod	A-588-843	8/26/97	7/29/98	Daido	34.21%	HM mixed
Japan	Stainless steel wire rod	A-588-843	8/26/97	7/29/98	Nippon Steel	21.18%	HM mixed
Japan	Stainless steel wire rod	A-588-843	8/26/97	7/29/98	Hitachi Metals	0.00%	CV
Japan	Stainless steel wire rod	A-588-843	8/26/97	7/29/98	Sanyo Special Steel	34.21%	FA
Japan	Stainless steel wire rod	A-588-843	8/26/97	7/29/98	Sumitomo	34.21%	FA
Korea	Stainless steel wire rod	A-580-829	8/26/97	7/29/98	Dongbng/Changwn/POSCO	5.19%	HM mixed
Korea	Stainless steel wire rod	A-580-829	8/26/97	7/29/98	Sammi Steel	28.44%	FA
Spain	Stainless steel wire rod	A-469-807	8/26/97	7/29/98	Roldan	4.73%	HM mixed
Sweden	Stainless steel wire rod	A-401-806	8/26/97	7/29/98	Fagersta	5.71%	HM mixed
Taiwan	Stainless steel wire rod	A-583-828	8/26/97	7/29/98	Walsin Cartech	8.29%	HM mixed
Taiwan	Stainless steel wire rod	A-583-828	8/26/97	7/29/98	Yieh Hsing	0.02%	HM mixed
Chile	Certain preserved mushrooms	A-337-804	2/2/98	10/22/98	Nature's Farm	148.51%	3C/CV
China	Certain preserved mushrooms	A-570-851	2/2/98	12/31/98	China Processed	121.47%	NME
China	Certain preserved mushrooms	A-570-851	2/2/98	12/31/98	Tak Fat	162.47%	NME
China	Certain preserved mushrooms	A-570-851	2/2/98	12/31/98	Shenzen Cofry	151.15%	NME
India	Certain preserved mushrooms	A-533-813	2/2/98	12/31/98	Agro Dutch	6.28%	3C mixed
India	Certain preserved mushrooms	A-533-813	2/2/98	12/31/98	Ponds	14.91%	3C/CV
India	Certain preserved mushrooms	A-533-813	2/2/98	12/31/98	Alpine Biotech	243.87%	FA
India	Certain preserved mushrooms	A-533-813	2/2/98	12/31/98	Mandeep	243.87%	FA
Indonesia	Certain preserved mushrooms	A-560-802	2/2/98	12/31/98	Dieng /Surya Jaya	7.94%	CV
Indonesia	Certain preserved mushrooms	A-560-802	2/2/98	12/31/98	Zeta	22.84%	CV

3. Dumping versus Price Discrimination

In the previous chapter we looked generally at the U.S. antidumping law's accuracy in targeting the effects of various market-distorting policies. Here we scrutinize in detail the specific nuts and bolts of the DOC's methodologies for calculating dumping. Specifically, we evaluate those methodologies according to their ability to identify and measure international price discrimination.

As we discussed in the previous chapter, antidumping supporters frequently contend that dumping can take the form of either international price discrimination or below-cost export sales. In practice, however, the U.S. antidumping law does not attempt to measure whether subject imports are sold below their cost of production. The closest that it ever comes is when U.S. prices are compared with constructed value—which equals cost of production plus some amount for profit. This artificial price is used as a surrogate for normal value when comparison-market prices are unavailable or have been deemed unusable; it is thus used as a "filler" and seldom serves as the exclusive basis of normal value. And even when all U.S. prices are compared with constructed value, what is measured is not whether the U.S. sales are below cost; what is measured, rather, is whether U.S. sales are below some designated benchmark of profitability.

Conversely, the typical U.S. antidumping case does involve voluminous and highly intricate comparisons of foreign producers' home-market and U.S. prices. According to antidumping supporters, such comparisons reveal dumping when a foreign producer charges lower prices in the United States than it charges at home. This kind of price discrimination supposedly demonstrates the existence of an unfair market distortion—in particular, a closed or "sanctuary" home market for the foreign producer. In a sanctuary market, trade barriers or other restrictions on competition allow the foreign producer to charge artificially high prices and earn artificially high profits with which it can cross-subsidize artificially low prices abroad. And because competition is restricted in the home market, the profit sanctuary cannot be arbitraged away by reimportation of dumped exports or retaliatory dumping by aggrieved foreign competitors.

In the previous chapter, we showed that the assumption that international price differences must be the result of underlying market distortions in the home market is highly questionable. Such price differences can have many innocent explanations that have nothing to do with unfair trade under any plausible definition of that term. Nevertheless, for purposes of this chapter, we will take for granted that imports sold at lower-than-home-market prices are indeed worth worrying about. Here, we will limit our analysis to this simple question: How well does the antidumping law actually measure international price discrimination?

The answer, unfortunately, is not well at all. In a depressingly wide variety of circumstances, a foreign producer can charge prices in the United States that are identical to or even higher than its home-market prices and still be found guilty of dumping. All too often, methodological quirks and biases in the U.S. law work to conjure dumping margins out of thin air.

The Effect of Price Fluctuations

Antidumping investigations compare average home-market and U.S. prices over the course of a year-long period of investigation. If prices fluctuate during that year, then differences in sales volumes can generate different average annual prices even if, at any given time, identical prices were charged in the two markets. Consider the hypothetical example shown in Table 3.1. Here, a foreign company sells widgets from a published price list and offers identical prices to all of its customers, domestic and foreign. For the first six months of the year, the price for a particular widget is $2.00. The price falls to $1.00 during the second half of the year. At both prices, demand is greater in the home market. But because U.S. customers respond more to the price decrease (i.e., U.S. demand is more elastic), the weighted-average price is lower in the United States ($1.33) than in the home market ($1.45). Comparison of these averages leads to a dumping margin (equal to the difference between home-market price and U.S. price divided by U.S. price) of 9.09 percent, even though there is no price discrimination whatsoever.

Table 3.1
PHANTOM DUMPING MARGINS ARISING FROM
PRICE LIST CHANGES

Month	Price List ($)	U.S. Market		Home Market	
		Quantity	Value ($)	Quantity	Value ($)
January	2	5	10	10	20
February	2	5	10	10	20
March	2	5	10	10	20
April	2	5	10	10	20
May	2	5	10	10	20
June	2	5	10	10	20
July	1	10	10	12	12
August	1	10	10	12	12
September	1	10	10	12	12
October	1	10	10	12	12
November	1	10	10	12	12
December	1	10	10	12	12
Total		90	$120.00	132	$192.00
Weighted-Average Price			$1.33		$1.45
Unit Margin					$0.12
% Margin					9.09%

Sales at identical prices generate dumping margins whenever a relatively larger volume is purchased in the export market at the lower price. If demand surges at different times in different markets, dumping can be found easily. Consider the example in Table 3.2, again showing sales made from the same price list. Because demand surged in the home market during June and U.S. demand surged in July, dumping margins of 5.26 percent are the result.

In these hypothetical examples the foreign producer does absolutely nothing wrong—it charges the same prices to everybody. But because its customers in the two different markets react to those prices differently, the company is found guilty of dumping. In these cases, then, determinations of dumping have nothing to do with unfair trade; they are simply artifacts of an imperfect methodology.

Excluding Below-Cost Sales

In the preceding examples, dumping margins emerge from identical prices simply because of the vagaries of market reactions.

Table 3.2
MORE PHANTOM DUMPING MARGINS ARISING FROM
PRICE LIST CHANGES

Month	Price List ($)	U.S. Market		Home Market	
		Quantity	Value ($)	Quantity	Value ($)
January	2	50	100	50	100
February	2	50	100	50	100
March	2	50	100	50	100
April	2	50	100	50	100
May	2	50	100	50	100
June	2	50	100	100	200
July	1	100	100	50	50
August	1	50	50	50	50
September	1	50	50	50	50
October	1	50	50	50	50
November	1	50	50	50	50
December	1	50	50	50	50
Total		650	$950.00	650	$1,000.00
Weighted-Average Price			$1.46		$1.54
Unit Margin					$0.08
% Margin					5.26%

In many other instances, however, the DOC actively skews the data to tilt the scale in favor of affirmative dumping determinations.

One of the most egregious methodological distortions in contemporary antidumping practice is the so-called cost test. The purpose of the cost test is to eliminate from consideration sales made in the home market at prices lower than the full cost of production. When below-cost sales are eliminated in this way, the result is that all U.S. sales are compared with only the highest-priced (that is, above-cost) home-market sales.

What possible purpose could be served by excluding below-cost home-market sales from normal value? Remember that the main theory behind the antidumping law is that the foreign producer is enjoying an artificial advantage because of a sanctuary market at home. According to this theory, trade barriers or other restrictions on competition cause prices (and profits) in the home market to be artificially high, thus allowing the foreign producer to cross-subsi-dize unfairly cheap export sales. Consequently, price differences between the export market and the home market are supposedly probative of unfair trade because they might indicate the existence of a closed sanctuary market in the foreign producer's home market. Whether those price differences exist, though, cannot be fairly deter-mined if all the lowest home-market prices are excluded from the comparison.

Indeed, the existence of below-cost sales in the home market is actually affirmative evidence of the absence of a sanctuary market. A sanctuary market, after all, is supposed to be an island of artificially high prices and profits. If home-market sales at a loss are found in significant quantities, isn't that a fairly compelling indication that there is no sanctuary market? But because of the cost test, it is precisely under these conditions that dumping margins are boosted significantly higher than they otherwise would be.

The cost test is thus fundamentally misconceived. And the way the test is applied only makes matters worse. Specifically, individual net prices are compared to average annual costs. But if unit costs fluctuate over the period of investigation—and they always do, if for no other reason than that varying levels of output continually change the denominator over which fixed costs are distributed—then the comparison of individual prices to average costs can yield perverse results. A company could make every single sale at prices above transaction-specific costs, but still some of those prices could be below average annual costs. Alternatively, a producer could recover all costs and make money over the course of a year, yet still charge below-cost prices on a significant fraction of sales.

The effect of the cost test on the dumping calculation can be dramatic. For example, in Table 3.3, there are five sales of widget Product 1 in the U.S. market at different prices ranging from $1.00 to $5.00. Likewise, in the home market there are five sales at the identical prices. Assuming the same volume is sold in each of the 10 transactions, the weighted-average price for Product 1 is $3.00 in both markets. The dumping margin for this comparison is zero. There is no price discrimination whatsoever. However, this is not how the calculation works.

The cost test imposes restrictions on the eligibility of home-market sales that factor into the average price. Sales made at prices below

Table 3.3
COST TEST

	Net U.S. Prices	Net H.M. Prices	Unit Costs	Cost Test	Net H.M. Prices (used)
	$1.00	$1.00	$2.50	Fail	—
	$2.00	$2.00	$2.50	Fail	—
	$3.00	$3.00	$2.50	Pass	$3.00
	$4.00	$4.00	$2.50	Pass	$4.00
	$5.00	$5.00	$2.50	Pass	$5.00
Average	$3.00	$3.00	$2.50		$4.00

the full cost of production are eliminated from consideration. In Table 3.3, the two home-market sales at prices below $2.50 are excluded, causing the average home-market price of Product 1 to rise to $4.00. This generates a dumping margin of 33 percent despite the fact that there are no price differences between markets.

In order to gauge the real-world impact of DOC methodological distortions, we were able to gain access to and analyze the proprietary records of actual U.S. antidumping determinations—14 in original investigations and 4 in administrative reviews.[1] For each of these 18 determinations, we were able to recreate the dumping margins determined by the DOC using the DOC's own dumping calculation computer programs. We then were able to alter those programs to measure the effect of various specific methodological distortions on the ultimate outcomes.

Table 3.4 reveals the significant effect of the cost test on dumping margins. In the 17 actual DOC dumping determinations that we examined in which the cost test was applied, the dumping margin decreased each and every time—by an average of 59.69 percent—when the cost test was eliminated from the protocol.[2] In two cases, one involving DRAMs from Taiwan and the other involving stainless steel sheet and strip from Japan, the margins were reduced all the way to zero. Margins in a review of preserved mushrooms from Indonesia and an investigation of polyester staple fiber from Taiwan decreased by more than 90 percent each. All but three cases showed double-digit declines and all but five decreased by more than 50 percent.

Table 3.4
ACTUAL DOC DETERMINATIONS—EFFECTS OF METHODOLOGICAL DISTORTIONS

Country	Case	Company	Proceeding	Sales	Matches	Zeroing	Zeroing *	Cost Test	CV Profit	CEP Profit	Indirect Selling Expenses
Moldova	Concrete reinforcing bars	1	Investigation	EP	CV	0.00%	0.00%	N/A	-22.80%	N/A	N/A
Japan	Cut-to-length plate	1	Investigation	EP/CEP	Price	-12.24%	-12.24%	-4.08%	N/A	-0.46%	-0.28%
Taiwan	DRAMs	1	Investigation	CEP	Price/CV	-1.07%	-1.07%	-89.52%	-13.91%	0.00%	-14.67%
Taiwan	DRAMs	2	Investigation	CEP	Price	-0.07%	-0.07%	-100.00%	N/A	0.00%	-12.98%
Taiwan	DRAMs	3	Investigation	CEP	Price/CV	-68.45%	-68.45%	-83.68%	-0.12%	0.00%	-3.05%
Japan	Hot-rolled steel	1	Investigation	EP/CEP	Price	-0.18%	-0.18%	-0.36%	N/A	-0.04%	-0.21%
Taiwan	Polyester staple fiber	1	Investigation	EP	Price	-13.99%	-13.99%	-64.46%	N/A	N/A	N/A
Taiwan	Polyester staple fiber	2	Investigation	EP	Price	-8.15%	-8.15%	-94.97%	N/A	N/A	N/A
Indonesia	Preserved mushrooms	1	Review	EP	Price	-411.82%	-100.00%	-92.64%	N/A	N/A	N/A
Germany	Stainless steel bar	1	Investigation	EP/CEP	Price	-29.74%	-29.74%	-35.91%	N/A	0.00%	-8.96%
Germany	Stainless steel bar	2	Investigation	EP/CEP	Price	-3.31%	-3.31%	-54.08%	N/A	-4.21%	-0.90%
Taiwan	Stainless steel plate in coils	1	Investigation	EP	Price	-2.60%	-2.60%	-63.96%	N/A	N/A	N/A
Taiwan	Stainless steel round wire	1	Investigation	EP	Price	-96.84%	-96.84%	-57.05%	N/A	N/A	N/A
Japan	Stainless steel sheet and strip	1	Review	EP	Price	-153.13%	-100.00%	-100.00%	N/A	N/A	N/A
Taiwan	SRAMs	1	Investigation	CEP	Price/CV	-296.83%	-100.00%	-66.27%	-18.25%	0.00%	-8.20%
India	Steel wire rope	1	Investigation	EP	Price	-48.32%	-48.32%	-31.35%	N/A	N/A	N/A
Japan	Tapered roller bearings (large)	1	Review	CEP	Price/CV	-231.23%	-100.00%	-68.39%	0.00%	-0.52%	-25.55%
Japan	Tapered roller bearings (small)	1	Review	CEP	Price	-177.47%	-100.00%	-7.95%	N/A	-7.11%	-15.84%
						-86.41%	-43.61%	-59.69%	-11.02%	-1.23%	-9.06%

* In some cases elimination of zeroing resulted in "negative" dumping margins. In this column the margin change is treated as -100 percent for those cases.

59

Use of Constructed Value

Application of the cost test systematically eliminates lower-priced sales in the home market, increasing the likelihood of finding positive dumping margins for two reasons. First, the sales remaining in the home-market database comprise only a higher-priced subset of all home-market sales. This translates into higher normal values. Second, the likelihood of matching any given U.S. CONNUM, or control number, to an identical or similar home-market CONNUM is diminished because the universe of potential matches is smaller. This increases the chances that constructed value—a cost-based approximation of normal value—will be used.

Constructed value is calculated by adding to the cost of producing the U.S. product an estimated amount for home-market selling expenses and profit. Both of these estimates are based on the averages of only those sales that pass both the arm's-length and cost tests. In other words, even though a substantial portion of the home-market sales may have been made at a loss—a fact that obviously tempers or even negates overall home-market profitability—only the expenses and profits of the profitable sales are used to calculate the averages for constructed value.

A comparison of U.S. prices to constructed value cannot indicate anything about the possible existence of price discrimination caused by a sanctuary market because constructed value is not based on price data. A cost-based normal value could be relevant only for assessing whether U.S. prices are below cost—but in that case, no profit amount should be included at all. Accordingly, a finding of dumping based on comparing U.S. prices to constructed value does not show that the U.S. sales are below cost; it shows only that they fall below some (arbitrary) benchmark for profitability. Such a finding has no relevance whatsoever to any plausible theory of unfair trade.

Five of the 18 actual DOC dumping determinations examined involved comparing U.S. sales to constructed value. Four of those five experienced reductions in dumping margins when the profit component was excluded from the calculation of constructed value (see Table 3.4). Although the overall average reduction was 11.02 percent, it was 22.8 percent in an investigation involving concrete reinforcing bars from Moldova, 18.25 percent for an investigation of SRAMs from Taiwan, and 13.91 percent in an investigation concerning DRAMs from Taiwan.

Model Matching

Dumping margins can also emerge from the technicalities of product definition and model matching. Specifically, the more potentially price-relevant product characteristics for a given product, the more intractable is the dilemma facing antidumping authorities.

On the one hand, if the DOC were to ignore certain characteristics as irrelevant for product definition, physically different products might be treated as identical. The more broadly identical products are defined, the greater the likelihood that phantom dumping margins could be generated, or real dumping margins could be masked, simply because of differences between the product mix sold in the United States and that sold in the home market. Consider a case in which a foreign producer manufactures widgets in two sizes (large, small) and three materials (rubber, plastic, vinyl). And let's say that only relatively low-priced rubber widgets are sold in the United States, while the mix sold in the home market includes rubber widgets as well as relatively high-priced plastic and vinyl widgets. If the DOC decided to ignore material as a matching characteristic, then large plastic and vinyl widgets sold in the home market would be treated as identical to large rubber widgets sold in the United States, and small plastic and vinyl widgets sold in the home market would be treated as identical to small rubber widgets sold in the United States. Consequently, price comparisons would show dumping simply because rubber widgets are less valuable merchandise. In other words, dumping margins would result simply because apples were compared with oranges.

Two model-match scenarios are presented in Table 3.5. Each outcome is based on the identical set of sales data. If both size and material are considered relevant product characteristics (Scenario A), there are no dumping margins whatsoever. In this scenario, the average net prices of small rubber widgets sold in the United States are compared to the average net prices of small rubber widgets sold in the home market. Likewise, large rubber widgets in the United States are matched to identical products in the home market. The average net prices of small and large rubber widgets are $1.25 and $2.55, respectively, in both markets, which generates zero dumping margins. All of the nonidentical home-market products are ignored.

Under Scenario B, only the size variable is considered a relevant product characteristic. In this case, the size variable has no effect on

Table 3.5
MODEL MATCHING—HOW DUMPING MARGINS CAN RESULT FROM PRODUCT DEFINITION

Abbreviated U.S. Sales List					Abbreviated H.M. Sales List				
OBSU	SIZEU	MATERIALU	QTYU	USPR	OBSH	SIZEH	MATERIALH	QTYH	NV
1	Small	Rubber	10	$1.20	1	Small	Rubber	10	$1.20
2	Small	Rubber	10	$1.20	2	Small	Rubber	10	$1.30
3	Small	Rubber	10	$1.20	3	Small	Plastic	10	$1.35
4	Small	Rubber	10	$1.30	4	Small	Plastic	10	$1.45
5	Small	Rubber	10	$1.30	5	Small	Vinyl	10	$1.45
6	Small	Rubber	10	$1.30	6	Small	Vinyl	10	$1.55
7	Large	Rubber	10	$2.30	7	Large	Rubber	10	$2.50
8	Large	Rubber	10	$2.40	8	Large	Rubber	10	$2.60
9	Large	Rubber	10	$2.50	9	Large	Plastic	10	$2.60
10	Large	Rubber	10	$2.60	10	Large	Plastic	10	$2.70
11	Large	Rubber	10	$2.70	11	Large	Vinyl	10	$2.80
12	Large	Rubber	10	$2.80	12	Large	Vinyl	10	$3.00

(continued)

"Scenario A"

If both characteristics are deemed relevant, average net prices and dumping margins are as follows:

SIZEU	MATERIALU	QTYU	USPR	VALUE	SIZEH	MATERIALH	QTYH	NV	UMARGIN	EMARGIN	TOTPUDD	PCTMARG
Small	Rubber	60	$1.25	$75.00	Small	Rubber	20	$1.25	$0.00	$0.00	$0.00	0.00%
Large	Rubber	60	$2.55	$153.00	Large	Rubber	20	$2.55	$0.00	$0.00	$0.00	0.00%
				$228.00							$0.00	0.00%

Conclusion: No Dumping

"Scenario B"

If only the size characteristic is deemed relevant, average net prices and dumping margins are as follows:

SIZEU	MATERIALU	QTYU	USPR	VALUE	SIZEH	MATERIALH	QTYH	NV	UMARGIN	EMARGIN	TOTPUDD	PCTMARG
Small	N/A	60	$1.25	$75.00	Small	N/A	60	$1.38	$0.13	$8.00	$8.00	10.67%
Large	N/A	60	$2.55	$153.00	Large	N/A	60	$2.70	$0.15	$9.00	$9.00	5.88%
				$228.00							$17.00	7.46%

Conclusion: Dumping Margins of 7.46%

the average net prices in the United States because only one material—rubber—is sold, so a small rubber is equivalent to a small, and a large rubber is equivalent to a large. The average net price for small widgets is $1.25, and for large widgets it is $2.55. However, results on the home-market side are much different under the one-characteristic specification. Now, rubber, plastic, and vinyl widgets of the same size group are averaged together. The average net price for small widgets in the home market is $1.38, and for large widgets it is $2.70. Although the data are identical under both scenarios, the mere change in product specification generates an overall dumping margin of 7.46 percent.

This example would seem to argue for making product definitions as specific as possible. But that approach creates problems as well. The more fine-grained the product definition, the higher the likelihood that dumping margins are the product of chance or arbitrary distinctions.

Table 3.6 demonstrates how subjective determinations about product definition affect the outcomes in dumping calculations. The average net U.S. price of 12 sales of medium rubber widgets is $2.25. In the home market, there are 6 sales of large rubber widgets, averaging $3.25 each, and 6 sales of small rubber widgets, averaging $1.25 each. Whether or not these sales are dumped hinges upon whether medium is deemed to be more similar to large or to small.

In Scenario A, comparing U.S. medium widgets to home-market small widgets generates a negative and therefore zero margin. The normal value is increased by the difference in merchandise (DIFMER), which is the difference in variable costs of manufacturing the nonidentical products (VCOMU-VCOMH). The result is FUPDOL, from which is subtracted USPR, generating a $-\$0.50$ unit margin.

In Scenario B, however, large is deemed more similar to medium, and the result is an affirmative dumping margin of 22 percent. In this case, the higher home-market price is slightly mitigated by a negative DIFMER of $-\$0.50$, but the resulting FUPDOL is still $0.50 higher than the U.S. price.

Furthermore, when products are defined very narrowly, the likelihood is greater that U.S. sales will be compared to a very small (and possibly unrepresentative) fraction of home-market sales. Thus, if all U.S. sales are of small rubber widgets, while small rubber widgets

Table 3.6
Model Matching—How Dumping Margins Can Result from Ranking Hierarchies

	Abbreviated U.S. Sales List						Abbreviated H.M. Sales List				
OBSU	SIZEU	MATERIALU	QTYU	USPR	VCOMU	OBSH	SIZEH	MATERIALH	QTYH	NV	VCOMH
1	Medium	Rubber	10	$2.00	$1.50	1	Small	Rubber	10	$1.00	$1.00
2	Medium	Rubber	10	$2.00	$1.50	2	Small	Rubber	10	$1.10	$1.00
3	Medium	Rubber	10	$2.10	$1.50	3	Small	Rubber	10	$1.20	$1.00
4	Medium	Rubber	10	$2.10	$1.50	4	Small	Rubber	10	$1.30	$1.00
5	Medium	Rubber	10	$2.20	$1.50	5	Small	Rubber	10	$1.40	$1.00
6	Medium	Rubber	10	$2.20	$1.50	6	Small	Rubber	10	$1.50	$1.00
7	Medium	Rubber	10	$2.30	$1.50	7	Large	Rubber	10	$3.00	$2.00
8	Medium	Rubber	10	$2.30	$1.50	8	Large	Rubber	10	$3.10	$2.00
9	Medium	Rubber	10	$2.40	$1.50	9	Large	Rubber	10	$3.20	$2.00
10	Medium	Rubber	10	$2.40	$1.50	10	Large	Rubber	10	$3.30	$2.00
11	Medium	Rubber	10	$2.50	$1.50	11	Large	Rubber	10	$3.40	$2.00
12	Medium	Rubber	10	$2.50	$1.50	12	Large	Rubber	10	$3.50	$2.00

(continued next page)

Table 3.6

MODEL MATCHING—HOW DUMPING MARGINS CAN RESULT FROM RANKING HIERARCHIES (*continued*)

"Scenario A"

If medium is deemed more similar to small, average net prices and dumping margins are as follows:

SIZEU	MATERIALU	QTYU	USPR	VALUE	SIZEH	MATERIALH	QTYH	NV	DIFMER	FUPDOL	UMARGIN	EMARGIN	TOTPUDD	PCTMARG
Medium	Rubber	120	$2.25	$270.00	Small	Rubber	60	$1.25	$0.50	$1.75	–$0.50	–$60.00	$0.00	0.00%

Conclusion: No Dumping

"Scenario B"

If medium is deemed more similar to large, average net prices and dumping margins are as follows:

SIZEU	MATERIALU	QTYU	USPR	VALUE	SIZEH	MATERIALH	QTYH	NV	DIFMER	FUPDOL	UMARGIN	EMARGIN	TOTPUDD	PCTMARG
Medium	Rubber	120	$2.25	$270.00	Large	Rubber	60	$3.25	–$0.50	$2.75	$0.50	$60.00	$60.00	22.22%

Conclusion: Dumping Margins of 22.22%

comprise only 1 percent of home-market sales, the existence or non-existence of price discrimination will be determined on the basis of a very small sample of home-market sales. Those sales may have uncharacteristically high or low prices and thus offer a poor measure of overall price levels in the home market. Nevertheless, all other sales in the home market will simply be excluded from the dumping calculation and ignored.[3] The situation gets worse when the sales of the U.S. product are compared to a tiny sample of nonidentical (but next most similar) sales in the home market.

Random chance and unavoidably arbitrary distinctions can thus play a major role in determining the final outcome of a dumping determination. In the preceding examples, the foreign company was not engaging in price discrimination, yet it was found guilty of dumping. The dumping margins reflect, not unfair trade, but methodological shortcomings.

Difference-in-Merchandise Adjustment

The problems caused by comparing prices of nonidentical products are amplified by the shortcomings of the DOC's DIFMER adjustment. When comparing prices of nonidentical products, the DOC adjusts normal value by the difference between the two CONNUMs' variable manufacturing costs (i.e., materials, direct labor, and variable factory overhead). Although the basis for this adjustment is logical enough—products that are more costly to produce generally have higher prices—the assumption that price differences exactly mirror cost differences is nonetheless totally artificial.

In all too many cases, wide variations in prices between products exist alongside little or no differences in costs of production. A case in point from the early 1990s involved fresh cut-roses from Colombia. The CONNUMs in that case reflected stem size, bulb size, and bulb color. Although long-stemmed and large-bulbed red roses commanded the highest prices, there were virtually no differences in the cost of production between this variety and the short-stemmed and small-bulbed yellow roses, which were the lowest priced. Because demand is seasonal and peaks at different times in each market (during Valentine's Day in the United States and Mother's Day in Canada, the third-country comparison market used in this case), identical products were often not available in the comparison pool. As a result, the next most similar product was selected on the basis of the relevant characteristics. But since production of all roses, regardless of variety, entailed the same basic costs for seed, fertilizer, land, and water, the DIFMER adjustment made for nonidentical matches was small and usually zero. As a result, low-priced, short-stemmed, small-bulbed yellow roses in the United States were matched to high-priced, long-stemmed, large-bulbed red roses in Canada during May without any significant adjustment. Although the opposite dynamic prevailed in February, the large negative dumping margins associated with the higher U.S. prices had no impact on the overall margin because they were zeroed out.

The inadequacy of the DIFMER adjustment combines with the unfairness of the cost test to generate large phantom dumping margins whenever "second-quality" merchandise is sold in the United States. Such flawed or off-spec products sell for a fraction of the price of prime merchandise, but they cost the same to produce. As a result, sales of second-quality merchandise are almost always made at prices below the cost of production. But because the cost test is administered on home-market sales only, the necessarily low-priced U.S. sales of second-quality merchandise must be compared to the higher-priced sales of prime products in the home market, or to constructed value. And because there is no appreciable cost difference between second-quality and prime merchandise, there can be no significant DIFMER adjustment. Accordingly, high-priced prime merchandise sold at home is compared to low-value second-quality merchandise in the United States—with big phantom dumping margins as the result.

Asymmetric Treatment of Indirect Selling Expenses

Calculation and deduction of indirect selling expenses introduce some potentially significant inequities into the process of determining dumping margins. Indirect selling expenses are expenses that do not vary directly with the volume of sales—sales staff salaries, sales department overhead, and so forth. In "export price" situations—that is, when the foreign producer sells directly to an unrelated purchaser in the U.S. market—no adjustment is made to export or home-market prices for such indirect selling expenses. But in "constructed export price" situations—when the foreign producer sells to unrelated U.S. customers through a related reseller in the United States—certain indirect expenses are deducted. Specifically, all indirect selling expenses incurred with respect to U.S. sales are deducted from the export price, but the adjustment to home-market price for home-market-related indirect selling expenses is capped at the amount of the U.S. indirect selling expenses. All home-market-related indirect selling expenses in excess of the cap are simply disregarded.

There is no possible justification for this asymmetry. The policy of deducting U.S. indirect expenses is apparently based on the assumption that resales by the reseller in the export market are on a different level of trade—and therefore that those resale prices include additional expenses—than direct sales by the foreign producer in the home market. That assumption, though, is completely arbitrary. It may be that the reseller's U.S. customers are large national distributors, while the foreign producer sells directly to small local wholesalers at home—in which case the home-market price actually has more of the distribution chain built into it than does the U.S. price. Why then should the adjustment for home-market indirect selling expenses be limited to the amount of similar expenses incurred in the United States?

This asymmetry—known as the CEP offset cap—skews dumping calculations in the direction of higher dumping margins. If U.S. indirect expenses are greater than equivalent home-market expenses, then both are fully taken into account. If, however, the home-market expenses are greater, they are capped. The result in that case is an artificially inflated normal value—and an artificially inflated dumping margin.

Of the 18 actual DOC determinations that were examined, 10 would have had lower dumping margins if the asymmetry of the CEP offset cap had been eliminated (see Table 3.4). For example, in two reviews involving tapered roller bearings from Japan (one review involved "large" bearings; the other review involved "small" bearings), if no indirect selling expenses had been deducted on either side, the dumping margin in the large bearings case would have been 25.55 percent lower, and the margin in the small bearings case would have been 15.84 percent lower.

In reality it makes no sense to adjust automatically for indirect selling expenses. No reasonable basis exists for assuming that such overhead costs are built directly into the selling price. Stripping them out of the price, rather than creating fairer price comparisons, instead produces price comparisons even more removed from the actual market reality of real sales prices. This artificiality is exacerbated by the asymmetry of always deducting all U.S. indirect selling expenses while only partially deducting equivalent home-market expenses.

CEP Profit

The misguided policy of deducting indirect selling expenses from the U.S. price in CEP situations is exacerbated by the further deduction of so-called CEP profit—the estimated profit attributable to U.S. selling operations.

What is the rationale for deducting such profit? As with the deduction of indirect selling expenses, the assumption apparently is that U.S. sales are on a lower level of trade—that is, closer to the ultimate end user—than the home-market sales to which they are compared. But this is a completely arbitrary assumption that may or may not be valid in any particular case. Accordingly, why deduct profit from U.S. sales without making any corresponding deduction from normal value? This asymmetry can have no effect but to drive up dumping margins artificially.

In 5 of the 10 actual DOC dumping determinations that were reviewed and that contained CEP sales, the margins decreased when the CEP profit deduction was eliminated. For the other 5 there was no impact. Overall, the average decrease was 1.23 percent (see Table 3.4). In these particular cases, then, the impact was relatively minor. The effect in other cases, though, could be significantly greater and, in any event, further contribute to the serious inflation of dumping margins caused by all the rest of the antidumping law's methodological distortions.

Zeroing

The final step in the dumping calculation includes one of the antidumping law's most egregious distortions: the practice of zeroing. By ignoring "negative" dumping margins (i.e., instances in which U.S. prices are higher than home-market prices), the DOC employs a "heads I win, tails you lose" strategy for maximizing dumping margins.

Table 3.7
ZEROING

Product Code	Net U.S. Price	Net H.M. Price	Unit Margin	U.S. Quantity	Total Margin	Total PUDD	Total Value
1	$1.00	$0.50	−$0.50	100	−$50	$0	$100
2	$1.00	$1.00	$0.00	100	$0	$0	$100
3	$1.00	$1.00	$0.00	100	$0	$0	$100
4	$1.00	$1.00	$0.00	100	$0	$0	$100
5	$1.00	$1.50	$0.50	100	$50	$50	$100
				Total Margin			$0
				Total PUDD			$50
				Total Value			$500
				Margin Percentage			10.00%

Consider the simple example in Table 3.7. Each product in this example is sold at identical net prices in both markets with the exception of Product 1 and Product 5. Product 1 is sold for $0.50 less in the home market than in the U.S. market, and Product 5 is sold for $0.50 more in the home market than in the U.S. market. The sum of the individual dumping margins (total margin) is zero because the price differences for Products 1 and 5 cancel each other out. Under U.S. antidumping rules, however, the negative dumping margin on Product 1 is given short shrift by denying it any impact on the overall margin. The total amount of negative dumping is always set equal to zero. Accordingly, in this case the DOC would find a dumping margin of 10 percent despite the lack of any difference in overall price levels between the two markets.

Zeroing, as this practice has come to be known, has been found to violate the WTO Antidumping Agreement in a case involving bed linen brought by the Indian government against the European Union.[4] The EU has since changed its practice (at least somewhat), but zeroing remains a controversial and significant component of U.S. antidumping methodology.

In the 18 actual DOC determinations that were examined, zeroing was the most significant cause of dumping margins. It affected the outcomes in 17 of the 18 cases. On average, eliminating the practice of zeroing caused the margins to decrease by 86.41 percent in these 18 cases[5] (see Table 3.4). The margins would have been entirely eliminated in 5 of the 18 cases had zeroing not been practiced. In a sixth case, the margin was reduced by 96.84 percent.

A Hypothetical Case Study

To put all the methodological issues in context and to show how they interact in practice, we have constructed a detailed, hypothetical case study. What follows is a thorough assessment of the entire dumping calculation process, using a fictitious widget case as an example.

Appendix 3.1 provides an abbreviated sample of an imaginary Section B home-market sales list. It is abbreviated because many of the expense fields have already been consolidated into aggregate expense groups like movement expenses and indirect selling expenses. This type of aggregation occurs during the course of running the margin program on the itemized database submissions, but to keep these examples relatively simple and compact, identification of each specific field is forgone. The realism of the case study, though, is not compromised by this shortcut.

Appendix 3.1 is a sample home-market sales database for a fictitious foreign widget producer. Each of the fields ends with the letter H, which indicates that the field is a home-market item. The first field, OBSH, corresponds to the sales observation and is sequential. There are 25 observations.[6]

The second field, CONNUMH, is the DOC control number or product code. In this example, the CONNUMH reflects the product characteristics, SIZEH and MATERIALH. The first digit in the CON-NUMH reflects the size of the widget, where a value of "1" corresponds to "small," and "2" corresponds to "large." The second digit reflects the widget's material content, where "1" equals "rubber," "2" equals "plastic," and "3" equals "vinyl." Under this CON-NUMH construction, there are six products, each of which is sold in the home market.

The field PRIMEH indicates whether the product sold was prime (designated by a "1") or second-quality (designated by a "2") merchandise. As explained earlier, prime merchandise is output that was manufactured without significant deviations from the intended quality specifications. Second-quality merchandise is output that, because of a flaw in the production process or in one or more of the input materials, exhibits significant deviations from the intended quality standards. As a result, second-quality merchandise is not as desirable to the customer because it usually cannot be used for its intended purpose. Although demand may still exist for the lesser-quality second-quality merchandise, it is usually sold at prices well below those for prime.

QTYH represents the number of units sold in the transaction. GRSUPRH is the gross selling price per unit. DISCREBH is the aggregated unit value of all discounts and rebates awarded on the transaction. Companies often grant volume discounts, early payment discounts, or rebate programs to their customers. MOVEH is the aggregated unit value of all transportation expenses incurred to get the merchandise from the factory to the customer. DIRSELH is the aggregated unit direct selling expenses associated with the transaction. It typically reflects commissions, warranties, advertising, technical assistance, and any other expenses associated directly with the sale in question. CREDITH is the unit credit expense associated with the specific transaction. It is an imputed expense, which ostensibly measures the opportunity cost of maintaining accounts receivable. When a sale is made, the merchandise usually leaves the producer's warehouse for the customer's destination. However, payment is often not received for some time. CREDITH attempts to measure the opportunity cost of not having received payment when the merchandise was shipped to the customer. Its value is based on the prevailing short-term interest rate, the number of days between shipment and receipt of payment, and the sales price.

INDSELLH represents the aggregated unit indirect selling expenses, which typically include general and administrative expenses incurred by the sales department that are not associated with any particular sale. Office supplies, managers' salaries, postage, rent incurred by the sales department, and other such items make up indirect selling expenses. INVCARH is another imputed expense, but unlike CREDITH, it is considered an indirect expense. It attempts to measure the opportunity cost of not selling merchandise on a just-in-time basis. Holding inventory is more expensive than selling straight off the production line because there is an opportunity cost of not having the cash available immediately. Like CREDITH, the INVCARH expense is based on the prevailing short-term interest rate, but here the cost of production (rather than sales price) and the days between production and sale (rather than between sale and receipt of payment) are used as the components of the calculation.

PACKH is the cost of packing materials, labor, and overhead. Many products are placed in some sort of packaging before they are shipped to the customer. PACKH measures the aggregated unit cost of packaging.

VCOMH is the unit variable cost (materials, labor, and variable overhead) of producing the merchandise. It is included in the Section B database because it is relevant to the model-matching procedure, which will be discussed below.

The fields in Appendix 3.1, although not a complete list of all the data typically reported in a Section B response, suffice to provide realistic examples of dumping calculation methodology.

Appendix 3.1 also contains some additional fields that are calculated for future reference. NETPRIH is the net home-market sales price, calculated as GRSUPRH – DISCREBH – MOVEH – DIRSELH – CREDITH – PACKH. The home-market net price equals the gross selling price minus discounts and rebates, movement expenses, direct selling expenses, credit, and packing. Indirect selling expenses are not deducted in the DOC's calculation of home-market net price. NETPRIH is the basis for normal value, which is compared to the average export price in the margin calculation.

NPRICOP is a different expression of the net home-market sales price, which is the net of all nonimputed selling expenses, both direct and indirect, and is used for the cost test to be discussed. It is calculated as GRSUPRH – DISCREBH – MOVEH – DIRSELH – INDSELH – PACKH. TOTCOP is the total cost of production (materials + labor + overhead + general and administrative expenses + interest expenses) for each CONNUMH reported in Section D of the questionnaire response. It is merged into the home-market sales database to perform the cost test and to calculate profit rates, as follows. REVENUE is the total net revenue, NPRICOP × QTYH. COST is the total cost, TOTCOP × QTYH. PROFIT is REVENUE – COST.

Note that the overall profit rate on home-market sales (the figure in the bottom right corner of the table in Appendix 3.2) is a negative 1.84 percent—in other words, a loss of 1.84 percent. The fact that the company lost money on its home-market sales should undercut any reasonable conclusion that it is dumping, since there is evidently no sanctuary market of high prices and high profits. The DOC's antidumping procedures, however, are not designed to reach reasonable conclusions.

Appendix 3.2 provides a summary of the weighted-average net prices per product (where product is a unique combination of CON-NUMH and PRIMEH), as well as the revenue, costs, and profit. Note that the average net home-market price is $6.09 per unit—or 15 percent *lower* than the average net U.S. price of $7.14 per unit.[7] In other words, far from dumping in the U.S. market, the producer in this hypothetical example is actually exporting to the United States at premium prices. This commercial reality, however, is ultimately turned on its head by the DOC's various procedures for massaging and skewing the data.

The first such procedure examined here is the screening of home-market sales under the cost test.[8] Sales at prices below the full cost of production, if they are made in sufficient quantities, are deemed outside the ordinary course of trade and eliminated from further consideration. The net selling price, as defined by NPRICOP, is compared to the cost of production, TOTCOP. If NPRICOP is less than TOTCOP, the selling price is below the cost of production. That sale does not necessarily fail the cost test, however. If the volume of all sales found to be priced below cost comprises less than 20 percent of the volume of all sales of that product (CONNUMH/ PRIMEH combination), then despite being priced below cost, those sales pass the cost test.

Appendix 3.3 shows how the cost test is performed. The field TOTCOP, or total cost of production, comes from the Section D cost database. Typically, the DOC will merge the Sections B and D databases by CONNUMH to extract the unit cost information, which is used for the cost test and to calculate profit rates for constructed value comparisons as well as for the CEP profit deduction.

As shown in Appendix 3.3, the cost test in this hypothetical case results in the exclusion of a number of home-market sales. Note that even though Observation 1 is priced below cost, the collective volume of above-cost sales of that product (CONNUMH 11/PRIMEH 1) exceeds 80 percent. Thus, all sales of that product pass the cost test. Nonetheless, a significant portion of the home-market sales database (13 of the 25 sales) fails the cost test and is dropped from further consideration. Appendix 3.4 lists the sales that passed the cost test, and Appendix 3.5 shows the bottom line: the average home-market price rises from $6.09 to $6.54, and the profit rate increases from − 1.84 percent to 19.06 percent.

The three calculated variables presented at the bottom of Appendix 3.5, DSELLH, ISELLH, and CVPROF, are used in the calculation of constructed value, which serves as normal value when no viable price comparisons are available. DSELLH is the average amount of home-market direct selling expenses incurred on sales made in the ordinary course of trade. ISELLH is the average amount of indirect selling expenses incurred on sales made in the ordinary course of trade. CVPROF is the profit rate on sales made in the ordinary course of trade.

Appendix 3.6 is an abbreviated sample of the Section C U.S. sales list for the same fictitious foreign widget producer. As in the home-market examples, certain fields have been consolidated to facilitate illustration of the relevant points. In this table, which reflects the company's sales in the United States, there are 45 sales observations of subject merchandise. These observations include sales of a unique product, CONNUMU 34, which is a large aluminum widget.

Most of the fields represent the same variables as in the home-market exhibits (although they each end with a U for U.S., rather than an H for home market). Fields not appearing on the home-market side, which are important to the dumping calculations, include TCOMU and SALEU. In addition, in the U.S. database, when there are CEP sales, indirect expenses are divided into those incurred domestically and accruing to all sales (DINDIRSU and DINVCARU) and those incurred in the United States as well as accruing specifically to U.S. sales (INDIRSU and INVCARU).

TCOMU represents the total cost of manufacturing (not to be confused with the more inclusive TOTCOP or total cost of production). Although a cost variable, TCOMU is relevant to the sales list because it comes into play when selecting the appropriate products to compare. Ideally, identical CONNUMs are available in both markets, which allows for the most reasonable price comparisons. However, because of the product exclusions caused by the arm's-length and cost tests, as well as the fact that different markets demand different products, U.S. products frequently do not have identical home-market matches. Under these circumstances, the most similar, nonidentical product is selected from the remaining home-market options for price comparison. Under DOC procedures, any product is considered similar provided that the differences in variable costs (VCOMU − VCOMH) do not exceed 20 percent of the total cost

(TCOMU). Hence, TCOMU serves as a benchmark in determining whether product comparisons are appropriate.

SALEU indicates whether the sale is an export price (EP) or constructed export price (CEP) transaction. An EP sale is generally defined as an arm's-length transaction between the exporter and an unaffiliated importer with the terms of the sale (price, quantity, etc.) having been agreed on before importation of the merchandise. A CEP sale is generally a sale made after importation to an unaffiliated customer by an importer or reseller that is related to the exporter. The terms of CEP sales are generally agreed upon after importation of the merchandise. Big exporters with subsidiary operations in the United States often conduct business this way. Their U.S. subsidiaries are often the importers of record and maintain warehouse facilities, sales operations, and even manufacturing capabilities in the United States. Transactions between the exporter and a related importer are considered to be unreliable benchmarks for export price because the prices may not reflect true market prices.

Under U.S. antidumping rules, EP and CEP sales are treated differently in the process of calculating net prices. Net prices on EP sales are calculated by deducting only discounts, rebates, and movement expenses from the gross selling price. The selling expenses and packing costs that are still reflected in the U.S. net prices are added back to the net prices on the home-market side, which are already net of the home-market selling and packing expenses. Indirect selling expenses are not deducted from either side in the dumping calculations for EP transactions. In CEP transactions, on the other hand, home-market and U.S. movement, packing, and direct selling expenses are deducted from each side, respectively. In addition, indirect selling expenses are deducted from U.S. prices—and also from home-market prices, up to the amount of U.S. indirect expenses (the so-called CEP offset cap). CEP profit is deducted as well.

To calculate CEP profit, the DOC tallies profits on home-market and U.S. sales by calculating the revenues and expenses on all arm's-length transactions, as depicted in Appendix 3.7. This table shows that the overall CEP profit ratio is 3.58 percent, which is applied to all CEP selling expenses and then deducted from the gross U.S. price.

Appendix 3.8 is derived from the original U.S. sales database and shows the net prices (NETPRIU) along with total amounts for direct selling expenses (DIREXPU) and packing (PACKINGU). These values are carried forward to conduct the dumping margin calculations.

Note that on EP sales, the net price equals the gross price (GRSUPRU) minus discounts and rebates (DISCREBU) and movement expenses (MOVEU). On CEP sales, the net price equals the gross price minus discounts and rebates, movement expenses, direct selling expenses (DIRSELLU), credit expenses (CREDITU), U.S. indirect selling expenses (INDSELU and INVCARU), and CEP profit (CEPPROFIT). As a final step before conducting the margin calculations, the net prices, direct selling expenses, and packing costs are weight-averaged by CONNUMU, PRIMEU, and SALEU. Those figures appear in Appendix 3.9.

With average prices and expenses calculated in both markets, the DOC determines which prices to compare by following its model-matching procedure. For each U.S. CONNUMU, the most similar home-market CONNUMH is selected as the basis for the comparison. Although identical matches are always the most similar, they are not always available for reasons already discussed. Appendix 3.10 summarizes the outcome of the model match as well as the calculated dumping margins for this hypothetical example.

Note that most of the U.S. CONNUMUs were matched to identical home-market CONNUMHs. Despite the cost test, at least some home-market sales of these products (namely, the higher-priced sales) remained in the database. CONNUMU 34, which was unique to the U.S. market, did not match an identical home-market product. The most similar home-market product was CONNUMH 33, a large vinyl widget. The difference in variable costs, or DIFMER (VCOMU − VCOMH), was less than 20 percent of the total cost to manufacture CONNUMU 34 (TCOMU), so the match passed that requirement.

U.S. CONNUMU 32, however, found no eligible matches from the available pool of home-market CONNUMHs. All home-market sales of the identical CONNUMH were dropped after the cost test, and none of the remaining CONNUMHs passed the cost requirement. The closest matches physically, CONNUMH 31 and 33, have variable costs of $5.30 and $8.10, respectively (see VCOMH in Appendix 3.1). With a variable cost of $6.70 and a total cost of $6.90 for CONNUMU 32 (see VCOMU and TCOMU in Appendix 3.6), the differences in variable costs between the U.S. model and the two home-market models exceed 20 percent of the total cost of CONNUMU 32. As a result, the price of this CONNUMU was matched to constructed value, as indicated by CV in the field CONNUMH.

The dumping margin is calculated by comparing the net U.S. price (NETPRIU) to the foreign unit price in dollars (FUPDOL). For price-to-price comparisons, FUPDOL is based on the net home-market price (NETPRIH). For price-to-constructed-value comparisons, FUPDOL is based on cost (TOTCOP). In either case, FUPDOL contains elements in addition to these main components.

For price-to-price comparisons involving EP sales, FUPDOL equals NETPRIH + DIFMER + DIREXPU + PACKU. DIFMER is the difference-in-merchandise adjustment or the difference in variable costs, which is zero for identical matches. DIREXPU refers to the average U.S. direct selling expenses, and PACKU is the average U.S. packing expense. For price-to-price comparisons involving CEP sales, FUPDOL equals NETPRIH + DIFMER + PACKU.

For price-to-constructed-value comparisons involving EP sales, FUPDOL equals CV + DIREXPU, and for price-to-constructed-value comparisons involving CEP sales, FUPDOL equals CV. In either case, CV equals TOTCOP + HMISEL + PACKU + CVPROF. HMISEL is the average amount of home-market indirect selling expenses on sales made in the ordinary course of trade. CVPROF is the estimated profit, which is based on the profit rate of sales made in the ordinary course of trade, converted to an absolute figure by multiplying by TOTCOP.

Ultimately, the unit margin (UMARGIN) is the difference between FUPDOL and NETPRIU. That unit margin is multiplied by the quantity sold of each U.S. product (CONNUMU/PRIMEU/SALEU combination) to calculate the extended margin, or EMARGIN. If EMARGIN is less than zero, it is set equal to zero in the field TOTPUDD, which stands for total potentially uncollected dumping duties. This practice of zeroing, as discussed previously, contributes, in some cases substantially, to the exaggeration of dumping margins. The field VALUE is the total net value of U.S. sales, which equals NETPRIU times QTYU. The bottom-line dumping margin is calculated as the sum of the TOTPUDD field ($259.00) divided by the sum of the VALUE field ($2,499.31), which in this case equals 10.36 percent.

Table 3.8 shows what the dumping margins would be if various methodological distortions were corrected. If there were no cost test, NETPRIH values would be lower, and there would have been no CV comparisons. The dumping margin would fall to zero. If indirect selling expenses were not deducted in CEP transactions, margins

Table 3.8
HYPOTHETICAL CASE STUDY: EFFECT OF METHODOLOGICAL DISTORTIONS ON DUMPING MARGINS

	Dumping Margin
Using DOC methodology	10.36%
Exclude cost test	0.00%
Exclude CEP indirect selling expense deduction only	10.05%
Exclude CEP profit deduction only	10.29%
Exclude Both CEP asymmetric adjustments	9.98%
Exclude zeroing only	8.94%
Exclude all methodological distortions	−5.54%

would fall to 10.05 percent. If no CEP profit deduction were made, the dumping margin would decrease to 10.29 percent. If the practice of zeroing were eliminated, the dumping margin would fall to 8.94 percent. And if all these methodological flaws were eliminated, this fictitious widget maker would have a dumping margin of −5.54 percent. In other words, it would be cleared of all charges of dumping.

This example illustrates how a fictitious company that sells at significantly higher prices in the United States than in its home market can nonetheless be found to be dumping under U.S. rules. In short, findings of dumping under the current U.S. antidumping law are barely worth the pages of the *Federal Register* they are printed on. All too often they convey no useful information about a company's selling practices for the simple reason that the underlying procedures for evaluating those practices are fatally flawed.

Conclusion

This examination of the U.S. antidumping law's "tricks of the trade" reveals a sharp divergence between the law's inner workings and its wholesome public image. The antidumping law is hailed by supporters across the political spectrum as the guarantor of a level playing field for U.S. industry and import competition. In fact, however, the law systematically discriminates against foreign goods with skewed rules that generate dumping margins out of thin air.

The antidumping law imposes trade-restrictive duties, yet its supporters claim that it is not protectionist. They contend that antidumping measures target only "unfair trade"—in particular, artificially low-priced products exported from sanctuary markets where normal competitive forces are suppressed. Because of the underlying distortions of a sanctuary market, prices in the home market are abnormally high, which then allows foreign producers to sell here in the United States at abnormally low prices. The antidumping law, by imposing duties on imports sold at prices lower than those charged in the home market, counteracts the distortions caused by sanctuary markets without interfering in normal, healthy foreign competition.

Or so the story goes. The reality, though, is very different. For purposes of this chapter, we put aside the deeper question of whether price differences between national markets are, in and of themselves, reliable evidence of market distortions. Instead, we examine the more basic issue of whether the antidumping law accurately measures differences between U.S. prices and foreign-market prices. Unfortunately, the law as it currently stands fails to meet that basic test—and fails badly. Comparisons of average prices can be skewed by something as simple and common as price fluctuations over the period of investigation. The existence or nonexistence of dumping margins can turn on unavoidably arbitrary definitions of the products being compared. Comparisons of nonidentical products, even with difference-in-merchandise adjustments, can easily produce dumping margins that reflect nothing more than different commercial values.

Compounding these problems, the law then proceeds to make matters worse—much worse—with rules that skew the calculation and comparison of net prices in the direction of higher dumping margins. The cost test eliminates low-priced sales in the home market when they are found to be below cost, thus boosting dumping margins in precisely those situations where the evidence for a sanctuary market (which is supposedly highly profitable) is weakest. Indirect selling expenses are fully deducted from U.S. prices in CEP transactions, but not from the home-market prices to which they are compared. CEP profit is also deducted from U.S. prices in these situations, but no corresponding deduction is made on the home-market side. Constructed value, which sometimes serves as the benchmark for judging the fairness of U.S. prices, is inflated by the unjustifiable

81

addition of an amount for profit—an amount that is then exaggerated by being based only on above-cost home-market sales. Finally, the practice of zeroing ensures that dumping margins are routinely much higher than the actual differences in net-price levels.

In sum, the antidumping law does not do what its supporters say it does. It does not accurately measure the differences between U.S. prices and foreign-market prices. It is therefore incapable of distinguishing between unfair trade and normal, healthy competition. As a result, normal, healthy competition from abroad is all too often stifled in the name of fighting dumping. In other words, the antidumping law, while pretending to secure a level playing field, in fact indulges in old-fashioned protectionism. That protectionism is no less real because it is obscured by technical complexity. Indeed, its complexity makes the law all the more effective as a protectionist vehicle by shielding it from scrutiny.

Glossary of Terms

TERM	DEFINITION	ELABORATION
CEPPROFIT	Constructed export price profit	Per-unit amount of profit attributed to and deducted from constructed export price sales.
CONNUMH	Home-market control number	Each product is defined according to the product characteristics deemed relevant by the Department of Commerce. The CONNUMH reflects the product's relevant characteristics.
CONNUMU	U.S. control number	Each product is defined according to the product characteristics deemed relevant by the Department of Commerce. The CONNUMU reflects the product's relevant characteristics.
CREDITH	Home-market credit expense	Per-unit opportunity cost of not receiving immediate payment for delivery of merchandise.
CREDITU	U.S. credit expense	Per-unit opportunity cost of not receiving immediate payment for delivery of merchandise.
CV	Net constructed value	Final constructed value used for comparison to U.S. price.
CVPROF	Constructed value profit	Per-unit profit calculated and added to constructed value to derive a surrogate normal value.
DIFMER	Difference in merchandise adjustment	Difference in variable costs of production used as price adjustment when the prices of nonidentical products are compared.
DINDSELU	U.S. indirect selling expenses (incurred in home market)	Per-unit indirect selling expenses associated with the U.S. sale, incurred before U.S. importation of the merchandise.
DINVCARU	U.S. inventory carry cost (incurred in home market)	Per-unit opportunity cost of not receiving immediate payment upon production of merchandise. Portion of expense associated with days in inventory before U.S. importation.
DIREXPU	U.S. direct selling expenses	Per-unit, average direct selling expenses.

DIRSELH	Home-market direct selling expenses	Per-unit expenses directly incurred when selling the merchandise, such as commissions, warranties, advertising, and technical assistance.
DIRSELU	U.S. direct selling expenses	Per-unit expenses directly incurred when selling the merchandise, such as commissions, warranties, advertising, and technical assistance.
DISCREBH	Home-market discounts and rebates	Per-unit discounts and rebates awarded on sale.
DISCREBU	U.S. discounts and rebates	Per-unit discounts and rebates awarded on sale.
DSELLH	Home-market average direct selling expenses	Per-unit average amount of direct selling expense incurred on sales in the "ordinary course of trade" (sales remaining after the cost test).
EMARGIN	Extended dumping margin	Unit margin times quantity of U.S. sale.
FUPDOL	Foreign unit price in dollars	Normal value (whether price-based or constructed value) converted from foreign currency to dollars.
GRSUPRH	Home-market gross price	Per-unit gross sale price.
GRSUPRU	U.S. gross price	Per-unit gross sale price.
HMDSEL	Average home-market direct selling expenses	Average home-market direct selling expenses used for CV calculations.
HMISEL	Average home-market indirect selling expenses	Average home-market indirect selling expenses used for CV calculations.
INDSELH	Home-market indirect selling expenses	Per-unit expenses associated indirectly with selling the merchandise, such as office supplies, managers' salaries, postage, and rent incurred by a sales department.
INDSELU	U.S. indirect selling expenses (incurred in United States)	Per-unit indirect selling expenses associated with the U.S. sale, incurred after U.S. importation of the merchandise.
INVCARH	Home-market inventory carrying cost	Per-unit opportunity cost of not receiving immediate payment upon production of merchandise.
INVCARU	U.S. inventory carry cost (incurred in United States)	Per-unit opportunity cost of not receiving immediate payment upon production of merchandise. Portion of expense associated with days in inventory before U.S. importation.

ISELLH	Home-market average indirect selling expenses	Per-unit average amount of indirect selling expense incurred on sales in the "ordinary course of trade" (sales remaining after the cost test).
MATERIALH	Home-market widget material characteristic	Identifies the material (rubber, plastic, vinyl) of the widget.
MATERIALU	U.S. widget material characteristic	Identifies the material (rubber, plastic, vinyl) of the widget.
MOVEH	Home-market movement expenses	Per-unit transportation, freight, warehousing, insurance and other expenses associated with moving the merchandise to the customer.
MOVEU	U.S. movement expenses	Per-unit transportation, freight, warehousing, insurance, and other expenses associated with moving the merchandise to the customer.
NETPRIH	Home-market net price	Per-unit price net of direct selling expenses, movement expenses, and packing costs. In Appendix 3.10 this field is the average net price per CONNUMH sold in the ordinary course of trade.
NETPRIU	U.S. net price	Per-unit, net U.S. price.
NPRICOP	Home-market net price (for the cost test)	Per-unit price net of certain selling expenses, movement expenses, and packing costs.
OBSH	Home-market observation number	Each sales transaction reported to the Department of Commerce is identified by a unique record number.
OBSU	U.S. observation number	Each sales transaction reported to the Department of Commerce is identified by a unique record number.
PACKH	Home-market packing cost	Per-unit cost of materials, labor and overhead associated with packing the merchandise destined for the home market.
PACKINGU	U.S. packing cost	Per-unit, average packing costs.
PACKU	U.S. packing cost	Per-unit cost of materials, labor and overhead associated with packing the merchandise destined for the U.S.
PCTMARG	Percent dumping margin	TOTPUDD divided by VALUE.

PRIMEH	Home-market quality of merchandise identifier	Indicates whether product sold was within-specification (prime) or off-specification (secondary) merchandise.
PRIMEU	U.S. quality of merchandise identifier	Indicates whether product sold was within-specification (prime) or off-specification (secondary) merchandise.
QTYH	Quantity sold in home-market transaction	Quantity sold.
QTYU	Quantity sold in U.S. transaction	Quantity sold.
SALEU	U.S. sale type indicator	Identifies whether the U.S. sale is an "export price" ("EP") or a "constructed export price" ("CEP") transaction.
SIZEH	Home-market widget size characteristic	Identifies the size (small, medium, large) of the widget.
SIZEU	U.S. widget size characteristic	Identifies the size (small, medium, large) of the widget.
TCOMU	Total cost of manufacturing the product sold in the U.S.	Per-unit total cost of manufacturing the specific CONNUMU sold in the transaction.
TOTCOP	Total cost of production	Per-unit cost of producing the specific CONNUMH sold in the transaction.
TOTCV	Total constructed value	Gross constructed value (including profit and certain expenses that are ultimately deducted).
TOTPUDD	Total potentially uncollected dumping duties	Sum of the positive extended margins.
UMARGIN	Unit dumping margin	Net foreign price (FUPDOL) minus net U.S. price (NETPRIU).
VALUE	Net U.S. sales value	Net U.S. price times U.S. quantity.
VCOMH	Variable cost of manufacturing the product sold in the home market	Per-unit variable cost of manufacturing the specific CONNUMH sold in the transaction.
VCOMU	Variable cost of manufacturing the product sold in the U.S.	Per-unit variable cost of manufacturing the specific CONNUMU sold in the transaction.

Appendix 3.1
Hypothetical Home-Market Sales List

OBSH	CONNUMH	PRIMEH	SIZEH	MATERIALH	QTYH	GRSUPRH	DISCREBH	MOVEH	DIRSELH	CREDITH	INDSELH	INVCARH	PACKH	VCOMH	NETPRIH	NPRICOP	TOTCOP	REVENUE	COST	PROFIT
1	11	1	Small	Rubber	3	$4.25	$0.21	$0.15	$0.04	$0.20	$0.25	$0.05	$0.10	$3.40	$3.55	$3.50	$4.25	$10.49	$12.75	-$2.27
2	11	1	Small	Rubber	8	$6.50	$0.33	$0.40	$0.07	$0.25	$0.25	$0.05	$0.10	$3.40	$5.36	$5.36	$4.25	$42.88	$34.00	$8.88
3	11	1	Small	Rubber	9	$6.75	$0.34	$0.45	$0.07	$0.25	$0.25	$0.05	$0.10	$3.40	$5.55	$5.55	$4.25	$49.91	$38.25	$11.66
4	11	2	Small	Rubber	8	$4.00	$0.20	$0.40	$0.04	$0.30	$0.25	$0.05	$0.10	$3.40	$2.96	$3.01	$4.25	$24.08	$34.00	-$9.92
5	12	1	Small	Plastic	10	$7.00	$0.35	$0.50	$0.07	$0.15	$0.25	$0.05	$0.10	$3.60	$5.83	$5.73	$4.50	$57.30	$45.00	$12.30
6	12	1	Small	Plastic	4	$5.25	$0.26	$0.20	$0.05	$0.25	$0.25	$0.05	$0.10	$3.60	$4.39	$4.39	$4.50	$17.54	$18.00	-$0.46
7	12	1	Small	Plastic	8	$5.50	$0.28	$0.40	$0.06	$0.15	$0.25	$0.05	$0.10	$3.60	$4.52	$4.42	$4.50	$35.36	$36.00	-$0.64
8	13	1	Small	Vinyl	8	$7.50	$0.38	$0.40	$0.08	$0.15	$0.25	$0.06	$0.10	$4.40	$6.40	$6.30	$5.50	$50.40	$44.00	$6.40
9	13	1	Small	Vinyl	7	$7.75	$0.39	$0.35	$0.08	$0.30	$0.25	$0.06	$0.10	$4.40	$6.54	$6.59	$5.50	$46.10	$38.50	$7.60
10	21	1	Medium	Rubber	12	$7.25	$0.36	$0.60	$0.07	$0.35	$0.25	$0.07	$0.10	$4.80	$5.77	$5.87	$6.00	$70.38	$72.00	-$1.62
11	21	1	Medium	Rubber	4	$8.50	$0.43	$0.20	$0.09	$0.30	$0.25	$0.07	$0.10	$4.80	$7.39	$7.44	$6.00	$29.76	$24.00	$5.76
12	21	1	Medium	Rubber	9	$8.25	$0.41	$0.45	$0.08	$0.35	$0.25	$0.07	$0.10	$4.80	$6.86	$6.96	$6.00	$62.60	$54.00	$8.60
13	21	1	Medium	Rubber	8	$8.25	$0.41	$0.40	$0.08	$0.10	$0.25	$0.07	$0.10	$4.80	$7.16	$7.01	$6.00	$56.04	$48.00	$8.04
14	22	1	Medium	Plastic	5	$8.00	$0.40	$0.25	$0.08	$0.25	$0.25	$0.07	$0.10	$5.00	$6.92	$6.92	$6.25	$34.60	$31.25	$3.35
15	22	2	Medium	Plastic	9	$1.00	$0.05	$0.45	$0.01	$0.25	$0.25	$0.07	$0.10	$5.00	$0.14	$0.14	$6.25	$1.26	$56.25	-$54.99
16	23	1	Medium	Vinyl	8	$9.00	$0.45	$0.60	$0.09	$0.35	$0.25	$0.08	$0.10	$5.20	$7.61	$7.71	$6.50	$61.68	$52.00	$9.68
17	23	1	Medium	Vinyl	12	$7.25	$0.36	$0.60	$0.07	$0.10	$0.25	$0.08	$0.10	$5.20	$6.02	$5.87	$6.50	$70.38	$78.00	-$7.62
18	23	1	Medium	Vinyl	4	$9.25	$0.46	$0.20	$0.09	$0.30	$0.25	$0.08	$0.10	$5.20	$8.10	$8.15	$6.50	$32.58	$26.00	$6.58
19	31	1	Large	Rubber	10	$7.00	$0.35	$0.50	$0.07	$0.25	$0.25	$0.08	$0.10	$5.30	$5.73	$5.73	$7.00	$57.30	$70.00	-$12.70
20	31	1	Large	Rubber	7	$9.25	$0.46	$0.35	$0.09	$0.25	$0.25	$0.08	$0.10	$5.30	$8.00	$8.00	$7.00	$55.97	$49.00	$6.97
21	31	1	Large	Rubber	5	$7.00	$0.35	$0.25	$0.07	$0.35	$0.25	$0.08	$0.10	$5.30	$5.88	$5.98	$7.00	$29.90	$35.00	-$5.10
22	32	1	Large	Plastic	10	$8.25	$0.41	$0.50	$0.08	$0.25	$0.25	$0.10	$0.10	$6.70	$6.91	$6.91	$7.50	$69.05	$75.00	-$5.95
23	32	1	Large	Plastic	10	$7.75	$0.39	$0.50	$0.08	$0.25	$0.25	$0.10	$0.10	$6.70	$6.44	$6.44	$7.50	$64.35	$75.00	-$10.65
24	33	1	Large	Vinyl	10	$9.00	$0.45	$0.50	$0.09	$0.10	$0.25	$0.12	$0.10	$8.10	$7.76	$7.61	$8.25	$76.10	$82.50	-$6.40
25	33	1	Large	Vinyl	2	$10.00	$0.45	$0.10	$0.10	$0.05	$0.25	$0.12	$0.10	$8.10	$9.20	$9.00	$8.25	$18.00	$16.50	$1.50

Appendix 3.2
HYPOTHETICAL HOME-MARKET SALES SUMMARY

CONNUMH	PRIMEH	SIZEH	MATERIALH	QTYH	Weighted-Average Net Price	Total Revenue	Total Cost	Profit
11	1	Small	Rubber	20	$5.17	$103.27	$85.00	$18.27
11	2	Small	Rubber	8	$2.96	$24.08	$34.00	–$9.92
12	1	Small	Plastic	22	$5.09	$110.20	$99.00	$11.20
13	1	Small	Vinyl	15	$6.46	$96.50	$82.50	$14.00
21	1	Medium	Rubber	33	$6.60	$218.78	$198.00	$20.78
22	1	Medium	Plastic	5	$6.92	$34.60	$31.25	$3.35
22	2	Medium	Plastic	9	$0.14	$1.26	$56.25	–$54.99
23	1	Medium	Vinyl	24	$6.89	$164.64	$156.00	$8.64
31	1	Large	Rubber	22	$6.48	$143.17	$154.00	–$10.84
32	1	Large	Plastic	20	$6.67	$133.40	$150.00	–$16.60
33	1	Large	Vinyl	12	$8.00	$94.10	$99.00	–$4.90
				190	$6.09	$1,123.99	$1,145.00	–$21.02
						Profit Rate		–1.84%

Appendix 3.3
COST-TEST RESULTS

OBSH	CONNUMH	PRIMEH	QTYH	NETPRIH	NPRICOP	TOTCOP	Status	Model-Specific Quantity Above Cost	Result
1	11	1	3	$3.55	$3.50	$4.25	Below	85.00%	Pass
2	11	1	8	$5.36	$5.36	$4.25	Above	85.00%	Pass
3	11	1	9	$5.55	$5.55	$4.25	Above	85.00%	Pass
4	11	2	8	$2.96	$3.01	$4.25	Below	0.00%	Fail
5	12	1	10	$5.83	$5.73	$4.50	Above	45.45%	Pass
6	12	1	4	$4.39	$4.39	$4.50	Below	45.45%	Fail
7	12	1	8	$4.52	$4.42	$4.50	Below	45.45%	Fail
8	13	1	8	$6.40	$6.30	$5.50	Above	100.00%	Pass
9	13	1	7	$6.54	$6.59	$5.50	Above	100.00%	Pass
10	21	1	12	$5.77	$5.87	$6.00	Below	63.64%	Fail
11	21	1	4	$7.39	$7.44	$6.00	Above	63.64%	Pass
12	21	1	9	$6.86	$6.96	$6.00	Above	63.64%	Fail
13	21	1	8	$7.16	$7.01	$6.00	Above	63.64%	Fail
14	22	1	5	$6.92	$6.92	$6.25	Above	100.00%	Pass
15	22	2	9	$0.14	$0.14	$6.25	Below	0.00%	Fail
16	23	1	8	$7.61	$7.71	$6.50	Above	50.00%	Pass

(continued next page)

Appendix 3.3
Cost-Test Results *(continued)*

OBSH	CONNUMH	PRIMEH	QTYH	NETPRIH	NPRICOP	TOTCOP	Status	Model-Specific Quantity Above Cost	Result
17	23	1	12	$6.02	$5.87	$6.50	Below	50.00%	Fail
18	23	1	4	$8.10	$8.15	$6.50	Above	50.00%	Pass
19	31	1	10	$5.73	$5.73	$7.00	Below	31.82%	Fail
20	31	1	7	$8.00	$8.00	$7.00	Above	31.82%	Pass
21	31	1	5	$5.88	$5.98	$7.00	Below	31.82%	Fail
22	32	1	10	$6.91	$6.91	$7.50	Below	0.00%	Fail
23	32	1	10	$6.44	$6.44	$7.50	Below	0.00%	Fail
24	33	1	10	$7.76	$7.61	$8.25	Below	16.67%	Fail
25	33	1	2	$9.20	$9.00	$8.25	Above	16.67%	Pass

Appendix 3.4
Hypothetical Home-Market Sales List after Cost Test

OBSH	CONNUMH	PRIMEH	SIZEH	MATERIALH	QTYH	GRSUPRH	DISCREBH	MOVEH	DIRSELH	CREDITH	INDSELH	INVCARH	PACKH	VCOMH	NETPRIH	NPRICOP	TOTCOP	REVENUE	COST	PROFIT
1	11	1	Small	Rubber	3	$4.25	$0.21	$0.15	$0.04	$0.20	$0.25	$0.05	$0.10	$3.40	$3.55	$3.50	$4.25	$10.49	$12.75	−$2.27
2	11	1	Small	Rubber	8	$6.50	$0.33	$0.40	$0.07	$0.25	$0.25	$0.05	$0.10	$3.40	$5.36	$5.36	$4.25	$42.88	$34.00	$8.88
3	11	1	Small	Rubber	9	$6.75	$0.34	$0.45	$0.07	$0.25	$0.25	$0.05	$0.10	$3.40	$5.55	$5.55	$4.25	$49.91	$38.25	$11.66
5	12	1	Small	Plastic	10	$7.00	$0.35	$0.50	$0.07	$0.15	$0.25	$0.05	$0.10	$3.60	$5.83	$5.73	$4.50	$57.30	$45.00	$12.30
8	13	1	Small	Vinyl	8	$7.50	$0.38	$0.40	$0.08	$0.15	$0.25	$0.06	$0.10	$4.40	$6.40	$6.30	$5.50	$50.40	$44.00	$6.40
9	13	1	Small	Vinyl	7	$7.75	$0.39	$0.35	$0.08	$0.30	$0.25	$0.06	$0.10	$4.40	$6.54	$6.59	$5.50	$46.10	$38.50	$7.60
11	21	1	Medium	Rubber	4	$8.50	$0.43	$0.20	$0.09	$0.30	$0.25	$0.07	$0.10	$4.80	$7.39	$7.44	$6.00	$29.76	$24.00	$5.76
14	22	1	Medium	Plastic	5	$8.00	$0.40	$0.25	$0.08	$0.25	$0.25	$0.07	$0.10	$5.00	$6.92	$6.92	$6.25	$34.60	$31.25	$3.35
16	23	1	Medium	Vinyl	8	$9.00	$0.45	$0.40	$0.09	$0.35	$0.25	$0.08	$0.10	$5.20	$7.61	$7.71	$6.50	$61.68	$52.00	$9.68
18	23	1	Medium	Vinyl	4	$9.25	$0.46	$0.20	$0.09	$0.30	$0.25	$0.08	$0.10	$5.20	$8.10	$8.15	$6.50	$32.58	$26.00	$6.58
20	31	1	Large	Rubber	7	$9.25	$0.46	$0.35	$0.09	$0.25	$0.25	$0.08	$0.10	$5.30	$8.00	$8.00	$7.00	$55.97	$49.00	$6.97
25	33	1	Large	Vinyl	2	$10.00	$0.45	$0.10	$0.10	$0.05	$0.25	$0.12	$0.10	$8.10	$9.20	$9.00	$8.25	$18.00	$16.50	$1.50

Appendix 3.5

HYPOTHETICAL HOME-MARKET SALES SUMMARY AFTER COST TEST

CONNUMH	PRIMEH	SIZEH	MATERIALH	QTYH	Weighted-Average Net Price	Total Revenue	Total Cost	Profit
11	1	Small	Rubber	20	$5.17	$103.27	$85.00	$18.27
12	1	Small	Plastic	10	$5.83	$57.30	$45.00	$12.30
13	1	Small	Vinyl	15	$6.46	$96.50	$82.50	$14.00
21	1	Medium	Rubber	4	$7.39	$29.76	$24.00	$5.76
22	1	Medium	Plastic	5	$6.92	$34.60	$31.25	$3.35
23	1	Medium	Vinyl	12	$7.77	$94.26	$78.00	$16.26
31	1	Large	Rubber	7	$8.00	$55.97	$49.00	$6.97
33	1	Large	Vinyl	2	$9.20	$18.00	$16.50	$1.50
				75	$6.54	$489.65	$411.25	$78.40

Profit Rate 19.06%

To Be Used for CV Calculations

Direct Selling Expenses	DSELLH	$0.33
Indirect Selling Expenses	ISELLH	$0.32
Profit	PROFIT	19.06%

Appendix 3.6
Hypothetical U.S. Sales List

OBSU	CONNUMU	PRIMEU	SIZEU	MATERIALU	SALEU	QTYU	GRSUPRU	DISCREBU	MOVEU	DIRSELU	CREDITU	DINDSELU	DINVCARU	INDSELU	INVCARU	PACKU	VCOMU	TCOMU
1	11	1	Small	Rubber	EP	5	$5.50	$0.42	$0.45	$0.05	$0.20	$0.25	$0.05	$0.00	$0.00	$0.15	$3.40	$3.91
2	11	1	Small	Rubber	EP	7	$6.20	$0.00	$0.55	$0.00	$0.25	$0.25	$0.05	$0.00	$0.00	$0.15	$3.40	$3.91
3	11	1	Small	Rubber	EP	5	$5.20	$0.00	$0.45	$0.00	$0.35	$0.25	$0.05	$0.00	$0.00	$0.15	$3.40	$3.91
4	11	1	Small	Rubber	CEP	8	$5.70	$0.00	$0.65	$0.05	$0.25	$0.25	$0.05	$0.10	$0.01	$0.15	$3.40	$3.91
5	11	2	Small	Rubber	EP	8	$4.00	$0.22	$0.60	$0.00	$0.30	$0.25	$0.05	$0.00	$0.00	$0.15	$3.40	$3.91
6	12	1	Small	Plastic	EP	10	$7.20	$0.62	$0.70	$0.10	$0.15	$0.25	$0.05	$0.00	$0.00	$0.15	$3.60	$4.14
7	12	1	Small	Plastic	EP	12	$6.20	$0.00	$0.80	$0.00	$0.10	$0.25	$0.05	$0.00	$0.00	$0.15	$3.60	$4.14
8	12	1	Small	Plastic	EP	9	$7.20	$0.00	$0.65	$0.00	$0.25	$0.25	$0.05	$0.00	$0.00	$0.15	$3.60	$4.14
9	12	1	Small	Plastic	EP	4	$6.20	$0.00	$0.40	$0.00	$0.25	$0.25	$0.05	$0.00	$0.00	$0.15	$3.60	$4.14
10	12	1	Small	Plastic	CEP	8	$6.60	$0.52	$0.65	$0.10	$0.15	$0.25	$0.05	$0.10	$0.01	$0.15	$3.60	$4.14
11	13	1	Small	Vinyl	EP	5	$7.20	$0.00	$0.45	$0.00	$0.30	$0.25	$0.06	$0.00	$0.00	$0.15	$4.40	$5.06
12	13	1	Small	Vinyl	EP	8	$8.20	$0.00	$0.60	$0.00	$0.25	$0.25	$0.06	$0.00	$0.00	$0.15	$4.40	$5.06
13	13	1	Small	Vinyl	EP	5	$8.20	$0.72	$0.45	$0.10	$0.30	$0.25	$0.06	$0.00	$0.00	$0.15	$4.40	$5.06
14	13	1	Small	Vinyl	EP	8	$8.20	$0.72	$0.60	$0.00	$0.15	$0.25	$0.06	$0.00	$0.00	$0.15	$4.40	$5.06
15	13	1	Small	Vinyl	CEP	7	$8.50	$0.72	$0.60	$0.00	$0.30	$0.25	$0.06	$0.10	$0.01	$0.15	$4.40	$5.06
16	21	1	Medium	Rubber	EP	10	$9.20	$0.00	$0.70	$0.00	$0.35	$0.25	$0.07	$0.00	$0.00	$0.15	$4.80	$5.52
17	21	1	Medium	Rubber	EP	12	$8.20	$0.72	$0.80	$0.00	$0.35	$0.25	$0.07	$0.00	$0.00	$0.15	$4.80	$5.52
18	21	1	Medium	Rubber	EP	4	$9.20	$0.00	$0.40	$0.10	$0.30	$0.25	$0.07	$0.10	$0.01	$0.15	$4.80	$5.52
19	21	1	Medium	Rubber	CEP	9	$8.35	$0.72	$0.70	$0.00	$0.35	$0.25	$0.07	$0.10	$0.01	$0.15	$4.80	$5.52
20	21	1	Medium	Rubber	CEP	8	$8.35	$0.00	$0.65	$0.00	$0.10	$0.25	$0.07	$0.10	$0.01	$0.15	$4.80	$5.52
21	22	1	Medium	Plastic	EP	8	$9.20	$0.00	$0.60	$0.00	$0.10	$0.25	$0.07	$0.00	$0.00	$0.15	$5.00	$5.75
22	22	1	Medium	Plastic	EP	7	$8.20	$0.00	$0.55	$0.10	$0.10	$0.25	$0.07	$0.00	$0.00	$0.15	$5.00	$5.75
23	22	1	Medium	Plastic	EP	10	$8.20	$0.00	$0.70	$0.00	$0.25	$0.25	$0.07	$0.10	$0.01	$0.15	$5.00	$5.75
24	22	1	Medium	Plastic	CEP	5	$8.35	$0.72	$0.50	$0.00	$0.25	$0.25	$0.07	$0.10	$0.01	$0.15	$5.00	$5.75
25	22	2	Medium	Plastic	EP	9	$4.20	$0.00	$0.65	$0.00	$0.25	$0.25	$0.07	$0.00	$0.00	$0.15	$5.00	$5.75
26	23	1	Medium	Vinyl	EP	8	$8.20	$0.00	$0.60	$0.10	$0.30	$0.25	$0.08	$0.00	$0.00	$0.15	$5.20	$5.98
27	23	1	Medium	Vinyl	EP	5	$9.20	$0.82	$0.45	$0.00	$0.15	$0.25	$0.08	$0.00	$0.00	$0.15	$5.20	$5.98

(continued next page)

93

Appendix 3.6
Hypothetical U.S. Sales List (continued)

OBSU	CONNUMU	PRIMEU	SIZEU	MATERIALU	SALEU	QTYU	GRSUPRU	DISCREBU	MOVEU	DIRSELU	CREDITU	DINDSELU	DINVCARU	INDSELU	INVCARU	PACKU	VCOMU	TCOMU
28	23	1	Medium	Vinyl	EP	12	$10.20	$0.00	$0.80	$0.00	$0.35	$0.25	$0.08	$0.00	$0.00	$0.15	$5.20	$5.98
29	23	1	Medium	Vinyl	EP	8	$9.00	$0.00	$0.60	$0.00	$0.10	$0.25	$0.08	$0.00	$0.00	$0.15	$5.20	$5.98
30	23	1	Medium	Vinyl	CEP	4	$9.35	$0.00	$0.45	$0.00	$0.30	$0.25	$0.08	$0.10	$0.02	$0.15	$5.20	$5.98
31	31	1	Large	Rubber	EP	9	$8.20	$0.72	$0.65	$0.00	$0.20	$0.25	$0.08	$0.00	$0.00	$0.15	$5.30	$6.44
32	31	1	Large	Rubber	EP	8	$9.20	$0.00	$0.60	$0.00	$0.30	$0.25	$0.08	$0.00	$0.00	$0.15	$5.30	$6.44
33	31	1	Large	Rubber	EP	10	$5.20	$0.42	$0.70	$0.10	$0.25	$0.25	$0.08	$0.00	$0.00	$0.15	$5.30	$6.44
34	31	1	Large	Rubber	EP	7	$11.20	$0.00	$0.55	$0.00	$0.25	$0.25	$0.08	$0.00	$0.00	$0.15	$5.30	$6.44
35	31	1	Large	Rubber	CEP	5	$8.50	$0.00	$0.50	$0.00	$0.35	$0.25	$0.08	$0.10	$0.02	$0.15	$5.30	$6.44
36	32	1	Large	Plastic	EP	5	$9.20	$0.00	$0.45	$0.00	$0.25	$0.25	$0.09	$0.00	$0.00	$0.15	$6.70	$6.90
37	32	1	Large	Plastic	EP	9	$8.20	$0.72	$0.65	$0.00	$0.30	$0.25	$0.09	$0.00	$0.00	$0.15	$6.70	$6.90
38	32	1	Large	Plastic	EP	8	$9.20	$0.82	$0.60	$0.00	$0.30	$0.25	$0.09	$0.00	$0.00	$0.15	$6.70	$6.90
39	32	1	Large	Plastic	CEP	7	$6.00	$0.42	$0.60	$0.00	$0.10	$0.25	$0.09	$0.10	$0.02	$0.15	$6.70	$6.90
40	32	1	Large	Plastic	CEP	10	$8.35	$0.00	$0.75	$0.00	$0.25	$0.25	$0.09	$0.10	$0.02	$0.15	$6.70	$6.90
41	34	1	Large	Aluminum	EP	12	$11.20	$0.00	$0.80	$0.00	$0.15	$0.25	$0.10	$0.00	$0.00	$0.15	$8.25	$8.50
42	34	1	Large	Aluminum	EP	10	$10.20	$0.92	$0.70	$0.10	$0.35	$0.25	$0.10	$0.00	$0.00	$0.15	$8.25	$8.50
43	34	1	Large	Aluminum	EP	10	$10.20	$0.00	$0.70	$0.00	$0.10	$0.25	$0.10	$0.00	$0.00	$0.15	$8.25	$8.50
44	34	1	Large	Aluminum	EP	7	$10.20	$0.00	$0.55	$0.00	$0.20	$0.25	$0.10	$0.00	$0.00	$0.15	$8.25	$8.50
45	34	1	Large	Aluminum	CEP	5	$10.35	$0.00	$0.50	$0.00	$0.15	$0.25	$0.10	$0.10	$0.02	$0.15	$8.25	$8.50

Appendix 3.7
CEP Profit Calculations

		From U.S. Sales List						From Home-Market Sales List			
OBSU	CONNUMU	Total Revenue	Total Selling Exp.	Total Move Exp.	Total COP	OBSH	CONNUMH	Total Revenue	Total Selling Exp.	Total Move Exp.	Total COP
1	11	$27.50	$3.60	$2.25	$22.00	1	11	$12.75	$1.52	$0.45	$13.05
2	11	$43.40	$1.75	$3.85	$30.80	2	11	$52.00	$5.12	$3.20	$34.80
3	11	$26.00	$1.25	$2.25	$22.00	3	11	$60.75	$5.90	$4.05	$39.15
4	11	$45.60	$3.20	$5.20	$35.20	4	11	$32.00	$3.92	$3.20	$34.80
5	11	$32.00	$3.76	$4.80	$35.20	5	12	$70.00	$6.70	$5.00	$46.00
6	12	$72.00	$9.70	$7.00	$46.50	6	12	$21.00	$2.26	$0.80	$18.40
7	12	$74.40	$3.00	$9.60	$55.80	7	12	$44.00	$4.64	$3.20	$36.80
8	12	$64.80	$2.25	$5.85	$41.85	8	13	$60.00	$5.60	$3.20	$44.80
9	12	$24.80	$1.00	$1.60	$18.60	9	13	$54.25	$5.01	$2.45	$39.20
10	12	$52.80	$7.76	$5.20	$37.20	10	21	$87.00	$8.22	$7.20	$73.20
11	13	$36.00	$1.25	$2.25	$28.25	11	21	$34.00	$3.04	$0.80	$24.40
12	13	$65.60	$2.00	$4.80	$45.20	12	21	$74.25	$6.71	$4.05	$54.90
13	13	$41.00	$5.35	$2.25	$28.25	13	21	$66.00	$5.96	$3.20	$48.80
14	13	$65.60	$7.76	$4.80	$45.20	14	22	$40.00	$3.65	$1.25	$31.75
15	13	$59.50	$7.49	$4.20	$39.55	15	22	$9.00	$2.79	$4.05	$57.15
16	21	$92.00	$2.50	$7.00	$61.50	16	23	$72.00	$6.32	$3.20	$52.80
17	21	$98.40	$11.64	$9.60	$73.80	17	23	$87.00	$8.22	$7.20	$79.20
18	21	$36.80	$1.40	$1.60	$24.60	18	23	$37.00	$3.22	$0.80	$26.40
19	21	$75.15	$9.63	$6.30	$55.35	19	31	$70.00	$6.70	$5.00	$71.00
20	21	$66.80	$2.80	$5.20	$49.20	20	31	$64.75	$5.64	$2.45	$49.70
21	22	$73.60	$2.00	$4.80	$51.20	21	31	$35.00	$3.35	$1.25	$35.50
22	22	$57.40	$2.45	$3.85	$44.80	22	32	$82.50	$7.45	$5.00	$76.00

(continued next page)

Appendix 3.7
CEP Profit Calculations *(continued)*

| | | From U.S. Sales List | | | | | | From Home-Market Sales List | | | |
OBSU	CONNUMU	Total Revenue	Total Selling Exp.	Total Move Exp.	Total COP	OBSH	CONNUMH	Total Revenue	Total Selling Exp.	Total Move Exp.	Total COP
23	22	$82.00	$2.50	$7.00	$64.00	23	32	$77.50	$7.15	$5.00	$76.00
24	22	$41.75	$5.35	$2.50	$32.00	24	33	$90.00	$7.90	$5.00	$83.50
25	22	$37.80	$2.25	$5.85	$57.60	25	33	$20.00	$1.60	$0.20	$16.70
26	23	$65.60	$2.80	$4.80	$53.20						
27	23	$46.00	$5.35	$2.25	$33.25						
28	23	$122.40	$3.00	$9.60	$79.80						
29	23	$72.00	$2.00	$4.80	$53.20						
30	23	$37.40	$1.40	$1.80	$26.60						
31	31	$73.80	$8.73	$5.85	$64.35						
32	31	$73.60	$2.00	$4.80	$57.20						
33	31	$52.00	$7.70	$7.00	$71.50						
34	31	$78.40	$1.75	$3.85	$50.05						
35	31	$42.50	$1.75	$2.50	$35.75						
36	32	$46.00	$1.25	$2.25	$38.25						
37	32	$73.80	$8.73	$5.85	$68.85						
38	32	$73.60	$8.56	$4.80	$61.20						
39	32	$42.00	$5.39	$4.20	$53.55						
40	32	$83.50	$3.50	$7.50	$76.50						
41	34	$134.40	$3.00	$9.60	$106.80						
42	34	$102.00	$12.70	$7.00	$89.00						

(continued)

From U.S. Sales List

OBSU	CONNUMU	Total Revenue	Total Selling Exp.	Total Move Exp.	Total COP
43	34	$102.00	$2.50	$7.00	$89.00
44	34	$71.40	$1.75	$3.85	$62.30
45	34	$51.75	$1.75	$2.50	$44.50
Total		$2,836.85	$189.25	$221.40	$2,260.50

From Home-Market Sales List

OBSH	CONNUMH	Total Revenue	Total Selling Exp.	Total Move Exp.	Total COP
		$1,352.75	$128.57	$81.20	$1,164.00

CEP Profit Summary

	Total Revenue	Total Selling Exp.	Total Move Exp.	Total COP	Total Profit
U.S. Total	$2,836.85	$189.25	$221.40	$2,260.50	$165.70
H.M. Total	$1,352.75	$128.57	$81.20	$1,164.00	−$21.02
Total	$4,189.60	$317.82	$302.60	$3,424.50	$144.69

CEP Profit Rate — 3.58%

Appendix 3.8
Hypothetical U.S. Sales—Net Price Calculations

OBSU	CONNUMU	PRIMEU	SALEU	QTYU	GRSUPRU	DISCREBU	MOVEU	DIRSELU	CREDITU	DINDSELU	DINVCARU	INDSELU	INVCARU	PACKU	CEPPROFIT	NETPRIU	DIREXPU	PACKINGU
1	11	1	EP	5	$5.50	$0.42	$0.45	$0.05	$0.20	$0.25	$0.05	$0.00	$0.00	$0.15	$0.000	$4.63	$0.25	$0.15
2	11	1	EP	7	$6.20	$0.00	$0.55	$0.00	$0.25	$0.25	$0.05	$0.00	$0.00	$0.15	$0.000	$5.65	$0.25	$0.15
3	11	1	EP	5	$5.20	$0.00	$0.45	$0.00	$0.35	$0.25	$0.05	$0.00	$0.00	$0.15	$0.000	$4.75	$0.35	$0.15
4	11	1	CEP	8	$5.70	$0.00	$0.65	$0.05	$0.25	$0.25	$0.05	$0.00	$0.01	$0.15	$0.015	$4.63	$0.30	$0.15
5	11	2	EP	8	$4.00	$0.22	$0.60	$0.00	$0.30	$0.25	$0.05	$0.00	$0.00	$0.15	$0.000	$3.18	$0.25	$0.15
6	12	1	EP	10	$7.20	$0.62	$0.70	$0.10	$0.15	$0.25	$0.05	$0.00	$0.00	$0.15	$0.000	$5.88	$0.30	$0.15
7	12	1	EP	12	$6.20	$0.00	$0.80	$0.00	$0.10	$0.25	$0.05	$0.00	$0.00	$0.15	$0.000	$5.40	$0.10	$0.15
8	12	1	EP	9	$7.20	$0.00	$0.65	$0.00	$0.25	$0.25	$0.05	$0.00	$0.00	$0.15	$0.000	$6.55	$0.25	$0.15
9	12	1	EP	4	$6.20	$0.00	$0.40	$0.00	$0.25	$0.25	$0.05	$0.00	$0.00	$0.15	$0.000	$5.80	$0.25	$0.15
10	12	1	CEP	8	$6.60	$0.52	$0.65	$0.10	$0.15	$0.25	$0.05	$0.10	$0.01	$0.15	$0.032	$5.04	$0.25	$0.15
11	13	1	EP	5	$7.20	$0.00	$0.45	$0.00	$0.30	$0.25	$0.06	$0.00	$0.00	$0.15	$0.000	$6.75	$0.30	$0.15
12	13	1	EP	8	$8.20	$0.00	$0.60	$0.00	$0.25	$0.25	$0.06	$0.00	$0.00	$0.15	$0.000	$7.60	$0.25	$0.15
13	13	1	EP	5	$8.20	$0.72	$0.45	$0.10	$0.30	$0.25	$0.06	$0.00	$0.00	$0.15	$0.000	$7.03	$0.40	$0.15
14	13	1	EP	8	$8.20	$0.72	$0.60	$0.00	$0.15	$0.25	$0.06	$0.00	$0.00	$0.15	$0.000	$6.88	$0.15	$0.15
15	13	1	CEP	7	$8.50	$0.72	$0.60	$0.00	$0.30	$0.25	$0.06	$0.10	$0.01	$0.15	$0.041	$6.73	$0.30	$0.15
16	21	1	EP	10	$9.20	$0.00	$0.70	$0.00	$0.35	$0.25	$0.07	$0.00	$0.00	$0.15	$0.000	$8.50	$0.35	$0.15
17	21	1	EP	12	$8.20	$0.72	$0.80	$0.10	$0.35	$0.25	$0.07	$0.00	$0.00	$0.15	$0.000	$6.68	$0.35	$0.15
18	21	1	EP	4	$9.20	$0.00	$0.40	$0.00	$0.30	$0.25	$0.07	$0.00	$0.00	$0.15	$0.000	$8.80	$0.40	$0.15
19	21	1	CEP	9	$8.35	$0.72	$0.70	$0.00	$0.35	$0.25	$0.07	$0.10	$0.01	$0.15	$0.042	$6.42	$0.35	$0.15
20	21	1	CEP	8	$8.35	$0.00	$0.65	$0.00	$0.10	$0.25	$0.07	$0.10	$0.01	$0.15	$0.008	$7.48	$0.10	$0.15
21	22	1	EP	8	$9.20	$0.00	$0.60	$0.00	$0.10	$0.25	$0.07	$0.00	$0.00	$0.15	$0.000	$8.60	$0.10	$0.15
22	22	1	EP	7	$8.20	$0.00	$0.55	$0.10	$0.10	$0.25	$0.07	$0.00	$0.00	$0.15	$0.000	$7.65	$0.20	$0.15
23	22	1	EP	10	$8.20	$0.00	$0.70	$0.00	$0.25	$0.25	$0.07	$0.10	$0.01	$0.15	$0.039	$7.50	$0.25	$0.15
24	22	1	CEP	5	$8.35	$0.72	$0.50	$0.00	$0.25	$0.25	$0.07	$0.00	$0.00	$0.15	$0.000	$6.73	$0.25	$0.15
25	23	2	EP	9	$4.20	$0.00	$0.65	$0.10	$0.30	$0.25	$0.08	$0.00	$0.00	$0.15	$0.000	$3.55	$0.25	$0.15
26	23	1	EP	8	$8.20	$0.00	$0.60	$0.00	$0.15	$0.25	$0.08	$0.00	$0.00	$0.15	$0.000	$7.60	$0.40	$0.15
27	23	1	EP	5	$9.20	$0.82	$0.45	$0.00	$0.35	$0.25	$0.08	$0.00	$0.00	$0.15	$0.000	$7.93	$0.15	$0.15
28	23	1	EP	12	$10.20	$0.00	$0.80	$0.00	$0.35	$0.25	$0.08	$0.00	$0.00	$0.15	$0.000	$9.40	$0.35	$0.15
29	23	1	EP	8	$9.00	$0.00	$0.60	$0.00	$0.10	$0.25	$0.08	$0.00	$0.00	$0.15	$0.000	$8.40	$0.10	$0.15

(continued)

OBSU	CONNUMU	PRIMEU	SALEU	QTYU	GRSUPRU	DISCREBU	MOVEU	DIRSELU	CREDITU	DINDSELU	DINVCARU	INDSELU	INVCARU	PACKU	CEPPROFIT	NETPRIU	DIREXPU	PACKINGU
30	23	1	CEP	4	$9.35	$0.00	$0.45	$0.00	$0.30	$0.25	$0.08	$0.10	$0.02	$0.15	$0.015	$8.47	$0.30	$0.15
31	31	1	EP	9	$8.20	$0.72	$0.65	$0.00	$0.20	$0.25	$0.08	$0.00	$0.00	$0.15	$0.000	$6.83	$0.20	$0.15
32	31	1	EP	8	$9.20	$0.00	$0.60	$0.00	$0.30	$0.25	$0.08	$0.00	$0.00	$0.15	$0.000	$8.60	$0.30	$0.15
33	31	1	EP	10	$5.20	$0.42	$0.70	$0.10	$0.25	$0.25	$0.08	$0.00	$0.00	$0.15	$0.000	$4.08	$0.35	$0.15
34	31	1	EP	7	$11.20	$0.00	$0.55	$0.00	$0.25	$0.25	$0.08	$0.00	$0.00	$0.15	$0.000	$10.65	$0.25	$0.15
35	31	1	CEP	5	$8.50	$0.00	$0.50	$0.00	$0.35	$0.25	$0.08	$0.10	$0.02	$0.15	$0.017	$7.52	$0.35	$0.15
36	32	1	EP	5	$9.20	$0.00	$0.45	$0.00	$0.25	$0.25	$0.09	$0.00	$0.00	$0.15	$0.000	$8.75	$0.25	$0.15
37	32	1	EP	9	$8.20	$0.72	$0.65	$0.00	$0.30	$0.25	$0.09	$0.00	$0.00	$0.15	$0.000	$6.83	$0.30	$0.15
38	32	1	EP	8	$9.20	$0.82	$0.60	$0.00	$0.10	$0.25	$0.09	$0.10	$0.02	$0.15	$0.023	$7.78	$0.10	$0.15
39	32	1	CEP	7	$6.00	$0.42	$0.60	$0.00	$0.25	$0.25	$0.09	$0.10	$0.02	$0.15	$0.013	$4.74	$0.25	$0.15
40	32	1	CEP	10	$8.35	$0.00	$0.75	$0.00	$0.15	$0.25	$0.10	$0.00	$0.00	$0.15	$0.000	$7.22	$0.15	$0.15
41	34	1	EP	12	$11.20	$0.00	$0.80	$0.10	$0.35	$0.25	$0.10	$0.00	$0.00	$0.15	$0.000	$10.40	$0.45	$0.15
42	34	1	EP	10	$10.20	$0.92	$0.70	$0.00	$0.10	$0.25	$0.10	$0.00	$0.00	$0.15	$0.000	$8.58	$0.10	$0.15
43	34	1	EP	10	$10.20	$0.00	$0.70	$0.00	$0.20	$0.25	$0.10	$0.00	$0.00	$0.15	$0.000	$9.50	$0.20	$0.15
44	34	1	EP	7	$10.20	$0.00	$0.55	$0.00	$0.20	$0.25	$0.10	$0.00	$0.00	$0.15	$0.000	$9.65	$0.20	$0.15
45	34	1	CEP	5	$10.35	$0.00	$0.50	$0.00	$0.15	$0.25	$0.10	$0.10	$0.02	$0.15	$0.010	$9.57	$0.15	$0.15

Appendix 3.9
AVERAGE NET U.S. PRICES

CONNUMU	PRIMEU	SALEU	QTYU	Weighted Average Price	Weighted Average Direct Exp.	Weighted Average Pack Exp.
11	1	CEP	8	$4.63	$0.30	$0.15
11	1	EP	17	$5.09	$0.28	$0.15
11	2	EP	8	$3.18	$0.30	$0.15
12	1	CEP	8	$5.04	$0.25	$0.15
12	1	EP	35	$5.88	$0.20	$0.15
13	1	CEP	7	$6.73	$0.30	$0.15
13	1	EP	26	$7.11	$0.26	$0.15
21	1	CEP	17	$6.92	$0.23	$0.15
21	1	EP	26	$7.71	$0.36	$0.15
22	1	CEP	5	$6.73	$0.25	$0.15
22	1	EP	25	$7.89	$0.19	$0.15
22	2	EP	9	$3.55	$0.25	$0.15
23	1	CEP	4	$8.47	$0.30	$0.15
23	1	EP	33	$8.50	$0.27	$0.15
31	1	CEP	5	$7.52	$0.35	$0.15
31	1	EP	34	$7.22	$0.28	$0.15
32	1	CEP	17	$6.20	$0.19	$0.15
32	1	EP	22	$7.61	$0.29	$0.15
34	1	CEP	5	$9.57	$0.15	$0.15
34	1	EP	39	$9.57	$0.22	$0.15
			350	$7.14		

Appendix 3.10
Hypothetical Dumping Margin Calculations

CONNUMU	PRIMEU	SALEU	QTYU	NETPRIU	CONNUMH	PRIMEH	NETPRIH	TOTCOP	DIFMER	HMDSEL	HMISEL
11	1	CEP	8	$4.63	11	1	$5.17	N/A	$0.00	N/A	N/A
11	1	EP	17	$5.09	11	1	$5.17	N/A	$0.00	N/A	N/A
11	2	EP	8	$3.18	11	1	$5.17	N/A	$0.00	N/A	N/A
12	1	CEP	8	$5.04	12	1	$5.83	N/A	$0.00	N/A	N/A
12	1	EP	35	$5.88	12	1	$5.83	N/A	$0.00	N/A	N/A
13	1	CEP	7	$6.73	13	1	$6.46	N/A	$0.00	N/A	N/A
13	1	EP	26	$7.11	13	1	$6.46	N/A	$0.00	N/A	N/A
21	1	CEP	17	$6.92	21	1	$7.39	N/A	$0.00	N/A	N/A
21	1	EP	26	$7.71	21	1	$7.39	N/A	$0.00	N/A	N/A
22	1	CEP	5	$6.73	22	1	$6.92	N/A	$0.00	N/A	N/A
22	1	EP	25	$7.89	22	1	$6.92	N/A	$0.00	N/A	N/A
22	2	EP	9	$3.55	22	1	$6.92	N/A	$0.00	N/A	N/A
23	1	CEP	4	$8.47	23	1	$7.77	N/A	$0.00	N/A	N/A
23	1	EP	33	$8.50	23	1	$7.77	N/A	$0.00	N/A	N/A
31	1	CEP	5	$7.52	31	1	$8.00	N/A	$0.00	N/A	N/A
31	1	EP	34	$7.22	31	1	$8.00	N/A	$0.00	N/A	N/A
32	1	CEP	17	$6.20	CV	N/A	N/A	$7.50	$0.00	0.33	0.32
32	1	EP	22	$7.61	CV	N/A	N/A	$7.50	$0.00	0.33	0.32
34	1	CEP	5	$9.57	33	1	$9.20	N/A	$0.15	N/A	N/A
34	1	EP	39	$9.57	33	1	$9.20	N/A	$0.15	N/A	N/A

(continued next page)

101

Appendix 3.10

HYPOTHETICAL DUMPING MARGIN CALCULATIONS *(continued)*

CONNUMU	DIREXPU	PACKU	CVPROF	TOTCV	CV	FUPDOL	UMARGIN	EMARGIN	TOTPUDD	VALUE	PCTMARG
11	$0.30	$0.15	N/A	N/A	N/A	$5.32	$0.69	$5.52	$5.52	$37.04	14.90%
11	$0.28	$0.15	N/A	N/A	N/A	$5.60	$0.51	$8.74	$8.74	$86.45	10.11%
11	$0.30	$0.15	N/A	N/A	N/A	$5.62	$2.44	$19.52	$19.52	$25.44	76.73%
12	$0.25	$0.15	N/A	N/A	N/A	$5.98	$0.94	$7.52	$7.52	$40.32	18.65%
12	$0.20	$0.15	N/A	N/A	N/A	$6.18	$0.30	$10.50	$10.50	$205.75	5.10%
13	$0.30	$0.15	N/A	N/A	N/A	$6.61	−$0.12	−$0.84	$0.00	$47.11	0.00%
13	$0.26	$0.15	N/A	N/A	N/A	$6.87	−$0.24	−$6.18	$0.00	$184.74	0.00%
21	$0.23	$0.15	N/A	N/A	N/A	$7.54	$0.62	$10.54	$10.54	$117.64	8.96%
21	$0.36	$0.15	N/A	N/A	N/A	$7.90	$0.19	$4.88	$4.88	$200.46	2.43%
22	$0.25	$0.15	N/A	N/A	N/A	$7.07	$0.34	$1.70	$1.70	$33.65	5.05%
22	$0.19	$0.15	N/A	N/A	N/A	$7.26	−$0.64	−$15.90	$0.00	$197.35	0.00%
22	$0.25	$0.15	N/A	N/A	N/A	$7.32	$3.77	$33.93	$33.93	$31.95	106.20%
23	$0.30	$0.15	N/A	N/A	N/A	$7.92	−$0.55	−$2.20	$0.00	$33.88	0.00%
23	$0.27	$0.15	N/A	N/A	N/A	$8.19	−$0.31	−$10.14	$0.00	$280.45	0.00%
31	$0.35	$0.15	N/A	N/A	N/A	$8.15	$0.63	$3.15	$3.15	$37.60	8.38%
31	$0.28	$0.15	N/A	N/A	N/A	$8.43	$1.20	$40.93	$40.93	$245.62	16.66%
32	$0.19	$0.15	$1.58	$9.88	$9.55	$9.55	$3.35	$56.98	$56.98	$105.40	54.06%
32	$0.29	$0.15	$1.58	$9.88	$9.55	$9.84	$2.23	$49.03	$49.03	$167.46	29.28%
34	$0.15	$0.15	N/A	N/A	N/A	$9.50	−$0.07	−$0.35	$0.00	$47.85	0.00%
34	$0.22	$0.15	N/A	N/A	N/A	$9.72	$0.16	$6.05	$6.05	$373.15	1.62%
							$0.16	$223.39	$259.00	$2,499.31	10.36%

Calculated AD Margin 10.36%
Non-zeroed Margin 8.94%

4. The Antidumping Contagion

The U.S. debate over antidumping policy has been a woefully lopsided affair, dominated overwhelmingly by the industries that use the law against foreign competition and their champions in Congress and the executive branch. But despite antidumping supporters' success in framing the issue in "us-vs.-them" terms—with American import-competing industries on one side and foreign "unfair traders" and their governments on the other—the fact is that many vitally important American constituencies have a strong stake in antidumping reform.

Most obviously, American import-using industries and consumers suffer when antidumping measures increase the price or interfere with the availability of foreign-sourced raw materials, equipment, components, and goods. Their interests, and the overall national interest in strong economic performance, would be well served by new restraints on antidumping abuses.

Another powerful constituency also stands to benefit from improved antidumping rules. Although this group is usually at the very center of U.S. trade policy concerns, its interests with respect to antidumping have up to now been almost completely ignored. The constituency in question is U.S. exporters, whose interest lies, not in the U.S. law, but in the proliferating tangle of foreign antidumping laws and the growing threat they pose to market access abroad.

It is therefore imperative that the focus of the antidumping debate here in the United States be broadened. Policymakers need to lift their sights and recognize that more than 70 countries now have antidumping laws. They should recognize further that, as a result, U.S. exports—and the vitality of the world trading system—are increasingly being cut up in the crossfire.

Backdoor Protectionism

Antidumping laws have been around a long time. The U.S. law dates back to 1921, and laws in Canada, Australia, New Zealand,

Great Britain, and France go back even further.[1] But until the past couple of decades, those laws were sparingly invoked and even more stingily applied. In the United States, for example, there was a total of 706 antidumping investigations between 1921 and 1967, or about 15 per year, but a mere 75 of them resulted in relief for the petitioning industries.[2]

Changes in the laws during the 1970s and 1980s expanded antidumping protectionism dramatically. The big breakthrough occurred in 1974, when the U.S. law was amended to provide for use of the cost test, the exclusion of below-cost sales in the comparison market, and the use of constructed value when too many sales are excluded. This change made it much easier to find dumping, and it produced substantially higher dumping margins.[3] Other countries followed suit, and the result was an explosion of antidumping cases in the 1980s. The United States initiated 398 investigations between January 1980 and June 1989, or roughly 40 per year; Australia, the European Community, and Canada combined initiated 1,091 new cases over the same period.[4]

Despite the dramatic surge in cases, the number of jurisdictions resorting to antidumping protectionism remained small. The antidumping fraternity was almost exclusively a rich countries' club: the United States, the European Community (now Union), Canada, Australia, and New Zealand accounted for virtually all antidumping activity worldwide. Between January 1980 and June 1987, a mere seven investigations were initiated by developing countries.[5]

The major reason for this exclusivity was that antidumping measures would have been superfluous in most countries. Until the 1980s, developing countries typically maintained extremely protectionist trade policies: not only high tariffs, but also quotas and restrictive import-license schemes. Under the old General Agreement on Tariffs and Trade, such policies were winked at with the excuse that they were a necessary response to balance-of-payment difficulties.[6] Accordingly, there was no need to employ a protectionist tool as complicated, cumbersome, and difficult to use as antidumping.

Over the past couple of decades, however, many developing countries have engaged in sweeping trade liberalization. Furthermore, they have "locked in" many of their reforms by making them binding commitments under WTO agreements. Meanwhile, import-competing industries in those countries have had to contend with unprecedented competitive pressure from abroad. Faced with demands from

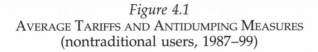

Figure 4.1
AVERAGE TARIFFS AND ANTIDUMPING MEASURES
(nontraditional users, 1987–99)

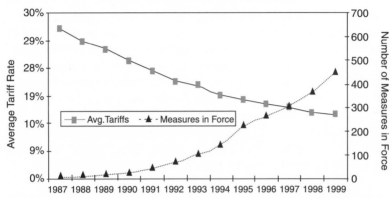

SOURCE: Tariff data, World Bank; Antidumping data, WTP Reports in
G/ADP/N series

struggling domestic industries to alleviate that pressure, but constrained by their WTO commitments, governments in the developing world have turned to the backdoor protectionism of antidumping measures.

Figure 4.1 tells the story. Antidumping measures by countries other than the traditional users[7] have skyrocketed as tariff levels in those countries have fallen. Country after country has charged through the antidumping loophole. The number of antidumping users shot up from 12 at the end of 1993 to 38 as of June 2002.[8] As of October 2002, a total of 71 jurisdictions (including the 15 countries of the European Union as a single jurisdiction) reported having antidumping legislation in their books.[9] As developing and postcommunist countries have rushed to join the antidumping club, the result has been another quantum leap in antidumping activity. A total of 2,483 investigations were initiated worldwide during 1990–99—a more than 50 percent increase over the record of the 1980s.[10]

The proliferation of antidumping protectionism began in the late 1980s as Mexico, Brazil, Argentina, and other countries joined the traditional users at the antidumping banquet table. The number of antidumping measures has accelerated greatly, though, since the

105

completion of the Uruguay Round in 1994. During the period of 1990 through 1994, 1,254 antidumping cases were initiated around the world.[11] The traditional users accounted for 63 percent of those initiations. The remaining 37 percent were initiated by numerous developing countries, most notably Mexico, Brazil, and Argentina.

During the second half of the decade, the user profile changed significantly. While the number of initiations trailed off slightly to 1,229,[12] traditional users accounted for a far smaller percentage of the total, several new users surfaced, and a few developing nations emerged as prominent users of antidumping. From 1995 to 1999, nontraditional users accounted for 59 percent (up from 37 percent) and traditional users accounted for 41 percent (down from 63 percent). New users such as Venezuela, Peru, Egypt, Israel, Malaysia, and the Philippines accounted for 108 initiations collectively.

Perhaps most noteworthy during this period, however, is the flurry of cases filed by India, South Africa, and Argentina. In the first half of the decade, India initiated 15 cases. In the second half it initiated 140, propelling it to the second largest user behind the European Union and ahead of the United States. Between those two periods, South Africa's case initiations increased eightfold from 16 to 129, making it the fourth largest user. And by increasing its case initiations, by more than 50 percent, to 96 in the second half of the decade, Argentina became the sixth largest user.[13]

Thus far we have been examining trends in new investigations— some fraction of which do not result in protectionism. But when we look instead at actual antidumping measures in force, a similar picture emerges.[14] The total number of definitive antidumping measures[15] in force increased by 26 percent between 1995 and 2000. Table 4.1 shows the top 10 antidumping users during this period. The most prolific was the United States, with an average of 323 measures in force during the period, followed by the European Union with 143, Canada with 88, Mexico with 84, and South Africa with 59.

The number of measures imposed by new users more than doubled between 1995 and 2000, while the figure for traditional users declined by 4.5 percent. The upward sloping trajectory was particularly steep for India and South Africa, whose measures increased by 654 percent and 518 percent, respectively. Whereas new users accounted for roughly 26 percent of all measures in 1995, their share of the total had increased to about 44 percent by 2000.

Table 4.1
TOP TEN ANTIDUMPING USERS
TOTAL MEASURES IN PLACE (1995–2000)

Country	1995	1996	1997	1998	1999	2000	Average
United States	309	313	321	327	342	323	322.50
EU	138	137	138	139	150	154	142.67
Canada	95	96	93	77	79	87	87.83
Mexico	92	90	82	83	77	77	83.50
South Africa	17	31	47	58	94	105	58.67
Australia	84	64	42	44	41	45	53.33
India	13	15	20	44	62	98	42.00
Argentina	19	31	35	37	42	43	34.50
Turkey	37	37	35	34	35	13	31.83
Brazil	20	26	24	31	37	41	29.83
All Others	50	59	84	102	122	117	89.00
Total	874	899	921	976	1,081	1,103	975.67
Traditional Users	651	636	618	611	631	622	628.16
Nontraditional	223	263	303	365	450	481	347.50

SOURCE: Compiled from WTO Reports in G/ADP/N series

Each of the top 10 users had measures in force against multiple countries, refuting any notion that antidumping measures target only a few notorious "unfair traders" (Table 4.2). The United States, once again, led the way, with antidumping measures in force against 58 different countries during 1995–2000. Many of the new users experienced rapid growth in the number of countries their laws target: between 1995 and 2000, South Africa leaped from 13 to 33, India from 7 to 30, and Brazil from 12 to 23. Unsurprisingly, as antidumping protectionism increases, many of the heaviest users have also become popular targets. Four of the top 10 targets during 1995–2000 (the United States, Brazil, Germany, and France) also number among the top 10 users; furthermore, an additional 4 of the top 10 antidumping users (India, Canada, Mexico, and the United Kingdom) are included among the 20 leading antidumping targets (Appendix 4.2).

The virulence of antidumping protectionism can be measured, not just by the number of countries targeted, but also by the range of industries affected. Nineteen of 21 broad industry groups were the subject of antidumping measures during 1995–2000[16] (Table 4.3). The

Table 4.2
TOP TEN ANTIDUMPING USERS
NUMBER OF TARGETED COUNTRIES PER YEAR (1995–2000)

Country	1995	1996	1997	1998	1999	2000	Total
United States	55	56	55	56	53	52	58
EU	32	32	33	33	35	37	43
Canada	34	34	34	32	33	35	41
Mexico	31	30	16	16	18	19	32
South Africa	13	16	21	25	33	33	33
Australia	29	24	18	19	22	22	32
India	7	7	9	19	23	30	30
Argentina	11	15	13	11	14	15	21
Turkey	17	17	17	16	17	10	21
Brazil	12	17	15	18	19	23	28
All Others	19	20	28	33	39	36	43
Total	75	75	76	76	78	80	87
Traditional Users	71	70	67	67	67	69	77
Nontraditional	56	57	50	54	61	60	74

SOURCE: Compiled from WTO Reports in G/ADP/N series

European Union maintained measures against 16 different industry groups during 1995–2000, followed closely by the United States and Mexico with 15 apiece. Note the rapid expansion of the scope of antidumping measures in India: from two industry groups targeted in 1995 to eight by 2000.

Although antidumping measures have left few industry groups unmolested, they are by no means evenly applied. Around the world, steel and other metal product industries are the most common and fastest growing targets of antidumping actions. In 2000 those industries accounted for roughly 36 percent of all outstanding measures in force. Chemical products (including pharmaceuticals) came in second, accounting for 21 percent of total measures in force as of June 2000 (Table 4.4).

Proliferation has become a self-reinforcing process. In other words, antidumping is contagious. If one country uses antidumping forcefully, it creates pressure from affected industries in other countries for similar measures at home. Measures to curtail competition in one country create excess supply, which is viewed as threatening

Table 4.3
TOP TEN ANTIDUMPING USERS
NUMBER OF INDUSTRY GROUPS TARGETED (PROTECTED)
BY YEAR (1995–2000)

Country	1995	1996	1997	1998	1999	2000	Total
United States	15	15	15	15	15	14	15
EU	10	12	16	15	15	15	16
Canada	11	11	10	10	10	11	12
Mexico	13	13	11	13	14	14	15
South Africa	7	8	8	9	9	10	10
Australia	9	8	8	9	8	8	10
India	2	2	4	6	7	8	8
Argentina	8	10	9	9	10	11	12
Turkey	9	8	8	8	8	3	9
Brazil	6	7	7	9	9	9	9
All Others	12	12	12	14	14	14	14
Total	17	17	18	19	18	18	19
Traditional Users	17	17	18	18	17	17	18
Nontraditional	15	15	14	16	16	16	16

SOURCE: Compiled from WTO Reports in G/ADP/N series

by industries in other countries. Consequently, they become more likely to petition their own governments for similar actions. Possible evidence of this domino effect is the fact that 12 of the 28 jurisdictions that reported definitive antidumping measures to the WTO during the period 1995–2000 had more measures in place against steel and steel-using products than against any other industries. Seven others targeted chemical and allied product industries more than any other industry.[17]

There is also evidence of a tit-for-tat motivation for antidumping actions. Twelve countries simultaneously targeted and protected the same industry group (steel and steel products) the most (Appendix 4.3). In 29 countries the very same products were subjected to anti-dumping duty orders both at home (against imports) and abroad (against exports) (Appendix 4.4). So much for the theory that anti-dumping measures merely ensure a level playing field: How can an industry that is injured by reason of unfairly priced imports from

Table 4.4
Antidumping Targets by Industry
Total Measures in Place (1995–2000)

HTS Section	1995	1996	1997	1998	1999	2000	Average
Base Metals, Articles of Base Metal	276	290	305	316	372	401	327
Chemical, Allied Industry Products	201	203	204	210	217	228	211
Machinery, Mechanical, Electr. Equip.	81	85	94	95	100	81	89
Textiles, Textile Articles	48	60	61	54	70	79	62
Plastics, Rubbers	53	54	55	53	66	74	59
Vehicles, Aircraft, Transport Equip.	42	40	40	42	43	30	40
Articles of Stone, Plaster, Cement	34	37	37	42	44	40	40
Wood Pulp, Paper, Paperboard	18	17	21	31	44	39	31
Prepared Foodstuffs	35	31	29	31	28	27	30
Vegetable Products	15	19	19	24	23	22	20
Footwear, Headgear, Umbrellas	21	16	9	17	13	16	15
Optical, Photo, Cinema Instruments	14	11	10	9	20	23	15
Miscellaneous Manufactured Articles	14	15	14	13	12	14	14
Wood, Articles of Wood	6	6	6	5	11	11	8
Live Animals, Animal Products	4	3	4	6	7	7	5
Animal, Vegetable Fats, Oils	9	9	9	2	1	1	5
Mineral Products	0	0	0	9	9	9	5
Arms, Ammunition, Parts Thereof	3	3	3	3	0	0	2
Raw Hides, Skins, Leather Products	0	0	1	1	1	1	1
Total	874	899	921	976	1,081	1,103	976

Source: Compiled from WTO Reports in G/ADP/N series

Country A itself be causing injury to that same industry in Country A?

The past decade has witnessed a sea change in the nature of antidumping protectionism. In short, it has gone global. Once the preserve of a few rich countries, antidumping is now spreading rapidly throughout the developing and postcommunist worlds. Indeed, all the considerable net growth in worldwide antidumping activity in recent years has come from new users. Leaders of developing countries complain, with justification, when rich countries preach free trade but use antidumping to block access to their markets. Those leaders need to recognize, however, that the use of antidumping laws increasingly pits one developing country against another. From 1995 to 1999, developing countries were targeted in 818, or 67 percent, of all actions taken. Nearly half of those actions, though, were taken by other developing countries.[18]

Meanwhile, the exports of rich countries are increasingly under antidumping attack. Antidumping measures in force against the exports of traditional users were up 46 percent between 1995 and 2000. Although the number of antidumping measures taken by traditional users against traditional users actually fell over this period, measures taken by new users against the old guard skyrocketed 192 percent—from 72 in 1995 to 210 in 2000[19] (Appendix 4.5). In a bit of poetic justice, rich countries have been hoist with their own petard. And no traditional user of the antidumping laws has been more victimized in recent years than the United States.

Targeting U.S. Exporters

From January 1995 to June 2000, the United States was the third most popular target of antidumping measures worldwide—trailing only China and Japan. Over that period, U.S. exports were the subject of 81 investigations by 17 different countries; in 51 of those cases antidumping measures were imposed (Appendices 4.6 and 4.7).[20] A total of 103 measures by 18 different countries were in effect against U.S. exports for at least some portion of the years in question. The exposure of U.S. exports to antidumping harassment has risen sharply: the average number of antidumping measures in force against U.S. goods during 1996–2000 was 41 percent higher than during 1991–95.[21]

111

U.S. exports were subject to an average of 65 antidumping measures worldwide at any given time during 1995–2000. That level of abuse put the United States well ahead of many countries commonly associated with allegations of "unfair trade": Korea (54), Taiwan (51), Brazil (47), and Russia (33). Measures were applied against U.S. exports by 13 of the 28 WTO members that reported having taken any measures during this period.[22] The United States was the first or second largest target of 7 of those 13 antidumping users. For anyone who believes that findings of dumping are meaningful evidence of unfair practices, the frequent targeting of U.S. exports is doubtless a deep mystery. But once it becomes clear that the connection between a finding of dumping and the existence of unfair practices is somewhere between tenuous and random, it is unsurprising that the United States—as the world's largest exporter—must endure a large number of antidumping complaints.

A broad range of U.S. exports has felt the sting of the antidumping backlash. Exports in 14 separate categories of 21 broad industry groups have been hit by antidumping measures. Only China's exports have been targeted more broadly. As Table 4.5 shows, the U.S. chemical industry has been most badly victimized, with an average of 24 measures against it at any given time. In partial repayment for its own exuberant pursuit of antidumping remedies, the U.S. steel industry—along with other metal producers—comes in second on the hit list.

Among the victims of antidumping protectionism are some of the best-known names in American industry: 3M, Amana, Bethlehem Steel, Bristol-Myers Squibb, Celotex, ConAgra, Domino Sugar, Dow Chemical, Exxon Chemical, FMC, Frigidaire, Gerber, Inland Steel, International Paper, Lone Star Steel, LTV Steel, Mallinckrodt, Monsanto, Occidental Chemical, Owens Corning, Union Carbide, USX, Weyerhaeuser, and Whirlpool. Table 4.6 provides the details of those companies' run-ins with antidumping abroad. And those big-name firms are only the tip of the iceberg: many hundreds of U.S. firms have lost sales and whole markets because of foreign antidumping actions.

The effects of antidumping measures on U.S. exports can be devastating. A Canadian investigation of U.S. refined sugar resulted in antidumping duties ranging from 41 to 46 percent. U.S. exports fell from $50.1 million the year before the antidumping duty to only

Table 4.5
ANTIDUMPING TARGETS BY INDUSTRY
MEASURES AGAINST U.S. EXPORTERS (1995–2000)

HTS Section	1995	1996	1997	1998	1999	2000	Average
Chemical, allied industry products	21	24	24	22	26	27	24.00
Base metals, articles of base metal	12	12	12	11	7	4	9.67
Plastics, rubbers	6	6	6	6	5	4	5.50
Vegetable products	4	5	4	6	6	5	5.00
Wood pulp, paper, paperboard	2	3	4	6	5	4	4.00
Machinery, mechanical, electr. equip.	3	5	5	4	3	3	3.84
Textiles, textile articles	3	3	4	4	4	4	3.66
Articles of stone, plaster, cement	3	3	4	4	4	4	3.66
Prepared foodstuffs	2	1	1	2	2	2	1.66
Vehicles, aircraft, transport equip.	1	1	1	1	1	1	1.00
Optical, photo, cinema instruments	1	1	1	1	1	1	1.00
Live animals, animal products	0	0	0	0	1	2	0.50
Mineral products	0	0	0	1	1	1	0.50
Wood, articles of wood	1	1	0	0	0	0	0.33
Miscellaneous manufactured articles	1	1	0	0	0	0	0.33
Total	60	66	66	68	66	62	64.67

Source: Compiled from WTO Reports in G/ADP/N series

Table 4.6

MAJOR U.S. EXPORTERS HIT BY ANTIDUMPING MEASURES

U.S. Exporter	Case	Original Date	Duty
Amana	Appliances (dishwashers) to Canada	2001	55.80%
Bristol-Myers Squibb Co.	X-ray contrast media to Canada	2000	74.00%
Celotex Corporation	Polyiso insulation board to Canada	1997	0.01–72.28% (avg. 36%)
ConAgra	Frozen pot pies and frozen dinners to Canada	1985	4.3–39.9%
Domino Sugar	Refined sugar to Canada	1995	45.90%
Dow Chemical Company	Ethanolamines to the EC	1994	Minimum price undertaking
	Ethanolamines to Korea	1996	23.13–33.94%
	Triethanolamine & mixtures to Australia	1992	3–30%
Dupont	Aniline to India	2001	7.88 rupees/kg
Exxon Chemical Company	Synthetic baler twine to Canada	1994	9.40%
FMC Corporation	Orthophosphoric acid to Colombia	1992	77.75%
	Sodium carbonate to the EC	1995	8.90%
Frigidaire	Appliances (dishwashers) to Canada	2001	15.90%
	Appliances (dryers) to Canada	2001	15.30%
	Appliances (refrigerators) to Canada	2001	5.90%

(continued)

U.S. Exporter	Case	Original Date	Duty
Gerber Products Company	Baby food to Canada	1998	59.76%
Inland Steel Company	Corrosion-resistant steel sheet to Canada	1994	5.1–12.4%
International Paper	A4 paper to Australia	1994	0–26%
	Bond paper to Mexico	1994	20.88%
LTV Steel Company	Corrosion-resistant steel sheet to Canada	1994	6.2–34.1%
Mallinckrodt, Inc.	X-ray contrast media to Canada	2000	74.00%
Minnesota Mining and Manufacturing	Wound closure strips to Australia	1998	91–419%
Monsanto Chemical Company	Orthophosphoric acid to Colombia	1992	77.75%
Occidental Chemical Corporation	Polyvinyl chloride to Australia	1992	0–20% (avg. about 10%)
	Triethanolamine & mixtures to Australia	1992	45.00%
Owens Corning Fiberglass Corporation	E-glass fiber to Korea	1994	12.4–37.4%
	Fiberglass pipe insulation to Canada	1993	60.00%
USX Corporation	Corrosion-resistant steel sheet to Canada	1994	2.2–17.0%
Union Carbide	Ethanolamines to the EC	1994	Minimum price undertaking

(*continued next page*)

115

Table 4.6
Major U.S. Exporters Hit by Antidumping Measures (continued)

U.S. Exporter	Case	Original Date	Duty
Union Carbide (cont.)	Ethanolamines to Korea	1996	20.07–28.67%
	Graphite electrodes to India	1998	19.41 rupees/kg
	Triethanolamine & mixtures to Australia	1992	14–43%
Weyerhaeuser Company	A4 paper to Australia	1994	0–20%
	Bond paper to Mexico	1994	20.88%
Whirlpool Corporation	Appliances (dishwashers) to Canada	2001	14.90%
	Appliances (dryers) to Canada	2001	18.90%
	Appliances (refrigerators) to Canada	2001	19.50%

$4.7 million two years after the order—a 91 percent drop. Exports of polyvinyl chloride were hit with a 19 percent duty in Colombia, and exports plummeted 80 percent in two years. An Indian investigation of acrylic fiber resulted in a 6 percent duty on one producer and a 43 percent duty on everyone else; exports dropped from $5.4 million the year before to zero two years afterward. In a Mexican case against regenerated cellulose film, U.S. firms received duty rates that averaged 31 percent. Exports of the product fell 81 percent in only three years. Details of those and other cases are provided in Appendix 4.8.[23]

Because of the enormous number of antidumping cases brought by U.S. steel producers against their foreign competitors, the United States enjoys the dubious distinction of being the world's most active user of antidumping measures. Even taking into account the significant and growing caseload against U.S. exports, the United States remains solidly a "net user"—more victimizer than victim. As of June 2000, there were 323 U.S. antidumping measures against foreign products, as opposed to only 62 foreign measures against U.S. goods. But when U.S. cases against steel imports are excluded, a different picture emerges: between 1995 and 1999, the United States initiated 58 nonsteel antidumping investigations, while the rest of the world initiated 79 antidumping investigations against U.S. exports.[24] Thus, leaving aside one small U.S. industry (of a total American workforce of 140 million people, fewer than 200,000 work in steel mills), the United States has become a net target of antidumping measures.

Even including steel, the United States is already a net target with respect to the 34 nations that would comprise a Free Trade Area of the Americas. According to a study released by the Organization of American States, U.S. exports were the subject of 260 antidumping measures by those countries during the period 1987–2000; by contrast, only 147 U.S. measures targeted goods from those countries during that same period.[25] Interestingly, the two biggest targeters of U.S. exports are located in the region: they are none other than Canada and Mexico, our North American Free Trade Agreement partners.

It would be difficult to think of a more telling indicator that current antidumping rules have little or nothing to do with offsetting unfair trade. Trade barriers have been reduced to a minimum within the North American market, and with them any possibility of sustaining "artificial" price differences in the face of cross-border arbitrage. Yet it is in this free-trade zone that U.S. firms are most frequently penalized for supposedly unfair practices. Again, only if one assumes that antidumping rules are designed to ensure a level playing field is the frequency of Canadian and Mexican actions against U.S. goods a mystery. Once it is understood that those rules are rigged against exporters, the paradox is resolved: Canadian and Mexican firms are maximally exposed to U.S. competition because of the elimination of tariffs and thus have the strongest incentives to bring antidumping cases.

Coming Home to Roost

In previous chapters we detailed how U.S. antidumping rules stack the deck against foreign exporters and in favor of protection-seeking domestic industries. Now, as antidumping laws spread around the world, U.S. companies are increasingly finding themselves on the receiving end of such protectionist abuses. A review of a few exemplary dumping determinations against U.S. exporters will help to illustrate how the chickens are coming home to roost.[26]

Dumping margins for U.S. exporters are routinely generated and inflated by creatively selective comparisons of home-market and export-market prices. For example, in the 1993 Canadian investigation of U.S. fiberglass pipe insulation, the authorities used only those home-market sales that surpassed a particular threshold of profitability. On a customer-by-customer basis, sales found insufficiently profitable over a 60-day period were excluded from the analysis. For two of the U.S. respondents (Schuller International and Knauf Fiber Glass), sales to a number of customers were excluded on that basis. Consequently, their dumping rates were determined by comparing all Canadian sales to only their highest-price U.S. sales. Knauf got a dumping rate of 44 percent; Schuller received a 52 percent rate.[27]

In a later Canadian investigation—the 1997 case on U.S. concrete panels—the standard for excluding low-price home-market sales had changed. Now, for home-market sales of a particular product to be used, there had to be profitable sales to at least two unrelated customers. Because there was only one home-market customer at the same level of trade as the importer, the authorities instead used sales at lower levels of trade (that is, closer to the ultimate consumer and therefore presumably at higher prices). The U.S. exporter, Custom Building Products, was hit with a dumping rate of 36 percent.[28]

A pair of Indian cases provides further examples of the mischief that can creep into price comparisons. In a 1997 case on acrylic fiber, the U.S. exporter, Cytec Industries, maintained a rebate program in the U.S. market under which it paid rebates to qualifying final consumers of yarn depending upon the end use of the yarn. Cytec offered no such rebates on its sales to India. Normally, rebates are deducted from the sales price to arrive at the net price, but in this case the Indian authorities refused—on the ground that the rebates weren't offered to Indian customers. Of course, any valid assessment of whether price discrimination was occurring would have to examine prices in both markets net of all discounts and rebates. Instead, the authorities ruled that a key difference in the terms of Indian and U.S. sales would be ignored solely because it was a difference. Cytec was given a dumping rate of 9.3 percent.[29]

In the 1997 investigation of graphite electrodes, Indian authorities compared Union Carbide's U.S. sales to its exports to India—not only from the United States but from several other countries as well. Of what possible relevance could it be that Union Carbide charges a different price in the United States than it does in India for goods made somewhere else? Such differences would not show that the same producer charges different prices in different markets, a fact that might possibly indicate the existence of a sanctuary home market. All it shows is that different (albeit affiliated) producers charge different prices in different markets—hardly an unusual state of affairs. Union Carbide was judged to be dumping 45 percent below "normal value."[30]

As discussed in previous chapters, findings of dumping are now frequently made without any comparison of actual prices. Instead, export-market prices are compared to artificial prices, or "constructed value," which is based on the cost of production plus some amount for profit. Such dumping findings say nothing about the possible existence of a sanctuary home market, since actual home-market price data are not used. Neither do those findings say anything about chronically below-cost export sales, since export sales prices are compared, not to the cost of production, but to cost plus profit.

The constructed-value methodology has no sound theoretical basis. Furthermore, the use of production costs in calculating normal value exposes U.S. exporters to additional forms of creative number crunching by foreign antidumping authorities. One more Canadian case—the 1995 investigation of refined sugar—is particularly interesting in this regard. Raw sugar prices in the United States are grossly inflated by a scheme of loan-based price supports and import restrictions. American sugar refiners are thus forced to pay roughly twice the world price for raw sugar when they produce for the domestic market. A special exemption, though, allows them to import raw sugar at world prices for production aimed at export markets. Since it is not practical to maintain physically separate inventories of high-price and world-price sugar, refiners keep detailed records to ensure that the quantity of refined sugar exported corresponds with the appropriate quantity of world-price raw sugar imported.

Under this system, the sugar refiners enjoy much lower costs for their export sales than for their domestic sales—thus allowing them to compete abroad despite the handicap of the U.S. sugar program. The Canadian antidumping authorities, however, decided that since high-price and low-price raw sugar are blended in inventory, it was not permissible for refiners to attribute only the lower cost of world-price sugar to their export sales. Accordingly, when calculating the constructed value of the exported merchandise, the authorities used a weighted average cost for raw sugar—thus substantially inflating constructed value and thereby the dumping margins. The ultimate dumping rates ranged from 41 to 46 percent.[31]

The South African investigation of U.S. chicken meat in 2000 also featured egregious manipulation of cost data. The exports under investigation were predominantly of dark meat and were at prices higher than the prices charged for dark meat in the United States. Indeed, it turns out that—contrary to the situation in the United States, where white meat is the premium product—in South Africa consumers prefer dark meat and will pay extra for it. On the face of things, therefore, it would appear that there could be no dumping: here was a case where exporters earned higher prices and profits abroad than they were able to manage at home.

The South African antidumping authorities would not be thwarted so easily. They reasoned that the American preference for white meat constituted a "particular market situation" that disqualified the use of U.S. prices as the basis of normal value. Anyway, they argued, the U.S. sales of dark meat were below the cost of production and therefore failed the cost test. They were able to reach this conclusion, however, only by disregarding American chicken producers' own accounting records and substituting their own methodology for allocating costs to different parts of the chicken.

In the American companies' normal methodology, costs are assigned to different parts on the basis of their revenue-generating power; in other words, high-value products are assigned higher costs and low-value products lower costs. The South African authorities decided instead to allocate costs on the basis of weight—thereby shifting costs away from white-meat parts and toward the dark-meat parts that were the subject of the investigation. This cost shifting achieved a dual purpose. First, it ensured that U.S. sales failed the cost test and therefore that constructed value would be used. Second, it ensured that constructed value—and therefore dumping margins—would be higher than otherwise. The two U.S. exporters—Tyson and Gold Kist—were found to be dumping by the whopping margins of 209 percent and 357 percent, respectively.[32]

In all of the cases mentioned above, dumping rates were at least based on the exporters' own data, however creatively massaged. All too often, however, U.S. exports are hit with determinations made on the basis of "facts available." The facts that are available, it turns out, are almost always harshly unfavorable to exporters (since typically they are supplied by the protection-seeking domestic industry). Consider the track records in India and South Africa, for example. Of the eight Indian determinations against U.S. exports between 1995 and 2000, five were based on facts available. The average dumping margin in those five cases was 83 percent.[33] In South Africa, three of the four determinations against U.S. exports during 1995–2000 were based on facts available, with an average dumping margin of 89 percent.[34]

Antidumping authorities have wide discretion regarding when to apply facts available. Minor errors or omissions in voluminous and complex responses can be enough to prompt authorities to disregard all the rest of the data provided by respondents and rely instead on figures concocted by the domestic industry. Often, though, U.S. companies do not even try to participate in foreign investigations. At best, they conclude it isn't worth the time and money to contest what they believe is a foregone conclusion; at worst, they fear that confidential price and cost data they supply to governments will somehow wind up in the hands of their competitors.

With its complexity and wide latitude for discretion, the anti-dumping law creates enormous potential for abuse in poorer countries that lack well-established traditions of transparency and procedural fairness—and, indeed, are prone to outright corruption. But procedural problems with antidumping enforcement, however severe, are a subsidiary issue. The fundamental problem with antidumping laws today is substantive: the present-day rules for defining unfair trade are hopelessly flawed and cannot help but generate arbitrary, protectionist outcomes.

The Looming Threat

The threat that the proliferation of antidumping measures poses to U.S. interests is likely to worsen as time goes on. There is every reason to expect that the number of countries using antidumping measures will continue to grow. As of 2002, 71 jurisdictions reported that they had antidumping legislation in place; only 38, however, have so far put their laws to use. The other 33 jurisdictions cannot be expected to remain dormant indefinitely. Other countries, meanwhile, are bound to enact their own laws.

Furthermore, the clear pattern among new antidumping users is for use to expand and broaden over time. Initially, only an intrepid few industries will brave the complexities and uncertainties of a new law. Eventually, though, other industries will catch on and take their place at the trough. The number of countries targeted tends to increase as well. To conserve on the expenses of preparing petitions, protection-seeking industries often target only their main foreign competitors at first. But antidumping measures against one country will create opportunities for third-country suppliers to fill the vacuum; domestic industries are then forced to file new petitions against additional countries to maintain the level of protection on which they have come to depend.

As antidumping activity trends up generally, U.S. exports are sure to feel the squeeze. Table 4.7 shows the disturbing overlap between the largest and fastest-growing U.S. export sectors and the hottest growth areas for antidumping actions. Note that, in potential FTAA partners Argentina and Brazil, three-quarters of U.S. exports are concentrated in those sectors most afflicted by antidumping activity.

Table 4.7
THE LOOMING THREAT:
COINCIDENCE OF THE MOST PROTECTED INDUSTRIES OF
NEW LARGE USERS AND U.S. EXPORTERS

	Top 4 Targeted/Protected Sectors	% of Total U.S. 2000 Exports Value to Country
Argentina	1. Base metals, articles of base metal 2. Machinery, mechanical, electr. equip. 3. Vehicles, aircraft, transport. equip. 4. Chemical, allied industry products	74.1%
Brazil	1. Base metals, articles of base metal 2. Chemical, allied industry products 3. Plastics and rubbers 4. Machinery, mechanical, electr. equip.	75.0%
India	1. Chemical, allied industry products 2. Plastics and rubbers 3. Textiles and textile articles 4. Base metals, articles of base metal	23.5%
Mexico	1. Base metals, articles of base metal 2. Chemical, allied industry products 3. Textiles and textile articles 4. Plastics and rubbers	25.4%
WORLD	1. Base metals, articles of base metal 2. Chemical, allied industry products 3. Machinery, mechanical, electr. equip. 4. Textiles and textile articles	54.8%

At the global level, more than half of U.S. exports are in the four industrial sectors in which antidumping protectionism is most common.

Broader American interests are also threatened by unchecked use of antidumping measures. The United States has an enormous economic stake in an open and stable world trading system—a stake that encompasses not only exports of goods but also services exports, investment in production facilities and business operations abroad, and cross-border financial flows. Furthermore, a free and prosperous world trading system undergirds U.S. national security by lending encouragement to free markets, the rule of law, and democratic values around the globe.

The continued spread and intensification of antidumping protectionism represent a real and serious threat to the integrity of the world trading system. First of all, antidumping measures are extremely unpredictable. Even if particular industries are known to be antidumping hot spots, the timing of cases, the exact products covered, the specific countries targeted, and the dumping rates ultimately imposed by the authorities are all swathed in uncertainty. Furthermore, antidumping measures are highly disruptive: duties are often so high as to knock affected exporters completely out of the protected market.

The combination of unpredictability and disruptiveness causes antidumping to have a chilling effect on international economic integration that transcends the visible interruptions in trade it causes. The relatively liberal world trading system has served as a bulwark of U.S. interests throughout the postwar era. Policymakers need to realize that the broadening scale and increasing frequency of antidumping actions pose a significant long-term threat to the health and integrity of that international economic order.

Appendix 4.1
NOTES ON METHODOLOGY

Unless otherwise noted, the data used pertaining to antidumping measures around the world were obtained from the website of the World Trade Organization (www.wto.org). Under the WTO Antidumping Agreement, members are required to report their antidumping activities semiannually to the WTO's antidumping authorities. These reports are published as official documents in the G/ADP series available from the website.

The primary data collection efforts that we undertook for this chapter included retrieving, reviewing, and analyzing all year-end reports filed by every antidumping jurisdiction[35] covering antidumping actions from 1995 through 1999 as well as the mid-year reports for the first half of 2000. For all jurisdictions that maintained any measures against U.S. exports, mid-year reports for 1995 through 1999 were examined as well.

In many cases, the reports were filed in accordance with a format prescribed by the WTO Antidumping Agreement. The format provides separate sections for information on new or recent antidumping actions, definitive duties in place at the end of the reporting period, and price undertakings ("suspension agreements") in place at the end of the reporting period. Some countries provided more tables and more data, but many reported fewer.

The section providing for information on new or recent actions contains cells for the following data: (1) target country or territory, (2) product under investigation or review, (3) initiation date, (4) provisional date and measures, (5) definitive date and measures, (6) undertaking date and measures, (7) reasons for no final measures, (8) trade volume, (9) dumped imports as a percentage of domestic consumption, (10) volume of trade investigated, and (11) basis of the determination. The sections pertaining to definitive duties and undertakings contain cells for (1) target country or territory, (2) product under definitive measure, and (3) date of definitive measure.

There is wide variation in the amount and quality of data presented in each WTO member's reports, and there is also variation within particular countries' reports over time. For example:

1. Some members reported only definitive measures in force, while others reported only current actions.
2. Some members listed separate definitive measures (undertaking and definitive duties) for the same case because some of the respondents were subject to the undertaking and others were not.
3. Some members referred to a particular product by one name in one report but by a slightly different name in other reports.
4. Some members listed current actions or definitive measures against the same products from the same countries but gave different names to the subject products.
5. Some members listed multiple antidumping measures against products that other countries ultimately bundled together under one action.
6. Some members listed actions or measures against the European Union, while others listed them against specific European Union member states. Related to this issue is the fact that the European Union brings antidumping actions collectively, but its member states are usually targeted individually.

Those inconsistencies are mentioned because they have the potential to affect the analysis. When the European Union is listed as opposed to its individual member states, the analysis of primary antidumping targets is potentially skewed. And since the European Union acts as one entity in bringing antidumping actions, whereas the United States, for example, brings cases against EU member states individually, comparing antidumping use of the two tends to exaggerate the relative U.S. use. When a country lists multiple measures for a product that another country consolidates under one, the analysis of primary users is potentially skewed. When different case names are assigned to the same product, the analysis of commonly targeted products is potentially skewed.

Most of these problems were addressed in our analysis of the data. Others remain but for purposes of the present analysis are largely innocuous. To the extent that statistics affected by underlying data problems are cited in the paper, appropriate reference is provided.

Appendix 4.2
ANTIDUMPING TARGETS OF WTO USERS
TOTAL MEASURES IN PLACE (1995–2000)

Rank	Country	1995	1996	1997	1998	1999	2000	Average
1	China	143	148	180	193	202	207	178.83
2	Japan	76	77	74	78	84	82	78.50
3	United States	60	66	66	68	66	62	64.67
4	Korea	53	54	44	49	57	65	53.67
5	Taiwan	40	41	45	52	61	66	50.83
6	Brazil	48	51	52	45	42	43	46.83
7	Germany	34	31	31	33	37	41	34.50
8	Russia	24	25	35	34	40	37	32.50
9	Thailand	19	23	25	32	31	34	27.33
10	France	19	19	22	23	33	36	25.33
11	Italy	21	18	21	25	32	30	24.50
12	Ukraine	19	19	21	21	26	26	22.00
13	India	15	15	15	21	29	35	21.67
14	Canada	19	19	19	19	20	18	19.00
15	United Kingdom	16	17	15	14	20	21	17.17
16	Mexico	11	15	17	17	19	21	16.67
17	Malaysia	13	15	16	16	17	17	15.67
18	Indonesia	10	11	12	17	20	21	15.17
19	Singapore	17	18	16	13	13	13	15.00
20	Netherlands	12	13	13	13	15	17	13.83
21	Romania	13	14	13	13	18	12	13.83
22	Spain	10	9	9	12	17	21	13.00
23	Belgium	11	10	9	10	16	17	12.17
24	South Africa	7	10	11	11	12	15	11.00
25	Sweden	9	9	8	12	14	14	11.00
26	Venezuela	12	11	10	11	10	11	10.83
27	Hong Kong	10	11	9	9	10	12	10.17
28	Poland	9	8	10	10	11	10	9.67
29	Turkey	9	9	6	8	10	13	9.17
30	Kazakhstan	8	8	8	8	10	8	8.33
31	Argentina	9	8	7	7	7	7	7.50
32	Finland	4	5	4	9	10	13	7.50
33	Hungary	9	7	8	5	7	6	7.00
34	Austria	3	2	2	6	8	12	5.50

(continued next page)

Appendix 4.2
ANTIDUMPING TARGETS OF WTO USERS
TOTAL MEASURES IN PLACE (1995–2000) *(continued)*

Rank	Country	1995	1996	1997	1998	1999	2000	Average
35	Denmark	5	4	4	5	6	9	5.50
36	Australia	5	6	5	6	5	5	5.33
37	Belarus	4	5	4	5	5	5	4.67
38	Greece	3	3	2	4	7	8	4.50
39	Bulgaria	4	4	5	4	5	3	4.17
40	Portugal	1	1	2	4	7	8	3.83
41	Chile	1	2	3	5	6	5	3.67
42	Czech Republic	3	3	4	2	4	6	3.67
43	Ireland	2	1	1	2	6	8	3.33
44	Yugoslavia	5	4	2	3	3	3	3.33
45	Philippines	4	3	3	3	3	3	3.17
46	New Zealand	3	3	3	4	2	2	2.83
47	Egypt	1	1	3	3	4	4	2.67
48	Luxembourg	1	1	1	2	4	6	2.50
49	Israel	3	2	2	2	3	2	2.33
50	Kyrgyzstan	3	3	2	2	2	2	2.33
51	Lithuania	3	3	2	2	2	2	2.33
52	Moldova	3	3	2	2	2	2	2.33
53	Uzbekistan	3	3	2	2	2	2	2.33
54	Croatia	1	3	2	2	2	3	2.17
55	Norway	2	2	3	2	2	2	2.17
56	Bangladesh	2	2	2	2	2	2	2.00
57	Latvia	2	2	1	1	3	3	2.00
58	Macedonia	3	3	2	1	1	2	2.00
59	Estonia	2	2	1	1	2	2	1.67
60	Pakistan	1	1	2	2	2	2	1.67
61	Slovak Republic	0	0	1	1	4	4	1.67
62	Armenia	2	2	1	1	1	1	1.33
63	Azerbaijan	2	2	1	1	1	1	1.33
64	Georgia	2	2	1	1	1	1	1.33
65	Tajikistan	2	2	1	1	1	1	1.33
66	Turkmenistan	2	2	1	1	1	1	1.33
67	Czechoslovakia	3	2	1	1	0	0	1.17
68	Slovenia	1	2	1	1	1	1	1.17
69	Colombia	1	1	1	1	1	1	1.00

(continued next page)

Appendix 4.2
ANTIDUMPING TARGETS OF WTO USERS
TOTAL MEASURES IN PLACE (1995–2000) *(continued)*

Rank	Country	1995	1996	1997	1998	1999	2000	Average
70	Iran	1	1	1	1	1	1	1.00
71	Kenya	1	1	1	1	1	1	1.00
72	Saudi Arabia	2	2	0	0	1	1	1.00
73	Bosnia	0	1	1	1	1	1	0.83
74	Ecuador	1	1	1	1	0	0	0.67
75	Liechtenstein	0	0	1	1	1	1	0.67
76	Montenegro	2	2	0	0	0	0	0.67
77	Serbia	2	2	0	0	0	0	0.67
78	Trinidad	0	0	1	1	1	1	0.67
79	Zimbabwe	0	0	1	1	1	1	0.67
80	Paraguay	1	1	0	0	0	1	0.50
81	Vietnam	0	0	0	1	1	1	0.50
82	Honduras	0	0	0	0	1	1	0.33
83	Uruguay	1	1	0	0	0	0	0.33
84	Algeria	0	0	0	0	0	1	0.17
85	Costa Rica	0	0	0	0	1	0	0.17
86	Cuba	0	0	0	0	0	1	0.17
87	Iceland	0	0	1	0	0	0	0.17
	Developed	315	315	315	350	408	427	355.00
	Developing	573	598	620	654	729	760	655.67
	Total	888	913	935	1,004	1,137	1,187	1,010.67

Appendix 4.3

ALL WTO ANTIDUMPING USERS

MOST PROTECTED AND MOST TARGETED INDUSTRIES BY COUNTRY

Country	Most Protected Industry	Avg. Number AD Measures In Force Per Period	Most Targeted Industry	Avg. Number AD Measures Against Per Period
Argentina*	Base metals, articles of base metal	10.33	Base metals, articles of base metal	7.00
Australia	Chemical, allied industry products	19.00	Base metals, articles of base metal	2.83
Austria	Base metals, articles of base metal	42.17	Wood pulp, paper, paperboard	2.00
Belgium	Base metals, articles of base metal	42.17	chemical, allied industry products	4.17
Brazil*	Base metals, articles of base metal	10.83	Base metals, articles of base metal	29.83
Canada*	Base metals, articles of base metal	44.50	Base metals, articles of base metal	10.33
Chile	Base metals, articles of base metal	1.00	Vegetable products	1.50
Colombia	Chemical, allied industry products	4.67	Vegetable products	0.67
Denmark	Base metals, articles of base metal	42.17	Prepared foodstuffs	1.67
Egypt*	Base metals, articles of base metal	2.00	Base metals, articles of base metal	1.67
Finland	Base metals, articles of base metal	42.17	Wood pulp, paper, paperboard	4.50
France	Base metals, articles of base metal	42.17	Chemical, allied industry products	7.67
Germany*	Base metals, articles of base metal	42.17	Base metals, articles of base metal	10.17
Greece	Base metals, articles of base metal	42.17	Wood pulp, paper, paperboard	1.33
Guatemala	Articles of stone, plaster, cement	0.67		0.00
India	Chemical, allied industry products	19.00	Base metals, articles of base metal	7.83
Indonesia	Base metals, articles of base metal	1.17	Wood pulp, paper, paperboard	2.50
Ireland	Base metals, articles of base metal	42.17	Wood pulp, paper, paperboard	1.33
Israel	Wood pulp, paper, paperboard	1.83	Chemical, allied industry products	1.00
Italy*	Base metals, articles of base metal	42.17	Base metals, articles of base metal	8.17
Japan	Textiles, textile articles	1.00	Machinery, mechanical, electr. equip.	19.17

(continued)

Country	Most Protected Industry	Avg. Number AD Measures In Force Per Period	Most Targeted Industry	Avg. Number AD Measures Against Per Period
Korea	Chemical, allied industry products	7.00	Base metals, articles of base metal	17.67
Luxembourg	Base metals, articles of base metal	42.17	Wood pulp, paper, paperboard	1.33
Malaysia	Wood pulp, paper, paperboard	3.50	Machinery, mechanical, electr. equip.	4.17
Mexico*	Base metals, articles of base metal	33.33	Base metals, articles of base metal	5.50
Netherlands	Base metals, articles of base metal	42.17	Prepared foodstuffs	3.00
New Zealand	Prepared foodstuffs	6.83	Base metals, articles of base metal	1.67
Nicaragua	Prepared foodstuffs	0.33		0.00
Peru	Textiles, textile articles	1.67		0.00
Philippines	Chemical, allied industry products	0.33	Plastics, rubbers	1.00
Poland	Chemical, allied industry products	0.50	Base metals, articles of base metal	5.50
Portugal	Base metals, articles of base metal	42.17	Wood pulp, paper, paperboard	1.67
Singapore	Base metals, articles of base metal	2.00	Machinery, mechanical, electr. equip.	3.50
South Africa	Chemical, allied industry products	22.83	Base metals, articles of base metal	6.67
Spain*	Base metals, articles of base metal	42.17	Base metals, articles of base metal	5.17
Sweden*	Base metals, articles of base metal	42.17	Base metals, articles of base metal	6.17
Thailand*	Base metals, articles of base metal	1.17	Base metals, articles of base metal	5.83
Trinidad	Live animals, animal products	0.50	Base metals, articles of base metal	0.67
Turkey	Machinery, mechanical, electr. equip.	6.33	Base metals, articles of base metal	4.50
United Kingdom*	Base metals, articles of base metal	42.17	Base metals, articles of base metal	5.33
United States	Base metals, articles of base metal	144.67	Chemical, allied industry products	24.00
Venezuela*	Base metals, articles of base metal	3.83	Base metals, articles of base metal	8.83

* An asterisk indicates that the country's most protected industry is also the most targeted abroad

131

Appendix 4.4
Products That Are Both Protected at Home and Targeted Abroad

Country	Product	Foreign Target	Foreign Plaintiff
Argentina	Cold-Rolled Plate/Cold-Rolled Sheet/Cold-Rolled Carbon Steel Flat Products	Australia, Brazil	United States
Australia	Portland Cement	Germany	Brazil
	Canned Pears	China	United States
Austria	Seamless Steel Pipes and Tubes	Croatia, Ukraine, Czech Republic, Hungary, Poland, Romania, Russia, Slovak Republic	India
Belgium	Sheets and Plates of Iron or Steel/Carbon Steel Plate	Macedonia, Montenegro, Serbia, Slovenia	Canada
	Thermal Paper/Thermal Sensitive Paper	Japan	India
Brazil	Bicycle Tires	China, Taiwan, Thailand	Argentina
	Polyvinyl Chloride	Mexico, United States	Australia
	Triethanolamine	United States	Australia
Canada	Corrosion-Resistant Steel Sheet/Corrosion-Resistant Steel Flat Products	Australia, Brazil, France, Germany, Japan, Korea, New Zealand, Spain, Sweden, United Kingdom, United States	United States

(continued)

Country	Product	Foreign Target	Foreign Plaintiff
Canada (cont.)	Hot-Rolled Carbon Steel Plate/Hot-Rolled Carbon Steel Flat Products	Brazil, China, Finland, India, Indonesia, Italy, Korea, Mexico, Russia, Singapore, Slovak Republic, South Africa, Spain, Thailand, Ukraine	United States
	Refined Sugar/Sugar and Syrup	Denmark, Germany, Netherlands, United Kingdom, United States	United States
Denmark	Sheets and Plates of Iron or Steel/Carbon Steel Plate	Macedonia, Montenegro, Serbia, Slovenia	Canada
	Thermal Paper/Thermal Sensitive Paper	Japan	India
Egypt	Stainless Steel Sinks	Greece, Spain	South Africa
Finland	Sheets and Plates of Iron or Steel/Carbon Steel Plate	Macedonia, Montenegro, Serbia, Slovenia	Canada
	Thermal Paper/Thermal Sensitive Paper	Japan	India
France	Ball Bearings/Antifriction Ball Bearings	Japan	United States
	Thermal Paper/Thermal Sensitive Paper	Japan	India

(continued next page)

Appendix 4.4
PRODUCTS THAT ARE BOTH PROTECTED AT HOME AND TARGETED ABROAD (continued)

Country	Product	Foreign Target	Foreign Plaintiff
Germany	Ball Bearings/Antifriction Ball Bearings	Japan	United States
	Photo Albums/Photo Albums with Pocket Sheets	China	Canada
	Seamless Steel Pipes and Tubes/Standard Seamless Line and Pressure Pipe	Croatia, Ukraine, Czech Republic, Hungary, Poland, Romania, Russia, Slovak Republic	United States
	Sheets and Plates of Iron or Steel/Carbon Steel Plate	Macedonia, Montenegro, Serbia, Slovenia	Canada
	Thermal Paper/Thermal Sensitive Paper	Japan	India
	Urea/Solid Urea	Russia, Venezuela	United States
Greece	Thermal Paper/Thermal Sensitive Paper	Japan	India
India	Hot-Rolled Coils, Sheets, Plates, Strips/Hot-Rolled Carbon Steel Plate/Hot-Rolled Coil	Kazakhstan, Russia, Ukraine	Canada, Philippines
	Potassium Permanganate	China	EU-15
Indonesia	Hot-Rolled Carbon Steel Plate	China, Russia, Ukraine	Canada

(continued)

Country	Product	Foreign Target	Foreign Plaintiff
Ireland	Thermal Paper/Thermal Sensitive Paper	Japan	India
Italy	Ball Bearings/Antifriction Ball Bearings	Japan	United States
	Polyester Staple Fiber/Polyester Synthetic Staple Fibers	Belarus	Turkey
	Sheets and Plates of Iron or Steel/Carbon Steel Plate	Macedonia, Montenegro, Serbia, Slovenia	Canada
	Thermal Paper/Thermal Sensitive Paper	Japan	India
Korea	Disposable Lighters	China	Argentina, EU-15
Luxembourg	Thermal Paper/Thermal Sensitive Paper	Japan	India
Mexico	Non-refillable Pocket Lighters/Disposable Lighters	China	EU-15
	Polyvinyl Chloride	United States	Argentina, Australia, Brazil
	Steel Plate in Sheets/Cut-to-Length Carbon Steel Plate	Brazil, Russia, Ukraine, United States	United States
Netherlands	Thermal Paper/Thermal Sensitive Paper	Japan	India

(continued next page)

Appendix 4.4
Products That Are Both Protected at Home and Targeted Abroad (*continued*)

Country	Product	Foreign Target	Foreign Plaintiff
Portugal	Thermal Paper/Thermal Sensitive Paper	Japan	India
South Africa	Flat-Rolled Steel Plates and Sheets	Russia, Ukraine	EU-15
	Self Copy Paper	Germany, United Kingdom	Australia
Spain	Potassium Permanganate	China, India, Ukraine	United States
	Sheets and Plates of Iron or Steel/Carbon Steel Plate	Macedonia, Montenegro, Serbia, Slovenia	Canada
	Thermal Paper/Thermal Sensitive Paper	Japan	India
Sweden	Ball Bearings/Antifriction Ball Bearings	Japan	United States
	Thermal Paper/Thermal Sensitive Paper	Japan	India
Thailand	Clear and Tinted Float Glass/Clear Float Glass/Float Glass	Indonesia	Australia, South Africa
Turkey	Polyester Synthetic Staple Fibers	Belarus, Indonesia, Italy, Korea, Russia, Taiwan, Romania	EU-15
United Kingdom	Ball Bearings/Antifriction Ball Bearings	Japan	United States

(continued)

Country	Product	Foreign Target	Foreign Plaintiff
United Kingdom (cont.)	Thermal Paper/Thermal Sensitive Paper	Japan	India
United States	3.5" Microdisks	Japan	EU-15
	Cold-Rolled Carbon Steel Flat Products	Argentina, Brazil, China, Germany, Indonesia, Japan, Korea, Netherlands, Russia, Slovak Republic, South Africa, Taiwan, Thailand, Turkey, Venezuela	Canada, Mexico
	Corrosion-Resistant Carbon Steel Flat Products	Australia, Canada, France, Germany, Japan, Korea	Canada
	Cylindrical Roller Bearings/ Roller Bearings	France, Germany, Italy, Japan, Sweden, United Kingdom	South Africa
	Oil Country Tubular Goods/ Oil and Gas Well Casing	Argentina, Canada, Israel, Italy, Japan, Korea, Mexico, Taiwan	Canada
	Sugar and Syrup	Belgium, France, Germany, Canada	Canada
Venezuela	Cold-Rolled Carbon Steel Flat Products	Kazakhstan, Russia, Ukraine	United States

Appendix 4.5
ANTIDUMPING MEASURES IN FORCE,
WTO ANTIDUMPING USERS AND TARGETS, 1995–2000

	1995	1996	1997	1998	1999	2000	Total	Percent of Change 1995–2000
New Users								
Targeting New	165	197	224	270	331	355	1,542	115.15%
Targeting Traditional	72	80	93	123	175	210	753	191.67%
Traditional Users								
Targeting New	485	479	474	463	481	484	2,866	−0.21%
Targeting Traditional	166	157	144	148	150	138	903	−16.87%
New (as target)	650	676	698	733	812	839	4,408	29.08%
New (as user)	237	277	317	393	506	565	2,295	138.40%
Traditional (as target)	238	237	237	271	325	348	1,656	46.22%
Traditional (as user)	651	636	618	611	631	622	3,769	−4.45%
Total	888	913	935	1,004	1,137	1,187	6,064	33.67%

Traditional = United States, Canada, European Union, Australia, New Zealand
New = Everyone else
Note = Measures for which target is identified as "EU" have been counted 15 times, one for each EU member.

Appendix 4.6
ANTIDUMPING INITIATIONS AGAINST U.S. EXPORTS,
JANUARY 1995–JUNE 2000

	Argentina	Australia	Brazil	Canada	Chile	China	Colombia	Costa Rica	EU
1995	3	1	0	3	0	0	0	0	2
1996	2	1	3	2	1	0	0	1	0
1997	2	0	0	1	0	1	0	0	3
1998	0	2	2	0	0	0	1	0	0
1999	1	0	2	2	0	1	0	0	1
2000	0	0	0	1	0	0	0	0	1
TOTAL	8	4	7	9	1	2	1	1	7

	India	Indonesia	Israel	Korea	Mexico	South Africa	Taiwan	Venezuela	TOTAL
1995	1	0	2	0	2	1	0	0	15
1996	3	0	1	3	2	4	0	0	23
1997	0	1	0	2	2	0	0	1	13
1998	1	0	1	0	4	1	0	0	12
1999	3	0	0	0	2	1	2	1	16
2000	0	0	0	0	0	0	0	0	2
TOTAL	8	1	4	5	12	7	2	2	81

139

Appendix 4.7
ANTIDUMPING MEASURES IN FORCE AGAINST U.S. EXPORTS, JANUARY 1995–JUNE 2000

	Argentina	Australia	Brazil	Canada	Chile	China	Colombia	Costa Rica	EU
Pre-1995	0	6	6	15	0	0	3	0	1
1995	1	0	0	3	0	0	1	0	1
1996	0	0	0	2	0	0	0	0	1
1997	0	0	0	2	0	0	0	0	0
1998	1	1	0	1	0	1	0	0	1
1999	0	1	1	0	0	0	1	0	0
2000	1	0	1	1	0	0	0	0	0
TOTAL	3	8	8	24	0	1	5	0	4

	India	Indonesia	Israel	Korea	Mexico	New Zealand	South Africa	Taiwan	Venezuela	TOTAL
Pre-1995	1	0	0	1	14	1	2	0	2	52
1995	0	0	0	0	2	0	0	0	0	8
1996	0	0	1	3	2	0	0	0	0	9
1997	2	0	0	0	2	0	2	0	0	8
1998	2	0	1	0	4	0	0	0	0	12
1999	1	0	1	0	1	0	1	0	0	7
2000	1	0	0	0	1	0	0	0	2	7
TOTAL	7	0	3	4	26	1	5	0	4	103

Appendix 4.8
EFFECT OF ANTIDUMPING MEASURES ON U.S. EXPORTS
(Values in US$)

Country	Product	HTS Codes	Year of AD Measure	Pre-Measure Export Value	Post-Measure Export Value	Change in Export Value	Method *
Argentina	Telephone cable	854420	1994	27,827,864	19,962,391	−28.26%	−1 to +1
Australia	Polyvinyl chloride	390410	1992	3,769,427	2,578,004	−31.61%	−1 to +1
Australia	Triethanolamine & mixtures	292213	1992	83,842	55,313	−34.03%	−1 to +1
Australia	Trifluralin techincal	292143	1993	670,716	0	−100.00%	−1 to +1
Brazil	Aluminium chloride anhydrous	282732	1992	355,251	0	−100.00%	−1 to +2
Brazil	Polyvinyl chloride	390410	1992	9,709,631	1,089,042	−88.78%	−1 to +1
Brazil	Triethanolamine	292213	1993	1,000,671	437,408	−56.29%	−1 to +1
Canada	Copper and brass pipe fittings	741210, 741220	1993	34,227,952	33,246,165	−2.87%	−1 to +1
Canada	Corrosion-resistant steel sheet	721030, 721049, 721220, 721230, 722591, 722592, 722599, 722693, 722694	1994	101,165,183	70,584,079	−30.23%	−1 to +1
Canada	Gypsum board	680911, 680919	1993	15,283,476	1,851,568	−87.89%	−1 to +2
Canada	Iceberg lettuce	070511	1992	82,893,779	79,235,797	−4.41%	−1 to +2
Canada	Machine tufted carpeting	570320	1992	194,330,621	149,439,895	−23.10%	−1 to +1
Canada	Polyiso insulation board	392113	1997	42,158,548	35,878,482	−14.90%	−1 to +2
Canada	Refined sugar	170191, 170199, 170290	1995	50,090,422	4,658,476	−90.70%	−1 to +2
Canada	Synthetic baler twine	560741	1994	5,902,159	485,580	−91.77%	−1 to +2

(continued next page)

Appendix 4.8
Effect of Antidumping Measures on U.S. Exports
(Values in US$) (continued)

Country	Product	HTS Codes	Year of AD Measure	Pre-Measure Export Value	Post-Measure Export Value	Change in Export Value	Method *
Colombia	Ethyl acetate	291531, 291535	1994	1,304,554	563,560	−56.80%	−1 to +1
Colombia	Homopolymer polypropylene	390210	1994	8,166,494	4,129,013	−49.44%	−1 to +2
Colombia	Orthophosphoric acid	280920	1992	215,816	0	−100.00%	−1 to +1
Colombia	Polyvinyl chloride	390410	1999	3,348,050	682,087	−79.63%	−1 to +1
EU	Microdisks (3.5 inch)	852230	1996	142,732,877	129,801,189	−9.06%	−1 to +2
EU	Polysulphide polymers	400299	1998	102,434,520	93,143,736	−9.07%	−1 to +2
EU	Sodium carbonate	283620	1995	25,689,031	18,574,293	−27.70%	−1 to +1
India	Acrylic fiber	550330	1997	5,424,778	0	−100.00%	−1 to +2
India	Bisphenol-A	290723	1997	669,320	40,807	−93.90%	−1 to +1
India	Graphite electrodes	854590	1998	48,701	6,033	−87.61%	−1 to +1
India	Newsprint	480100	1998	5,353,145	944,499	−82.36%	−1 to +2
Israel	Gypsum board	680911, 680919	1996	1,662,529	110,340	−93.36%	−1 to +2
Israel	Medium density fibreboard	441111, 441119, 441121, 441129, 441131, 441139, 441191, 441199	1998	3,701,277	360,780	−90.25%	−1 to +2
Israel	PVC	390410	1999	3,731,901	942,078	−74.76%	−1 to +1
Korea	Choline chloride	292310	1996	63,319	16,200	−74.42%	−1 to +2
Korea	E-Glass fibre	701911, 701912, 701919, 701931	1994	1,357,459	390,833	−71.21%	−1 to +1

(continued)

Country	Product	HTS Codes	Year of AD Measure	Pre-Measure Export Value	Post-Measure Export Value	Change in Export Value	Method *
Korea	Ethanolamines	292211, 292212, 292213	1996	2,993,379	1,598,405	−46.60%	−1 to +2
Mexico	Acrylic fiber	550330, 550630	1991	12,152,959	276,726	−97.72%	−1 to +2
Mexico	Bond paper	482351, 482359	1998	42,802,986	24,462,795	−42.85%	−1 to +1
Mexico	Caustic soda	281511	1995	1,383,829	833,681	−39.76%	−1 to +1
Mexico	High fructose corn syrup	170260	1998	59,584,824	43,332,734	−27.28%	−1 to +2
Mexico	Hydrogen peroxide	284700	1993	3,718,162	436,681	−88.26%	−1 to +1
Mexico	Plastic syringes	901831	1992	54,825,196	29,511,472	−46.17%	−1 to +2
Mexico	Polyvinyl chloride	390410	1991	7,051,154	4,141,519	−41.26%	−1 to +2
Mexico	Regenerated cellulose film, coated	392071, 392072, 392073, 392079, 392114	1997	28,109,516	5,395,680	−80.80%	−1 to +2
Mexico	Swine for slaughter	010310, 010391, 010392	1999	17,794,755	6,028,575	−66.12%	−1 to +1
Safrica	Acetaminophenol	292429	1999	1,677,003	849,518	−49.34%	−1 to +1
Safrica	Aldicarb	380810	1997	7,446,329	7,380,844	−0.88%	−1 to +2
Safrica	Suspension PVC	390410	1997	1,239,562	136,390	−89.00%	−1 to +2
Venezuela	Crystal polystyrene	390311	1994	497,975	0	−100.00%	−1 to +1
Venezuela	High impact polystyrene	390319	1994	3,168,846	111,377	−96.49%	−1 to +2

* Method indicates whether the export comparision was between one year prior to and one year after or one year prior to and two years after the measure.

5. Reforming the WTO Antidumping Agreement

In November 2001, representatives of 142 countries convened in Doha, Qatar, and launched a new round of global trade negotiations. Included on the agenda of the "Doha Round" of World Trade Organization talks was the arcane, highly technical, and intensely controversial subject of antidumping rules. Specifically, talks focused on possible changes to the existing WTO Antidumping Agreement, which governs what WTO member states can and cannot do to protect domestic industries from "dumped" or "unfairly priced" import competition.[1]

The WTO antidumping negotiations faced strong political opposition in the United States. According to that opposition, any change in the WTO Antidumping Agreement threatened to "weaken" the U.S. antidumping law and so expose American industries to unfair foreign competition. Such concerns were reflected in the "trade promotion authority" (TPA) legislation passed by Congress in August 2002. Language in the bill instructed the president, in any trade negotiations, to

> preserve the ability of the United States to enforce rigorously its trade laws, including the antidumping, countervailing duty, and safeguard laws, and avoid agreements which lessen the effectiveness of domestic and international disciplines on unfair trade, especially dumping and subsidies, in order to ensure that United States workers, agricultural producers, and firms can compete fully on fair terms and enjoy the benefits of reciprocal trade concessions.[2]

Nearly identical language was incorporated into a resolution passed by the House of Representatives on November 7, 2001, on the eve of the Doha ministerial conference. That resolution passed by a vote of 410 to 4.[3] And 62 senators signed a letter to the president in May 2001 warning him not to agree to any trade deals that would weaken the antidumping or other trade remedy laws. "Unfortunately, some of our trading partners, many of whom maintain serious unfair trade practices, continue to seek to weaken these laws," the letter stated.[4]

The TPA legislation almost included an amendment that would have provided for the denial of special "fast-track" voting procedures (i.e., an up-or-down vote by Congress without amendments and within specified time periods) to those parts of any trade agreement that made changes to antidumping rules. This so-called Dayton-Craig amendment passed in the original Senate TPA bill but was eventually dropped in conference committee.

Mindful of domestic political pressures, both the Clinton and Bush administrations strongly opposed inclusion of antidumping on the negotiating agenda for the new round. The Clinton administration refused to budge on the issue, and the resulting impasse between the U.S. government and other WTO members was one of the major contributors to the failure to launch a new round at the Seattle ministerial conference in 1999.[5] The Bush administration sought to continue its predecessor's position but ultimately bowed to overwhelming international pressure and agreed at Doha to put antidumping rules on the table.

Although the U.S. government made that important concession, it still sought to limit the scope of WTO negotiations. Specifically, at U.S. insistence, the provision in the Doha ministerial declaration that authorized antidumping talks read in relevant part:

> In light of experience and of the increasing application of these instruments by Members, we agree to negotiations aimed at clarifying and improving disciplines under the [Antidumping Agreement], while *preserving the basic concepts, principles and effectiveness of [the Agreement] and [its] instruments and objectives.* . . . In the initial phase of the negotiations, participants will indicate the provisions, including disciplines on trade distorting practices, that they seek to clarify and improve in the subsequent phase.[6]

The commitment to preserve the "basic concepts, principles and effectiveness" of the agreement and its "instruments and objectives" was inserted after an effort by the United States to limit the scope of permissible changes to antidumping rules.

146

The resistance to changes in the WTO Antidumping Agreement is based on a fundamental misunderstanding of what antidumping laws actually do in practice. Those laws are defended as necessary bulwarks against unfair trade practices. But, as we have argued throughout this book, antidumping laws have little to do with targeting unfair trade under any plausible definition of that term. Stiff antidumping duties are routinely imposed against products of foreign firms that are engaged in perfectly normal and unexceptionable commercial practices. At the root of the problem are serious flaws in the current rules for conducting antidumping investigations. Because of those flaws, there is at present very little connection between the stated objectives of antidumping policy and the actual effects of antidumping actions.

Accordingly, the fear that changes in WTO antidumping rules will expose American industries to unfair competition is entirely misplaced. Significant changes in those rules are needed, not to "weaken" national laws, but to improve them by closing the yawning gap between what they are supposed to do and what they actually do.

The Doha Round of WTO talks offers the chance to close that gap. Although the U.S. government attempted to limit the scope of negotiations with restrictive language in the Doha ministerial declaration, a proper reading of that language makes clear that far-reaching changes in antidumping rules are not precluded. Indeed, that language—with its emphasis on the basic concepts, principles, and objectives of the Antidumping Agreement—provides an excellent point of departure for productive negotiations.

In this chapter we attempt to outline a road map for WTO antidumping negotiations in the Doha Round. We begin with the language of the ministerial declaration and then proceed to identify the basic concepts, principles, and objectives of the Antidumping Agreement—as delineated, not by critics of antidumping practice, but by the U.S. government and policy experts who support the use of antidumping remedies. We then examine how antidumping laws actually work in practice and compare that reality with the purposes those laws are supposed to serve.

That examination defines the basic work program of current and future WTO antidumping negotiations: to reduce the gap between contemporary antidumping practice and the agreed-upon concepts, principles, and objectives of the Antidumping Agreement. We then elaborate upon that basic mission with detailed analysis of the specific changes that are needed in the Antidumping Agreement.

Identifying Antidumping's Objectives

WTO antidumping negotiations should begin at the beginning—by attempting to define the basic concepts, principles, and objectives of the Antidumping Agreement. No such definition has ever emerged from any previous WTO or General Agreement on Tariffs and Trade negotiations. That is an oversight whose correction is long overdue.

The oversight may be explained by the fact that antidumping has been around much longer than the multilateral trading system. Antidumping laws originated in the early years of the 20th century; the U.S. law, for example, dates back to 1921,[7] and laws in Canada, Australia, New Zealand, Great Britain, and France go back even further. These laws thus predate even the original 1947 GATT treaty, Article VI of which provides basic authority for national governments to apply antidumping remedies. Subsequent negotiations to elaborate multilateral standards for the use of antidumping remedies—the Kennedy Round talks that produced an Antidumping Code in 1967, the Tokyo Round talks that revised that code in 1979, and the Uruguay Round talks that produced the current 1994 WTO Antidumping Agreement—simply assumed the background fact of national antidumping laws without making any effort to establish a consensus on why such laws are needed or what purposes they are meant to serve.

With so much water under the bridge, why focus now on what might be considered abstract or theoretical issues? The most obvious reason lies in the language of the ministerial declaration that launched the Doha Round. That declaration authorizes negotiations to amend the existing Antidumping Agreement "while preserving the basic concepts, principles and effectiveness of [the Agreement] and [its] instruments and objectives." To ensure that negotiations do not exceed the scope of this limiting language, it is necessary for parties to determine in the first instance what the basic concepts, principles, and objectives actually are.

Furthermore, antidumping negotiations promise to play a critical role in determining the overall success of the Doha Round. In prior rounds, antidumping was at best a second-tier issue. The United States and what is now the European Union accounted for the overwhelming majority of antidumping cases, and they were united in opposing anything but marginal changes in their laws. Although many other countries may have had an interest in restricting antidumping abuses, none with any bargaining power made that interest a top priority. Consequently, the United States and the European Union were able to contain antidumping reform initiatives within narrow limits without any real sacrifice of their own major negotiating objectives.

This time, the situation is different. With the proliferation of antidumping laws in recent years, the threat that antidumping abuses pose to the world trading system has become an issue of intense and widespread concern. There was overwhelming support for the inclusion of antidumping on the agenda of the Doha Round; indeed, the United States was completely isolated in opposition. As negotiations proceed, many countries can be expected to push antidumping reform as one of their top priorities. Accordingly, the course of the antidumping negotiations is likely to have important implications for the overall outcome of the round. Even if the U.S. government persists in resisting major antidumping reforms, it has a compelling interest in avoiding a rancorous deadlock that jeopardizes its own negotiating priorities.

Unless some common ground is first established, negotiators with opposing interests will simply talk past each other. Antidumping negotiations are simultaneously highly technical and intensely controversial: the details are comprehensible only to experienced specialists, and the general subject matter is one on which views are sharply conflicting and strongly held. That combination is a recipe for impasse and acrimony, not productive results.

A preliminary focus on defining the basic concepts, principles, and objectives of the Antidumping Agreement could help avoid a deadlock that might wreck the whole round. In many other contentious sectors—for example, agriculture and services—parties have made progress by agreeing on basic principles with a commitment to gradual (if unspecified) implementation of those principles in the future. Such an approach might be the only way for the U.S. government to reconcile its present opposition to significant changes in the Antidumping Agreement with its overriding interest in a

149

successful round. If the United States were to accept a clear definition of the basic concepts, principles, and objectives of the Antidumping Agreement, other countries might be satisfied with fairly modest changes to it in the current round. The U.S. government could then remove the antidumping issue as an obstacle to its own major negotiating objectives and ultimately bring home an agreement that keeps controversial changes to U.S. law within tolerable limits.

Meanwhile, supporters of antidumping reform have a strong interest in initial discussions on basic concepts, principles, and objectives. Such discussions, if they were conducted properly, could significantly strengthen the reformers' bargaining position. Specifically, they could enable reformers to claim the rhetorical high ground of support for fairness and a level playing field.

At present, defenders of antidumping stake their case on the grounds of fairness and a level playing field. Any efforts to change current practice, they claim, are really just plots to weaken existing laws and create "loopholes" for unfair traders. Defenders of antidumping thus define the debate as a conflict between a level playing field on the one hand and unfair traders on the other. Those terms, needless to say, strongly favor maintenance of the status quo.

Defenders of antidumping have been able to create and hold this rhetorical advantage because they have never been required to define "fairness" and "level playing field" or explain how current antidumping rules advance those admirable-sounding goals. They simply assert the connection between current antidumping rules and fairness and rely on the complexities of the law's methodologies to shield their assertion from scrutiny. For decades that strategy has been tremendously successful.

Negotiations aimed at fleshing out the basic concepts, principles, and objectives of the Antidumping Agreement could allow antidumping reformers to call their opponents' bluff. If the much-invoked level playing field were actually defined—if the specific circumstances that supposedly give rise to unfair trade were spelled out and the criteria for distinguishing those circumstances from normal conditions of competition were clearly delineated—then antidumping reformers could argue with considerable force that the imposition of antidumping duties in any other circumstances amounts to simple protectionism. Antidumping reformers could turn their opponents' traditional rhetorical advantage against them and claim with justice that they, not defenders of the status quo, are the ones truly concerned with fairness.

They could, in other words, redefine the terms of the debate. Instead of a choice between the level playing field and unfair traders—with defenders of antidumping on the side of the angels—the debate would now offer a choice between a level playing field and old-fashioned protectionism. Supporters of antidumping would at last find themselves on the negotiating defensive.

The effects of changing the terms of debate would be felt within the WTO negotiations themselves, and also in U.S. domestic politics. Within the WTO, antidumping reformers would be better able to recruit allies and isolate their opponents. Their position would be both more attractive and easier to understand, and their ability to persuade fence sitters to join their cause would be correspondingly enhanced. Antidumping reformers were able to force the United States to accept antidumping negotiations in Doha only because they succeeded in isolating the United States diplomatically. If they hope to achieve significant reforms in the present negotiations, they will once again have to rally world opinion to their side. This time the task will be considerably more difficult. Building a consensus on what antidumping is supposed to do (and on the fact that it isn't doing its job properly) would aid the needed diplomatic effort immensely.

Meanwhile, in the United States, a debate that highlighted the contrast between antidumping's objectives and its current practice could drive a wedge between hard-core supporters of the status quo and more casual supporters. The hard core is concerned primarily with the interests of import-competing industries (notably the steel industry) that use the law regularly. To those supporters, results are all that count: anything that makes it easier for domestic industries to win protection makes the law better, and anything that makes protection harder to achieve is a step backward. That standard, of course, has nothing to do with any notions of fair trade; it is a protectionist standard, pure and simple.

On the other hand, many U.S. supporters of the antidumping law are not so blatantly results-oriented. Rather, they are attracted to the idea of a level playing field and believe that antidumping remedies work to secure that noble-sounding objective. If those casual supporters could be made aware of the disconnect between the law's appealing rhetoric and how the law really works, they might be more amenable to changes in antidumping rules—or at least less hostile to such changes. WTO negotiations that focused initially on antidumping's basic concepts, principles, and objectives would illuminate that disconnect, thereby helping to reduce casual supporters' attachment to the antidumping status quo. That change in the U.S. political climate could lead in turn to a more accommodating U.S. position at the negotiating table.

Defining the "Level Playing Field"

What are the basic concepts, principles, and objectives of the Antidumping Agreement? The agreement itself is silent on those matters. It establishes standards for how antidumping investigations are to be conducted and remedies imposed, but it says nothing about why dumping is a problem in the first place. The agreement, in other words, defines the "solution," but not the problem that it supposedly solves. We therefore must look outside the agreement for guidance.

We propose to look for that guidance in the statements of the U.S. government and prominent supporters of the U.S. antidumping law. There are many sound reasons why this approach makes sense. The United States is the world's leading antidumping user.[8] In the international arena, the U.S. government has been the leading defender of the need for "strong" antidumping remedies. In the current WTO negotiations, the United States is expected to be the most formidable opponent of any changes to the Antidumping Agreement that might "weaken" national laws. Accordingly, if it can be shown that existing antidumping rules do a bad job of addressing the problem of dumping as U.S. antidumping supporters define that problem, the strongest possible case for changing the rules will have been made.

The U.S. government recently issued a position paper on the "Basic Concepts and Principles of the Trade Remedy Rules" in the Doha Round antidumping negotiations.[9] This paper provides an excellent starting point for understanding the problem that antidumping laws supposedly solve.

The Bush administration's position paper adopts what has become the standard refrain of U.S. antidumping supporters: that antidumping measures are needed to offset artificial competitive advantages created by market-distorting government policies. According to the document, "Effective trade remedy instruments are important to respond to and discourage trade-distorting government policies and the market imperfections that result."[10] Specifically, the U.S. government argues, government policies can create "artificial" competitive advantages that may be distinguished from the "real" competitive advantages that arise in normal market competition:

> Ideally, companies and nations would compete in the international marketplace on the basis of real comparative advantages such as natural resource endowments, labor skills and abundance, availability of capital, and technological innovation. Faced with the true relative prices of these production factors, companies and nations would gravitate towards producing and exporting those products in which they have a relative cost advantage and buying/importing those products in which they do not have this advantage. . . .
>
> However, government attempts to create artificial advantages distort market signals indicating where the most profitable business opportunities are found. Such distortions can lead to chronic oversupply by inefficient producers on the one hand, and the closure of otherwise efficient and competitive facilities on the other. . . . In short, market-distorting practices reduce worldwide economic efficiency, thereby diminishing the gains to all Members from international specialization and exchange based on comparative advantage.[11]

This formulation of the problem that gives rise to antidumping laws differs somewhat from the others discussed below in that it focuses on efficiency rather than fairness. The Bush administration has focused on the losses to worldwide economic efficiency caused by market-distorting practices; the usual focus, however, is on the unfairness to national industries that must face foreign rivals with artificial (i.e., government policy–caused) competitive advantages. There is no necessary conflict between the differing emphases, however.[12] And in either case, the bottom line is the same: antidumping measures are needed to neutralize artificial competitive advantages and restore the so-called level playing field.

The Bush administration's paper goes on to identify dumping as particular pricing practices that reflect the underlying existence of government policy–caused market distortions. Specifically, the paper states that dumping takes the form of either "international price discrimination" or "export pricing at levels below the cost of production plus a reasonable amount for selling, general and administrative expenses and profit."[13] That definition tracks the one normally supplied by U.S. supporters of antidumping, although the second half of the Bush administration's definition is more expansive than the usual formulation. Typically, dumping is defined as either international price discrimination or sales below the cost of production.

The pricing practices that constitute dumping, however that term is precisely defined, are deemed to be problematic because they supposedly are the consequence of market-distorting government policies. The Bush administration's paper offers little detail here, but the one example it gives is typical of those provided by U.S. antidumping supporters:

> A government's industrial policies or key aspects of the economic system supported by government inaction can enable injurious dumping to take place. . . . For instance, these policies may allow producers to earn high profits in a home "sanctuary market," which may in turn allow them to sell abroad at an artificially low price. Such practices can result in injury in the importing country since domestic firms may not be able to match the artificially low prices from producers in the sanctuary market.[14]

As discussed previously in this book, the association between dumping and "sanctuary markets" figures prominently in the justifications for antidumping laws offered by supporters of the U.S. law.

The Bush administration's interpretation of the basic concepts, principles, and objectives of the Antidumping Agreement shows considerable continuity with the line taken by the Clinton administration in another document that attempted to justify the use of antidumping measures. That earlier document goes into greater depth than the Bush administration's position paper and also accords more closely with the formulations of antidumping policy made by other prominent supporters of the U.S. law. Accordingly, the Clinton administration's paper merits detailed analysis.

The document in question is a 1998 submission by the U.S. government to the WTO Working Group on the Interaction of Trade and Competition Policy.[15] Some members of that working group had asserted that antidumping laws should be judged by the standards of competition policy—in other words, on the basis of whether they promote consumer welfare by targeting anti-competitive conduct. In the submission in question, the Clinton administration argued vociferously against that approach:

> Stated simply, the antidumping rules and competition laws have different objectives and are founded on different principles, and they seek to remedy different problems. If the antidumping rules were eliminated in favor of competition laws or modified to be consistent with competition policy principles, the problems which the antidumping rules seek to remedy would go unaddressed.[16]

In making its case, the submission expounds at considerable length on antidumping rules' underlying objectives and principles by defining the problems that antidumping rules seek to address. Accordingly, the Clinton administration's paper offers illuminating insights into what the basic concepts, principles, and objectives of the Antidumping Agreement might be.

The Clinton administration's paper defines dumping as "a situation where an exporter sells its product abroad at lower prices than it does at home or at prices that are below cost, which causes 'material injury' to producers of the product in the importing country."[17] It then asserts that the need for antidumping rules arises from "imperfections in the multilateral trading system." Specifically, dumping is generally the result of government policies in the dumping exporter's home market:

> Although some dumping may be due to business advantages and market segmentation which have arisen in response to commercial forces, more typically it is a government's industrial policies or key aspects of the national economic system which a government has created, promoted or tolerated that enables injurious dumping to take place.[18]

The 1998 U.S. submission identifies the following industrial policies as possibly giving rise to dumping: high tariffs or nontariff barriers that exclude foreign competition, regulations that restrict domestic competition, the absence of adequate competition laws to counteract private anti-competitive conduct, price controls that set artificially high prices for home-market sales of the exported product or artificially low prices for inputs for the exported product, and government subsidies that give foreign producers an artificial cost advantage or that result in excess capacity. "Although these policies take on many different forms," the paper states, "they provide similar artificial advantages to the benefiting producers." The paper then elaborates:

> Specifically, these policies enable the benefiting producers to charge higher than competitive prices in their home market—what can be thought of as a "sanctuary market"—and, as a result, to realize increased profits. If the government's policies have the effect of lowering the producers' unit costs, the producers may benefit even when they maintain current home market prices. . . . Absent intervention by their own government, competing producers in export markets are at a disadvantage and often suffer injury, such as lost market share, because they cannot match the low pricing from producers in the home market.[19]

The 1998 paper goes on to address how differences in national economic systems can result in dumping. For example, in countries in which social pressures or policies inhibit layoffs during downturns, labor costs are more fixed than variable. In such settings, producers may choose to sell below full costs instead of laying off unneeded workers. In other words, they will "export [their] unemployment to the other country's industry."[20] In another scenario, producers rely more heavily on debt in countries with poorly developed equity markets. They may find it necessary to sell below cost to service their debt obligations, whereas producers with lower debt-equity ratios might cut back production during slumps. The paper also identifies other situations—the presence of large, conglomerate business groupings with noncommercial access to financing; cut-throat pricing encouraged by a policy of adopting "market stabilization" cartels on the basis of precartel production levels; state planning regimes with quantitative export targets—in which differences in national economic structures can lead to dumping.

In sum, the Clinton administration's paper traces the roots of dumping to anti-market policies and institutions. The resulting suppression or distortion of market competition yields either abnormally high prices in the home market or abnormally low prices in export markets—or both. Those artificial pricing patterns are the problem supposedly addressed by antidumping rules. According to the 1998 U.S. paper:

The antidumping rules simply seek to remove unfairness and create a "level playing field" for producers and workers. It therefore may be more appropriate to view the antidumping rules as a judgment by the importing country that it will not accept low-priced or below-cost imports—even if its immediate overall economic welfare would be enhanced— to the extent that acceptance means forcing its producers and workers to compete against, and be injured by, foreign producers receiving unfair advantages from government policies or actions which lead to significant differences in economic systems.[21]

Other prominent supporters of the U.S. antidumping law concur in the overall analysis put forward by the Clinton and Bush administrations. Alan Wolff, counsel to the U.S. steel industry and a leading lobbyist for the antidumping status quo, also identifies two types of dumping, "price-to-price dumping" and "below-cost dumping." In a 1995 speech before the Steel Manufacturers Association, he answered the question, "What gives rise to dumping?" as follows:

Price-to-price dumping. Price-to-price dumping can occur because the dumping industry enjoys some degree of market power in its domestic market which enables it to maintain a higher price in the home market than in export markets. This may arise out of protection of the home market from import competition . . . ; the relative absence of internal competition because of the existence of a monopolistic, oligopolistic or cartelized market structure; or some combination of these factors. Absent such elements, the domestic price and the world price will equalize.

Below-cost dumping. Below-cost dumping can occur because the industry which is dumping possesses a structural characteristic which enables it to export its products below the cost of production for a sustained period without going out of business. Such characteristics vary widely, but may include the existence of some form of government support, the ability to cross-subsidize losses in one product area with profits earned in other areas, or simply enormous resources which make it possible to sell at a loss for a long period of time.[22]

Terence Stewart, another prominent attorney who represents domestic industries in U.S. antidumping investigations, takes a similar line. The antidumping law, he argues, is "designed to offset any artificial advantage that flows from closed foreign markets, cross-subsidization by multiproduct producers, government largesse, or other factors having nothing to do with comparative advantage."[23]

Greg Mastel is an economist who supports active use of antidumping laws. His views on the need for antidumping rules align closely with those expressed in the two U.S. government papers as well as those of Wolff and Stewart. Mastel identifies government interventionism—whether targeted subsidies or the pervasive controls of nonmarket economies—as a major cause of dumping. In particular, he pays special attention to the interrelation between dumping and sanctuary markets:

> A secure closed home market or sanctuary market encourages companies to make aggressive production and expansion decisions because they can be certain of selling a percentage of their production at home at good prices. . . . From a sanctuary market, it is also possible to dump in the markets of foreign competitors to depress the profit margins of those competitors and reduce their funds available for investment in R&D and marketing.
>
> Companies from countries with open markets do not enjoy this luxury. . . . Over time, this puts companies in open-market countries, such as the United States, at a serious disadvantage in competition with companies with sanctuary home markets.[24]

According to Mastel, a closed home market allows a dumping strategy to work by maintaining a price differential between the home and export markets:

> If a company engages in dumping and its home market is open, the price differential will induce the company's competitors or other resellers to reexport dumped products to the dumper's home market. These reexports would quickly pull the home market price down to the dumped price and erase home market profits. Thus, a closed or restricted home market is also a virtual precondition to a successful dumping strategy.[25]

Mastel argues that sanctuary markets can be created either by government-imposed trade barriers or by government acquiescence in the "private-sector protectionism" of anti-competitive collusion.

The justification of antidumping rules advanced in these analyses differs sharply from the popular view that antidumping is a remedy for "predatory" private anti-competitive conduct. The Clinton administration's WTO submission states flatly that "antidumping rules are not intended as a remedy for the predatory practices of firms or as a remedy for any other private anti-competitive practices typically condemned by competition laws."[26] Mastel takes a similar view. "There are only a handful of cases in recent history," he writes, "in which it reasonably can be argued that such a systematic predatory strategy was being followed."[27]

Instead, the U.S. government, through two administrations, and leading supporters of the U.S. antidumping law argue that the law is needed primarily to offset the effects of distortions caused by the anti-market policies of foreign governments. Interventionist policies, it is argued, can confer an artificial or unfair competitive advantage on foreign producers, allowing them to charge lower prices in export markets than at home or to charge below their cost of production. Antidumping remedies offset that artificial advantage and thereby restore a level playing field.

This approach to defining the problem of dumping offers a justification for antidumping rules that can be distinguished from simple protectionism. Many forms of government interventionism do indeed distort markets and give particular firms an artificial competitive advantage. Although it remains highly debatable whether trade barriers are the proper response to such market distortions, at least it can be maintained plausibly that government policy–caused market distortions are a legitimate problem in international trade. The case for trade barriers narrowly targeted at artificially advantaged firms is clearly distinguishable from the case for across-the-board protectionism.

Some of the analyses cited above, however, suggest that dumping can also be the result of purely private conduct. Thus, Wolff suggests that price-discrimination dumping can occur because of oligopolistic market power and that below-cost dumping can be due to cross-subsidization by a multiproduct firm. Stewart also cites cross-subsidization as a possible cause of dumping.

This attempted extension of the definition of dumping's causes cannot survive careful scrutiny. Many manufacturing industries are characterized by oligopolistic competition, and virtually all manufacturing enterprises are multiproduct firms. Yet within the United

159

States, there is no regulation of price premiums earned by oligopolistic firms. For instance, it is not considered legally actionable that a company with a strong brand name can use the strength of its brand to command a higher price. Likewise, there is no general regulation of cross-subsidies by multiproduct firms. For example, a firm that makes razors and blades may sell the former at or even below cost in order to maximize revenue from the latter. If domestic firms are completely free to engage in such practices, one cannot argue plausibly that foreign producers who do exactly the same thing are engaging in unfair trade. Any resorting to antidumping remedies in such situations is indistinguishable from garden-variety protectionism.

Aligning Theory and Practice

Unfortunately, as documented in considerable detail throughout this book, there is little connection between what antidumping laws actually do in practice and what their supporters say they are supposed to do. There is, in other words, a yawning gap between contemporary antidumping laws and the basic concepts, principles, and objectives of the Antidumping Agreement—as antidumping supporters themselves define those concepts, principles, and objectives.

The fundamental problem with antidumping rules today is their failure to limit the application of antidumping remedies to instances of unfair trade under any plausible definition of that term. That failure defines the gap between the basic concepts, principles, and objectives of the Antidumping Agreement and current antidumping practice. Closing that gap by altering the provisions of the Antidumping Agreement ought to be the goal of WTO negotiations— in the present Doha Round and in future rounds if need be.

Below we offer a number of specific proposals for reforming the Antidumping Agreement—not to weaken national antidumping laws, but to improve them. For each proposal, we identify some element of current antidumping practice that conflicts with the basic concepts, principles, and objectives of the Antidumping Agreement. We explain why the element in question is in need of reform and then discuss how the proposed reform or reforms would help to reduce the gap between antidumping theory and antidumping practice.

Require Evidence of Market Distortions

Critics of the antidumping status quo have a long laundry list of complaints, but surely the fundamental problem with current antidumping practice is the failure to require any direct evidence of underlying market distortions.

The supposed justification for targeting antidumping remedies at price discrimination and below-cost sales is that those pricing practices reflect the existence of underlying, market-distorting government policies. And, indeed, unusually high home-market prices can indicate a closed sanctuary market, and sustained red ink can be a sign of subsidies or "soft budget constraints." But there is a host of other possible explanations for international price differences, most of which have nothing to do with unfair trade under any plausible definition of that term. Likewise with below-cost sales: losses can be found in healthy, competitive markets as well as in distorted markets.

Unfortunately, current antidumping practice includes no mechanism for weeding out "false positives"—for distinguishing between those instances of targeted pricing practices that actually reflect underlying market distortions and those that have a perfectly innocent explanation. Under present rules, sales at less than normal value are simply assumed to be unfair—an assumption that is often completely unsupportable. Consequently, antidumping remedies are frequently imposed on exporters for engaging in normal commercial conduct that has nothing at all to do with unfair trade or an unlevel playing field.

Antidumping remedies will routinely deviate from the basic concepts, principles, and objectives of the Antidumping Agreement so long as this fundamental flaw remains uncorrected. There are many possible approaches to addressing this problem, but we suggest the following reforms. First, domestic industries should be required to present evidence of underlying market distortions in their antidumping petitions:

> **Reform Proposal 1**: Article 5.2 of the Antidumping Agreement should be amended to require domestic industries to provide credible evidence of underlying market distortions in the antidumping petition. If price-discrimination dumping is alleged, the evidence must indicate the existence of (1) tariffs significantly higher than those in the export market

under investigation, (2) nontariff barriers significantly higher than those in the export market under investigation, (3) government restrictions on competition in the home market, or (4) government acquiescence in private anti-competitive conduct. If sales-below-cost dumping is alleged, the evidence must relate to the existence of (1) subsidies that allow persistent losses to continue or (2) other government policies that create a "soft budget constraint" that allows persistent losses to continue.

In addition, national antidumping authorities should be required to make a finding of underlying market distortions before initiating an investigation as well as in their final determination of sales at less than normal value:

> **Reform Proposal 2**: Article 5.3 of the Antidumping Agreement should be revised to require antidumping authorities, before they initiate an investigation, to find that the domestic industry has provided credible evidence of underlying market distortions. Furthermore, Article 2 of the Antidumping Agreement should be amended to provide that authorities may find dumping only if they determine, on the basis of credible evidence provided by the domestic industry, that the price discrimination or below-cost sales found during the investigation reflect the existence of underlying market distortions as alleged in the petition.

It should be noted that the reform proposal above does not confer any new investigatory powers on national antidumping authorities. Any open-ended mandate to investigate "hidden" trade barriers, anti-competitive conduct, or other market distortions could easily lead to abusive "fishing expeditions." Responding to antidumping questionnaires is already far too burdensome; requiring respondents, under the threatened use of facts available, to satisfy antidumping authorities' potentially limitless curiosity about conditions in the home market would make a bad situation immeasurably worse. Accordingly, in the above proposal, findings by antidumping authorities of underlying market distortions are to be based on evidence provided by the domestic industry in its petition and subsequent submissions—not on any independent fact-finding by the authorities themselves.

162

Procedural fairness dictates that respondents in antidumping investigations should be able to rebut the evidence of market distortions provided by the domestic industry. In particular, they should be allowed to provide affirmative defenses to refute any causal connection between distortions in the home market and the pricing practices under investigation:

> **Reform Proposal 3**: Article 6 of the Antidumping Agreement should be revised to give respondents the right to present evidence that the pricing practices under investigation are due to factors other than distortions in the home market. In investigations of price-discrimination dumping, respondents would have the right to show, for example, that (1) high home-market prices are due to normal commercial factors (for example, strong brand-name recognition); (2) notwithstanding the existence of high prices, the respondent does not enjoy unusually high home-market profits on sales of the subject merchandise (and thus does not enjoy any artificial competitive advantage); or (3) the respondent's home market is too small for high profits in that market to confer an artificial competitive advantage in the export market under investigation. In investigations of sales-below-cost dumping, respondents would have the right to show, for example, that below-cost sales were made (1) to maximize the contribution to fixed costs; (2) to maximize overall revenue of joint products, products that share overhead, or complementary goods; (3) to maximize long-term revenue by exploiting learning-curve effects or by building long-term market position; or (4) otherwise as part of a conscious strategy to maximize long-term profits. National antidumping authorities must take this evidence into account when determining whether the pricing practices under investigation actually reflect (rather than merely coincide with) the existence of underlying market distortions.

The reform proposals above, if adopted, would mark a significant departure from traditional antidumping policy. But the fact is that traditional policy has been sharply at odds with the basic concepts, principles, and objectives that it supposedly serves. If the enormous gap between antidumping rhetoric and antidumping reality is to be closed, proposals along the lines of those suggested above will be an essential element of the overall reform program.

Eliminate the Cost Test

Current antidumping rules fail to achieve their supposed objectives on two basic levels. First, as discussed above, they make no attempt to connect the targeted pricing practices of price discrimination and sales below cost to underlying market distortions. Second, they do a poor job of identifying actual instances of price discrimination and below-cost export sales. Because of methodological distortions in the rules that define dumping, findings of sales at less than normal value all too frequently have little or nothing to do with the presence of price discrimination or below-cost export sales.

The use of the "cost test" is probably the single most egregious methodological distortion in contemporary antidumping practice. Like many other distortions, it skews comparisons of home-market and export prices and thereby artificially inflates dumping margins. What is especially noteworthy about the cost test, though, is that it operates to inflate dumping margins under specific conditions that are the complete opposite of those that supposedly give rise to unfair trade.

The existence and extent of dumping are at present determined by a comparison of export prices to "normal value," which is typically based on prices in the foreign producer's home market. If adjusted export prices are lower than normal value, dumping is said to exist; the difference between normal value and net export prices, divided by net export prices, is the dumping margin or dumping rate.

Under the cost test, home-market sales found to be below the cost of production are excluded from the calculation of normal value. As a result, all export prices are compared to those of only the highest (that is, above-cost) home-market sales. This asymmetric comparison skews the calculation in favor of finding dumping.

In the U.S. antidumping cases we examined in Chapter 3, the effect on dumping margins was dramatic. As Table 3.4 indicates, each of the 17 cases against market-economy countries had margins that were inflated by the cost test (investigations of countries judged to be nonmarket economies use a different method for calculating dumping in which the cost test is irrelevant). In two cases, the calculated dumping margin would have been zero had the cost test not been administered. Most of the remaining 15 would have had margins at least 50 percent lower than the rate ultimately calculated.

164

On average, the 17 cases would have had margins 59.69 percent lower.

What possible purpose could be served by excluding below-cost home-market sales from normal value? Remember that the theory behind price-discrimination dumping is that the foreign producer is enjoying an artificial advantage because of a sanctuary market at home. According to the theory, trade barriers or other restrictions on competition cause prices (and profits) in the home market to be artificially high, thus allowing the foreign producer to unfairly cross-subsidize cheap export sales. Consequently, price differences between the export market and the home market are supposedly probative of unfair trade because they might indicate the existence of a closed sanctuary market in the foreign producer's home market. Whether those price differences exist, though, cannot be fairly determined if all the lowest home-market prices are excluded from the comparison.

Moreover, the existence of below-cost sales in the home market is actually affirmative evidence of the absence of a sanctuary market. A sanctuary market, after all, is supposed to be an island of artificially high prices and profits. If home-market sales at a loss are found in significant quantities, isn't that a fairly compelling indication that there is no sanctuary market? But because of the cost test, it is precisely under those conditions that dumping margins are boosted significantly higher than they otherwise would be.

This absurd methodology clearly flies in the face of the basic concepts, principles, and objectives of the Antidumping Agreement. Yet it is nonetheless specifically authorized under Article 2.2.1 of the current agreement. Under this authority, the cost test has become a central feature of antidumping investigations. The survey of U.S. antidumping cases over a three-year period discussed in Chapter 2 found that only 4 of 37 determinations in which home-market sales were available as a basis for normal value employed a pure comparison of home-market and U.S. prices. In 33 of 37 determinations, or 89 percent of the time, the DOC excluded some or all home-market sales through use of the cost test. The average dumping margin when the cost test was used was 16.14 percent; by comparison, in the four determinations when the cost test wasn't employed, the average dumping margin was only 4 percent.[28]

Because the cost test is explicitly authorized in the current agreement, and because it is such a regular feature of contemporary antidumping investigations, resistance to reform in this area will be fierce. And there is only one reform that is adequate: outright elimination of the cost test.

The pretext for excluding below-cost sales from normal value is that such sales are not in the "ordinary course of trade." While it might make sense to exclude certain aberrant sales—sales of obsolete inventory or damaged goods—there is no serious case that unprofitable sales are outside the ordinary course of trade. In normal, healthy, competitive markets, there is nothing extraordinary at all about red ink—especially on a product-specific rather than a company-wide basis. It is absolutely routine for companies to fail to cover full costs of production on particular products at particular times. Selling below full cost is often the rational, profit-maximizing strategy. As long as variable costs of production are covered by the selling price, any contribution that price makes to covering fixed costs is more than would be received if the product did not sell at all, which is often the alternative if the price is incrementally higher.

Accordingly, the Antidumping Agreement should be revised to prohibit use of the cost test:

> **Reform Proposal 4**: Article 2.2.1 of the Antidumping Agreement should be rewritten to make clear that exclusion of home-market sales from the calculation of normal value is permitted only in the case of specified aberrational sales. In particular, sales must not be categorized as outside the ordinary course of trade simply because they are made at less than the full cost of production.

Until this reform is made, antidumping practice will bear little relation to its stated justification of remedying market distortions.

Revise Criteria for Use of "Constructed Value"; Eliminate Profit Component

Supporters of antidumping generally contend that dumping takes two basic forms: price-discrimination dumping and below-cost dumping. For the former, the cost test discussed above and many other methodological distortions discussed below ensure that actual price discrimination is rarely targeted in antidumping investigations, since comparisons of prices are often badly skewed. Meanwhile, the inclusion of profit in the calculation of constructed value means that below-cost export sales are never directly targeted.

166

The closest that current antidumping rules come to examining whether export sales are below cost is when constructed value is used as the basis of normal value. Constructed value is the U.S. term for an artificial price that is determined by calculating the unit cost of production for a given product and then adding some amount for profit. Constructed value is used only when (1) virtually all the foreign producer's sales of the subject merchandise are to the export market under investigation (that is, no "viable" home market or third-country export markets exist); (2) there is a viable comparison market for the merchandise, but no models sufficiently similar to those sold in the export market are sold there; or (3) all sales of similar comparison-market models have been excluded by the cost test.

Accordingly, antidumping rules are egregiously misdesigned for the purpose of detecting below-cost export sales. First of all, export sales are compared to constructed value only under exceptional circumstances that bear no relationship whatsoever to the likelihood that export sales may be below cost. If the problem to be addressed is below-cost export sales, what does it matter whether there are viable comparison markets, or comparable comparison-market products, or above-cost comparison-market products? Those criteria are completely irrelevant and therefore should not be preconditions for comparing export prices to constructed value.

Accordingly, the Antidumping Agreement should be amended to revise the criteria for use of constructed value:

> **Reform Proposal 5**: Article 2 of the Antidumping Agreement should be revised to provide for two alternative bases of normal value: price-to-price comparisons of export and home-market sales (unmodified by any cost test in the home market) and cost of production (known in the United States as constructed value). Which basis is used will depend on the form of dumping alleged by the petitioner. In its petition the domestic industry will allege either price-discrimination dumping or below-cost dumping, with appropriate corroborating evidence. If a price-discrimination case is initiated, normal value will be based on home-market prices; if a below-cost case is initiated, normal value will be based on cost of production.

Furthermore, if the goal is to determine whether export sales are below cost, then export prices should be compared to actual unit costs of production—not cost plus profit. An ex-factory export price that is lower than the cost of production plus profit indicates only that the export price is below a certain level of profitability. Yet supporters of antidumping generally define dumping, not as "insufficiently profitable" sales, but as below-cost sales. The remedy should target the problem.

It should be noted that the U.S. 2002 position paper on trade remedy rules does define dumping more broadly to include "export pricing at levels below the cost of production plus a reasonable amount for selling, general and administrative expenses and profit"[29]—a formulation that tracks the definition of constructed value under U.S. law. In support of this more expansive definition, it can be argued that a "normal" profit is part of a company's cost of capital. In other words, a company earning a subnormal return is selling below its full economic costs, if above its full accounting costs. Nevertheless, the Bush administration's definition goes beyond the prevailing characterization of dumping—and is unwarranted in doing so, since any claim that low profitability is evidence of market distortions is much weaker than is the case with respect to outright losses. Determining exactly what constitutes a normal rate of profit for a given company in a given industry at a given time is significantly more difficult than determining whether or not that company is losing money. Moreover, low profits are generally sustainable over much longer periods than are outright losses. Persistent failure to earn competitive returns can undermine a company's ability to make necessary investments and thereby may lead eventually to outright losses; it may also threaten the employment security of the company's management. Unlike sustained losses, though, low profitability in and of itself does not imperil a company's solvency and future as a going concern. Accordingly, even chronically low profits are much less suggestive of "artificial" market conditions caused by government policies than is genuine red ink.

The present inclusion of profit in constructed value serves to inflate dumping margins inappropriately. In 5 of the 18 actual U.S. dumping determinations that we examined in Chapter 3, constructed value was used for at least some product comparisons. In 4 of those 5, the profit element influenced the outcome. Had profit not been added to constructed value, the average calculated dumping margin would have been 11.02 percent lower (Table 3.4). In particular, the margin reduction would have been 22.80 percent in an investigation involving concrete reinforcing bars from Moldova, 18.25 percent in an investigation of static random access memories (SRAMs) from Taiwan, and 13.91 percent in an investigation concerning dynamic random access memories (DRAMs) from Taiwan.

The Antidumping Agreement should therefore be amended as follows:

> **Reform Proposal 6**: Article 2.2 of the Antidumping Agreement should be revised to exclude profit from the calculation of cost of production (known in the United States as constructed value).

If negotiators are unable to make this reform, an alternative, "second best" proposal is to revise the way profit is calculated. Under current practice, profit is usually calculated on the basis of above-cost comparison-market sales only. Clearly, if an estimated amount for profit must be included in constructed value, then limiting consideration to only the profitable sales distorts the actual profitability picture, artificially inflating profits—and therefore normal value, and therefore dumping margins. Current practice can result in absurdly high amounts for profit. As discussed in Chapter 2, Chen Hao Taiwan was given a profit rate of 25.77 percent in the 1997 U.S. investigation of melamine institutional dinnerware from Taiwa; in the parallel investigation of dinnerware from Indonesia, PT Multi Raya was given a profit rate of 22.61 percent. The average profit rate for the U.S. plastic products industry, by contrast, was only 5.23 percent (Table 2.4). The methodology of using only above-cost sales for calculation of profit routinely yields such absurd results.

Accordingly, if constructed-value profit is retained, its calculation should be reformed:

> **Reform Proposal 7**: If profit is not excluded altogether from the calculation of cost of production, it should be based on actual representative profit rates for the subject merchandise. Specifically, profit rates should be based on average industry-wide profit rates derived from public sources. In any event, profit should never be calculated on the basis of the foreign producer's (or anyone else's) above-cost sales only.

While any inclusion of profit in constructed value is inconsistent with the basic concepts, principles, and objectives of the Antidumping

Agreement, the reform outlined above would at least curtail some of the most egregious abuses created by this methodological distortion.

Eliminate Use of Third-Country Sales in Calculating Normal Value

Article 2.2 of the present Antidumping Agreement provides for the use of third-country sales as the basis of normal value under specified circumstances—in particular, when the foreign producer under investigation does not sell the subject merchandise in its home market or sells in insufficient volumes there to "permit a proper comparison." Although expressly allowed under current antidumping rules, a comparison of third-country prices to export prices has no rational relation to the basic concepts, principles, and objectives of the Antidumping Agreement.

Dumping, once again, is supposed to consist of either international price discrimination that reveals the existence of a sanctuary market or below-cost sales that reveal some underlying, market-distorting government policies. A comparison of export and third-country prices is incapable of identifying either phenomenon. First, and most obviously, a comparison of prices in the export market under investigation to prices in other export markets says nothing about whether the investigated sales are below cost. Second, while differences between export-market prices and third-country prices can possibly show international price discrimination, they cannot reveal a sanctuary market. Any foreign producer under investigation is an "outsider" as far as all third-country markets are concerned; it is hindered, not helped, by any government barriers that block access to its export sales. If for some reason the company is earning higher prices in that third country, the reason clearly is not that government-imposed barriers are shielding it from competition. On the contrary, it had to overcome any barriers that were present in that third-country market to be selling there at all. Meanwhile, prices charged in a third country indicate nothing about whether a firm's home market is closed.

Since a comparison of export-market and third-country prices cannot possibly identify any of the practices supposedly targeted by antidumping policy, it follows that third-country prices are an inappropriate basis for normal value. Accordingly, the Antidumping Agreement needs to be revised along the following lines:

> **Reform Proposal 8**: Article 2.2 of the Antidumping Agreement should be amended to provide that, in the absence of sufficient home-market sales, there is no basis for an allegation of price-discrimination dumping.

After this reform, the petitioning domestic industries would still be able to allege below-cost dumping in those cases where there are insufficient home-market sales. But it would no longer be possible to allege price-discrimination or sanctuary-market dumping when the alleged sanctuary market doesn't even exist.

Prohibit "Zeroing"

The practice of "zeroing" is one of the most notorious distortions in current antidumping methodology. It occurs in the final dumping determination, when the foreign producer's export prices (whether individual transactions or model-specific averages) are compared to normal value (usually average prices of comparable home-market merchandise). When normal value is higher than the export price, the difference is treated as the dumping amount for that sale. When, however, the export price is higher, the dumping amount is treated as equal to zero. All dumping amounts are then added and divided by the aggregate export sales amount to yield the company's overall dumping margin.

Zeroing thus eliminates "negative dumping margins" from the dumping calculation. In so doing, it can create dumping margins out of thin air. Consider the results of the 18 U.S. dumping determinations that we examined in Chapter 3. All of the 17 determinations involving market economies had margins inflated by zeroing. In 5 of the cases, the overall dumping margin would have been negative. On average, the margin results of the 17 cases would have been 86.41 percent lower if zeroing had not been employed (see Table 3.4).

The practice of zeroing has been found to violate the current Antidumping Agreement. In a case brought by India against the European Union involving bed linen, the WTO Appellate Body ruled in March 2001 that the EU's practice was WTO-inconsistent.[30] The European Union has since changed its practice as a consequence of the Appellate Body's ruling, but it still has not abandoned zeroing completely.[31]

The practice of zeroing continues unabated in other jurisdictions, most notably the United States. The DOC has thus far refused to

171

alter its practice, dismissing the *EU-Bed Linen* case on the ground that the United States was not a party. Given the EU's continued (if limited) use of zeroing, the United States' complete intransigence, and the need generally to provide certainty for worldwide antidumping practice, a revision of the Antidumping Agreement to expressly prohibit zeroing is called for:

> **Reform Proposal 9**: Article 2 of the Antidumping Agreement should be revised to clarify that the practice of zeroing is prohibited. Specifically, when calculating dumping margins, negative dumping amounts (i.e., instances in which export prices are higher than normal value) should be treated as such and given their full weight in the calculation of the foreign producer's overall dumping margin.

Especially in light of the Appellate Body's decision in the *EU-Bed Linen* case, this reform would be in full accord with the basic concepts, principles, and objectives of the Antidumping Agreement. Any measurement of international price differences that recognizes differences in only one direction and systematically ignores differences in the other direction has no methodological validity whatsoever. Eliminating zeroing would help to ensure that the price differences targeted by antidumping remedies actually exist in reality and are not just artifacts of skewed methodologies.

To close the door on zeroing completely, it would be helpful to supplement the reform proposal above as follows:

> **Reform Proposal 10**: Article 2.4.2 of the Antidumping Agreement should be amended to require that, in both original investigations and administrative reviews, dumping margins must be calculated on the basis of comparing average export prices to average normal values or else transaction-specific export prices to transaction-specific normal values. Comparisons of individual export prices to average normal values are never allowed.

Under the current Antidumping Agreement, Article 2.4.2 provides that "in the investigation phase" dumping margins shall "normally" be established on the basis of comparing average prices to average prices or transaction-specific prices to transaction-specific prices. It does, however, allow comparisons of individual export prices to average normal values "if the authorities find a pattern of export prices which differ significantly among different purchasers, regions or time periods." The ostensible purpose of this exception is to address instances of so-called targeted dumping, in which unfairly low prices to specific customers or regions or at specific times are masked by higher prices otherwise.

The current wording of Article 2.4.2 creates possible openings for the continued use of zeroing notwithstanding the Appellate Body's opinion in the *EU-Bed Linen* case. As explained above (see note 31), the Appellate Body concluded that zeroing is WTO-inconsistent because it prevents true average-to-average comparisons as called for by Article 2.4.2. This reasoning leaves open the possibility that zeroing may be permissible when dumping is calculated another way. Indeed, since the agreement explicitly allows individual-to-average comparisons under certain circumstances, and since those comparisons would yield exactly the same results as average-to-average comparisons unless zeroing is employed for the former, there is a plausible argument that zeroing is implicitly permitted under current WTO rules whenever individual-to-average comparisons are allowed.

Thus, zeroing may be consistent with Article 2.4.2 as currently worded in targeted dumping cases. That is the EU's position at present.[32] In addition, the United States claims that the reference to "the investigation phase" in Article 2.4.2 implies that average-to-average comparisons are the rule only in investigations, and that individual-to-average comparisons are allowed generally in administrative reviews. Accordingly, the DOC currently uses average-to-average comparisons in investigations and individual-to-average comparisons in reviews—with zeroing used in both methodologies. Thus, even if the United States eventually loses a WTO challenge along the lines of the *EU-Bed Linen* case, it could continue to argue that zeroing remains permissible, not only in targeted dumping situations during original investigations, but also in all administrative reviews.[33]

A clear rule against individual-to-average comparisons under any circumstances is necessary to eliminate all uncertainty and ensure that zeroing is completely abolished. As to concerns about targeted dumping, allowing the imposition of customer-specific antidumping duty rates would be preferable to the exaggeration of overall duty rates that zeroing causes.

Eliminate Asymmetric Treatment of Indirect Selling Expenses

Dumping calculations are not based on a comparison of actual sales prices in the comparison and export markets. Rather, antidumping authorities perform numerous adjustments to actual sales prices and then compare the adjusted "net" prices. The adjustments are designed to produce "apples-to-apples" comparisons by taking into account differences in transportation costs, physical characteristics, credit terms, warranty terms, and other selling expenses. If, however, adjustments are made asymmetrically—that is, subtractions are made from the export price but not from the home-market price—dumping margins can be generated out of thin air.

At present, a glaring asymmetry exists in the treatment of indirect selling expenses in "constructed export price" situations. Under U.S. law, indirect selling expenses are expenses that do not vary directly with the volume of sales—sales staff salaries, sales department overhead, and the like. In export price situations—that is, when the foreign producer sells directly to an unrelated purchaser in the export market—no adjustment is made to export or home-market prices for such indirect selling expenses. But in "constructed export price" situations—when the foreign producer sells to unrelated customers through a related reseller in the export market—certain indirect expenses are deducted. Specifically, all indirect selling expenses incurred with specific respect to the export market are deducted from the export price, but the adjustment to home-market price for home-market-related indirect selling expenses is capped at the amount of the export-market indirect selling expenses. All home-market-related indirect selling expenses in excess of the cap are simply disregarded.

There is no possible justification for this asymmetry. The policy of deducting export-market indirect expenses is apparently based on the assumption that resales by the reseller in the export market are on a different level of trade—and therefore include additional expenses—than direct sales by the foreign producer in the home market. That assumption, though, is completely arbitrary. It may be that the reseller's customers are large national distributors, while the foreign producer sells directly to small local wholesalers—in which case the home-market price actually has more of the distribution chain built into it than does the export price.

This asymmetry—known as the "CEP offset cap"—skews dumping calculations in the direction of higher dumping margins. If export-market indirect expenses are greater than equivalent home-market expenses, then both are fully taken into account; if, however, the home-market expenses are greater, they are capped. The result in that case is an artificially inflated normal value—and an artificially inflated dumping margin.

Ten of the 18 actual U.S. cases we examined in Chapter 3 would have had lower dumping margins if the asymmetry of the CEP offset cap had been eliminated. For example, in two reviews involving tapered roller bearings from Japan (one review involved "large" bearings; the other involved "small" bearings), if no indirect selling expenses had been deducted on either side, the dumping margin in the large bearings case would have been 25.55 percent lower, and its rate in the small bearings case could have been 15.84 percent lower. For the 10 determinations involving CEP transactions, the average effect of eliminating the deduction of indirect selling expenses was to reduce the dumping margin by 9.06 percent (Table 3.4).

It makes no sense to adjust prices automatically for indirect selling expenses. There is no reasonable basis for assuming such overhead costs are built directly into the selling price. Stripping them out of the price, instead of creating fairer price comparisons, produces price comparisons even more removed from the actual market reality of real sales prices. This artificiality is exacerbated by the asymmetry of always deducting all export-market indirect selling expenses while only partially deducting equivalent home-market expenses. The proper approach would be to end the automatic deduction of any indirect selling expenses from either the constructed export price or the home-market price.

At present the Antidumping Agreement is silent on the specific issue of the CEP offset cap (although Article 2.4 does require a "fair comparison" between export price and normal value). Accordingly, supplemental language is necessary to make clear that this arbitrary and asymmetric distortion is prohibited:

> **Reform Proposal 11**: Article 2.3 of the Antidumping Agree-
> ment (which deals with constructed export price situations)
> should prohibit the automatic deduction of indirect selling
> expenses from either the constructed export price or the
> comparison-market price. In situations where the related
> reseller's sales in the export market are deemed to take place on

a different level of trade from sales in the home market, differences in indirect selling expenses might serve as one possible basis for quantifying the appropriate level-of-trade adjustment.

This reform would eliminate the asymmetry of the CEP offset cap by eliminating indirect-selling-expense deductions altogether in normal cases. As a result, price comparisons would be fairer and more realistic—and the chances of penalizing firms for normal commercial conduct simply because of flawed methodologies would be correspondingly reduced.

Special Consideration for Second-Quality Merchandise

The Antidumping Agreement is currently silent on the treatment of second-quality merchandise. This silence needs to be remedied, since export sales of second-quality merchandise now tend to generate large dumping margins—not because of any unfair trade, but simply as a result of methodological flaws in dumping calculations.

Production processes do not always yield exactly what was intended. If the output fails to meet desired specifications or tolerances, it is considered second-quality merchandise—and is consequently sold at steeply discounted prices. Under current antidumping rules, sales of second-quality merchandise in the export market almost always give rise to high dumping margins.

Ideally, such sales would be compared to equivalent sales in the home market. Such comparisons are usually precluded, however, by the operation of the cost test. Although second-quality merchandise must be sold at lower prices than the prime merchandise it was intended to be, it costs the same to produce as prime merchandise. As a result, second-quality merchandise is almost always sold at prices below the cost of production. With all home-market sales of second-quality goods eliminated by the cost test, export sales of second-quality merchandise must be compared to much higher priced home-market sales of prime merchandise.

Antidumping rules do provide for price adjustments for physical differences in products. When export sales are compared to home-market sales of nonidentical merchandise, a difference-in-merchandise, or DIFMER, adjustment is made to compensate for physical differences and thereby, presumably, ensure an "apples-to-apples" comparison. Unfortunately, however, DIFMER adjustments are typically calculated as the difference in the variable costs of the models being compared. While there are real and important physical differences between prime and second-quality merchandise, there are no cost differences, and therefore no basis for a DIFMER adjustment. Accordingly, when second-quality export sales are compared to prime home-market sales, typically there is no adjustment of the large price difference between them, and the end result is a large dumping margin on those sales.

Much of the problem with second-quality merchandise would disappear if the cost test were eliminated. Export sales of off-quality goods could be compared to equivalent home-market sales—provided such sales existed in the home market. But if the cost test is retained, something needs to be done about this specific problem. And even if the cost test is eliminated, the problem still arises whenever there are export sales of second-quality merchandise but no corresponding home-market sales.

Accordingly, even if the cost test is eliminated, but especially if it isn't, the Antidumping Agreement needs to be modified along the following lines:

> **Reform Proposal 12**: Article 2 of the Antidumping Agreement needs to include a special provision dealing with sales of second-quality merchandise in the export market. This provision should require national antidumping authorities either to (1) disregard sales of second-quality merchandise in their dumping calculations or (2) compare export sales of second-quality merchandise to corresponding comparison-market sales without regard to whether the comparison-market sales are below the full cost of production. If export sales of second-quality merchandise are included in the dumping calculation, but there are no corresponding home-market sales, comparisons of the export sales to comparison-market sales of prime merchandise should receive a special DIFMER adjustment that reflects the average price difference between prime and second-quality subject merchandise.

Under current rules, export sales of second-quality merchandise are virtually certain to generate dumping margins—simply because of quirks in dumping-calculation methodologies. As a result, companies are being punished for normal commercial practices that have nothing to do with unfair trade under any plausible definition of that term. Fidelity to the basic concepts, principles, and objectives of the Antidumping Agreement requires that this abuse be eliminated.

Tighten Standards on Causation of Injury

In keeping with traditional practice, the current Antidumping Agreement requires more than simply a finding of dumping before antidumping remedies may be imposed. In addition, it requires a finding that dumped imports are causing "material injury" (or threat of material injury) to a domestic industry. This injury requirement is in keeping with the basic concepts, principles, and objectives of the Antidumping Agreement—namely, that trade-restricting remedies be used to offset artificial competitive advantages caused by underlying market distortions. If imports are not materially affecting the competing domestic industry, then clearly there is no artificial competitive advantage to be offset—and thus no cause for antidumping remedies.

Unfortunately, implementation of the injury requirement is seriously flawed under current antidumping rules. The chief problem is the absence of clear standards for judging whether there is a causal link between dumped imports and injury to a domestic industry. Under U.S. law, for example, injury analysis all too often lacks even the semblance of analytical rigor. Any coincidence of significant or rising imports and poor industry performance can serve as the basis for imposing antidumping remedies. The analysis of causation is a "black box"—there is no way of predicting when the International Trade Commission will find injury, or even of being sure that commissioners don't secretly resort to extrastatutory criteria in making their determinations. That said, U.S. practice is a model of transparency and high analytical standards compared to what goes on in many other antidumping jurisdictions.

At a bare minimum, WTO rules should be amended to require, as a necessary but not sufficient condition for finding injury, the existence of a clearly established correlation between increased imports and declining domestic industry performance. Accordingly, we propose a change in the Antidumping Agreement along the following lines:

> **Reform Proposal 13**: Article 3.5 of the Antidumping Agreement should be revised to provide that no affirmative injury determination shall be made in the absence of a substantial

correlation between increased imports during the period of
investigation and declining operating profits for the domestic
industry during the corresponding period. The required
increase in imports may take the form of either an absolute
increase in import volume or a relative increase (i.e., an
increase in market share). In codifying this requirement, the
Antidumping Agreement should make clear that the mere
presence of such a correlation, standing alone, does not neces-
sitate an affirmative determination.

If imports have not increased (whether in absolute or market-
share terms) during the period of investigation, there is no analytically tenable basis for concluding that any woes suffered by the
domestic industry during that period are due to imports rather than
some other factor. Although there are many indicators of industry
performance besides operating profits (including sales volumes,
average prices, investment, and employment), operating profits go
to the heart of an industry's well-being. Profit levels reflect both
volumes and prices, and they have a direct impact on investment
and employment. A bright-line requirement of a substantial (i.e.,
statistically significant) correlation between increased imports and
declining operating profits is therefore eminently sensible on the
merits and has the added advantage of establishing some minimal
analytical transparency in the injury process.[34]

But appropriate standards for guiding injury determinations cannot stop here. It is not enough to show that imports could have been
responsible for the domestic industry's deteriorating condition. It is
necessary to push beyond mere correlation and require the establish-
ment of a causal link between imports and injury.

Current WTO rules do make some effort along these lines. Specifically, under the "nonattribution" requirement of Article 3.5, antidumping authorities are required to "examine any known factors
other than dumped imports which at the same time are injuring the
domestic industry, and the injuries caused by these other factors
must not be attributed to the dumped imports." In a Japanese challenge to the U.S. antidumping investigation of hot-rolled steel, the
WTO Appellate Body made clear that, under this provision, antidumping authorities are not allowed to lump imports with other
factors and determine that, collectively, all the factors are causing
injury. Rather, authorities must disentangle imports from other factors and judge their injurious effects separately:

We recognize, therefore, that it may not be easy, as a practical matter, to separate and distinguish the injurious effects of different causal factors. However, although this process may not be easy, this is precisely what is envisaged by the non-attribution language. If the injurious effects of the dumped imports and the other known factors remain lumped together and indistinguishable, there is simply no means of knowing whether injury ascribed to dumped imports was, in reality, caused by other factors. Article 3.5, therefore, requires investigating authorities to undertake the process of assessing appropriately, and separating and distinguishing, the injurious effects of dumped imports from those of other known causal factors.[35]

The Appellate Body's interpretation of the nonattribution requirement, though, threatens to lead antidumping investigations into intractable factual and analytical difficulties. In two opinions dealing with causation of injury in the context of the Agreement on Safeguards, the Appellate Body ruled that, once an administering authority isolates the injurious effects of imports from those of other causal factors, the authority need not find that increased imports alone are causing or threatening injury.[36] Rather, the authority need find only a "genuine and substantial relationship of cause and effect" between imports and injury that may be the result of many causes.[37]

How this murky formulation should be applied in practice is unclear. What the Appellate Body's standard appears to involve is some weighing of different causal factors—that is, assigning relative importance to all the various causal factors and then determining whether imports alone contribute "enough" to the combined injurious effect. In many cases, however, such a task would be so analytically daunting as to be impracticable.

There is an easier and better way. We suggest that the approach rejected by the Appellate Body in the context of the Safeguards Agreement be made an explicit requirement in the Antidumping Agreement:

Reform Proposal 14: Article 5.3 of the Antidumping Agreement should be revised to require that antidumping authorities must find that dumped imports, considered alone, are causing material injury or threat thereof.

How is this requirement to be administered when there are multiple causal factors involved? The proper approach is to require antidumping authorities to use basic tools of quantitative economic analysis to determine whether the domestic industry is materially worse off because of dumped imports—or, in other words, whether application of the proposed antidumping measures would make the domestic industry materially better off.

To make this determination, the administering authority would need to estimate the substitutability of subject and nonsubject imports, subject imports and domestic production, and domestic production and other goods. If nonsubject imports substitute easily for subject imports, then the effect of antidumping remedies will be limited, since nonsubject imports will simply fill the place formerly occupied by subject imports. If subject imports and domestic production are not good substitutes (for example, if there are quality differences or other forms of product differentiation), then the injurious effect of subject imports on the prices of domestically produced merchandise will be attenuated. And if other products are good substitutes for the subject merchandise, the effect of antidumping remedies will again be limited, because domestic producers will be constrained from increasing prices because of competition from substitute goods.

Here then is an analytically sound approach to determining causation of injury. Unlike the Appellate Body's muddled approach, it is straightforward and administrable. In the United States, some ITC commissioners in the past used quantitative economic analysis in their determinations; doing so did not prove administratively burdensome. Certainly, making reasonable estimates of substitutability is far easier than assessing individually several different causal factors and assigning to each some level of culpability for an industry's condition.

Use of quantitative economic analysis would not be mechanical: it would require judgment calls and interpretation of evidence. Accordingly, it would not eliminate controversy or conflicting interpretations. Nevertheless, such an approach would at least specify the factors that bear on causation and makes them transparent. It would, in other words, open up the black box of injury analysis. Revising the Antidumping Agreement to require such an approach would be a dramatic step toward making the injury requirement operational in a consistent, administrable, and intellectually credible manner.

Change Standards for "Negligibility"

Under the current Antidumping Agreement, national antidumping authorities are authorized to "cumulate" imports from multiple countries for purposes of making an injury determination. In other words, authorities can group together the imports from some or all countries under investigation and determine whether the combined effect of those imports is to cause or threaten injury. Consequently, imports from a particular country are frequently subject to antidumping duties even though those imports, considered alone, were never found to have caused any harm.

There are understandable reasons for allowing cumulation to some degree. Without it, artificial competitive advantages caused by market distortions might go completely unremedied simply because no one import source, on its own, is considered injurious. On the other hand, dumping is a company- and country-specific phenomenon: the artificial competitive advantages targeted by antidumping policy supposedly accrue to particular companies and arise out of government policies in those companies' particular home markets. Accordingly, if particular companies or even whole countries are such minor players in an export market that they have no significant impact on competitive conditions in that market, then they cannot be said to enjoy any real competitive advantage vis-à-vis the domestic industry—and therefore cannot be proper targets of antidumping remedies.

Current antidumping rules balance these competing considerations by prohibiting the cumulation of "negligible" imports— imports from countries whose combined market share falls below a designated threshold. Specifically, under Article 5.8 of the present Antidumping Agreement, imports from a particular country are considered negligible if they amount to less than 3 percent of total imports of the product under investigation—unless all the countries under investigation that individually fall under the 3 percent threshold together account for more than 7 percent of total imports.

While the general approach of allowing cumulation except for negligible imports seems basically sound, the current threshold for determining negligibility is indefensible. Specifically, determining negligibility on the basis of percentage of total imports makes no methodological sense. What matters is whether the arguably negligible imports are capable of contributing meaningfully to the injury being suffered by the domestic industry—that is, whether they can be said to enjoy any real competitive advantage relative to the domestic industry. The proper criterion for judging this question is, not share of total imports, but share of the overall export market.

Consider the difference between the two criteria in the context of a recent U.S. antidumping investigation. In the investigation of hot-rolled steel from Argentina, China, India, Indonesia, Kazakhstan, Netherlands, Romania, South Africa, Taiwan, Thailand, and Ukraine, five countries were considered and rejected for negligibility exclusions because they exceeded the collective threshold: Argentina, 1.74 percent of imports; Kazakhstan, 2.78 percent; South Africa, 2.26 percent; Thailand, 2.40 percent; and Ukraine, 2.65 percent. Although each of those countries fell below the normal negligibility threshold of 3 percent, collectively they accounted for 11.80 percent of imports—and thus their products did not qualify collectively as negligible imports.

In this particular case, however, all imports from all sources accounted for only 26.4 percent of the total U.S. merchant market for hot-rolled steel and only 11.15 percent of total U.S. domestic consumption of hot-rolled steel. Accordingly, the import sources in question had the following market shares: Argentina, 0.46 percent of the merchant market (0.19 percent of total domestic consumption); Kazakhstan, 0.74 percent (0.31 percent); South Africa, 0.60 percent (0.25 percent); Thailand, 0.63 percent (0.27 percent); and Ukraine, 0.70 percent (0.30 percent). Those countries thus had a combined market share of only 3.13 percent—or 1.32 percent, depending on how market share is measured for this particular industry.[38] This level of combined import penetration cannot seriously be considered evidence of an unfair competitive advantage—yet under current antidumping rules such imports can be swept into the maw of a multicountry antidumping duty order.

Furthermore, judging negligibility on the basis of import share makes the standard a variable one—indeed, one that varies in perverse ways. The higher the total level of import penetration, the greater the market share an import source can gain and still be considered negligible—despite the fact that overall high import penetration presumably means that the domestic industry is more vulnerable. Meanwhile, the lower the overall import penetration, the smaller the volume of imports that exceeds the negligibility cutoff—even though the domestic industry is presumably less affected by foreign competition under such circumstances.

Accordingly, Article 5.8 of the Antidumping Agreement should be revised along the following lines:

> **Reform Proposal 15**: Article 5.8 of the Antidumping Agreement should be revised to change the threshold for negligibility from 3 percent of total import volume (and 7 percent collectively) to 2 percent of domestic consumption (and 5 percent collectively).

This proposal would preserve the negligibility rule's tradeoff between cumulation and exemption of small import sources. However, by redefining the criterion for judging negligibility, it would decrease the likelihood that imports that by reason of small volume cannot materially injure a domestic industry get unfairly tangled in protracted antidumping proceedings. It would also discourage the increasingly popular but abusive "shotgun approach" to filing antidumping petitions, in which domestic industries pile up allegations against many small exporting countries, many of which are of no competitive concern whatsoever, just for the purpose of pushing past the collective negligibility threshold of 7 percent.

Raise Initiation Standards

We have already proposed a major change in the process of initiating antidumping investigations—namely, that credible evidence of underlying market distortions be made a requirement for initiation (see Reform Proposals 1 and 2). Even if such fundamental reform of the definition of dumping is not undertaken, there are less far-reaching but still valuable improvements that can be made in the initiation process. Here again, the guiding principle of reform should be to improve antidumping's aim and limit disruption of normal commercial conduct.

Lax initiation standards can be the cause of significant disruptions. This is so because mere allegations of dumping can wreak havoc with trade patterns. Under U.S. law, for example, importers are responsible for paying antidumping duties. Thus, from an importer's perspective, the initiation of an antidumping investigation raises the prospect of significant extra costs in the form of duty liabilities—a prospect that many importers, quite understandably, are anxious to avoid. Consequently, the mere act of launching an antidumping investigation tends to depress imports from investigated countries. And since investigations last for approximately one year, significant damage can be done to a foreign producer even if it is ultimately cleared of all charges.[39]

Under current rules, it is too easy to launch antidumping cases. Here in the United States, innocent companies are frequently harassed by ill-founded charges and unnecessary investigations. Consider, for example, the fact that about 35 percent of U.S. cases result in findings of no injury or no dumping. In other words, even assuming that all affirmative dumping and injury findings are justified, more than one-third of all U.S. investigations result in year-long disruptions in fairly traded imports' access to the U.S. market.

Furthermore, it is instructive to compare dumping margins alleged in U.S. antidumping petitions with the dumping margins actually found by the DOC. Although the DOC's calculations are rife with methodological distortions that inflate dumping margins, they generally result in dumping margins substantially lower than those alleged in the petition. For example, in original investigations during 2001 in which adverse facts available were not used, the DOC found an average dumping margin of 38.18 percent. By contrast, the average dumping margin alleged in the petitions in those cases was 100.80 percent—more than twice as high.[40] It is clear, then, that the evidentiary quality of dumping allegations in U.S. petitions is extremely low—yet it nonetheless passes muster with the DOC.

Hair-trigger initiation of antidumping cases is by no means an exclusively American problem. For example, a WTO dispute settlement action brought by Mexico against Guatemala addressed the issue of lax initiation standards. At the center of the dispute was Guatemala's decision to initiate an antidumping investigation of gray portland cement from Mexico on the basis of laughably flimsy evidence. The only evidence of dumping provided in the petition was two sets of invoices: two Mexican invoices for one bag of cement each and two invoices for Guatemalan imports from Mexico of thousands of bags each. Given the glaring differences in sales volumes and levels of trade of the two sets of invoices, it should have been

185

obvious that this documentation provided no evidence of dumping. Nevertheless, Guatemalan authorities initiated the case. Meanwhile, the two import invoices also served as the only evidence in support of the petitioner's allegation of threatened injury.

In this particular case, the WTO found that Guatemala's initiation of an investigation under these circumstances was improper.[41] We have no way of knowing, however, how frequently antidumping authorities around the world are initiating investigations in a similarly slipshod manner but are never held to account before the WTO.

The problem is that the current Antidumping Agreement provides no standards at all to constrain the initiation of bogus cases. Article 5.2 of the agreement requires antidumping petitions to provide evidence of dumping, injury, and a causal link between the two; the agreement also says that a "simple assertion, unsubstantiated by relevant evidence, cannot be considered sufficient." Even this nebulous language was enough to allow the WTO, after the fact, to rule Guatemala's egregious actions in the cement case out of bounds, but it does nothing to restrict abuses before they happen. Clear rules are needed to limit authorities' discretion or create incentives for responsible behavior.

Reform Proposals 1 and 2, which would require credible evidence of underlying market distortions before any investigation is initiated, would go a long way toward restricting baseless investigations. Those proposals, though, aim to go beyond mere initiation standards to rethinking the basic question of how dumping is defined. Even if such reforms are not adopted in the short term, greater specification of the evidentiary requirements for dumping as traditionally defined would help to limit abuses in the initiation process. We therefore suggest changes to the Antidumping Agreement along the following lines:

> **Reform Proposal 16**: Articles 5.2 and 5.3 of the Antidumping Agreement should be revised to specify concrete evidentiary standards for initiation. With respect to evidence of dumping, the petitioner must supply documentation on a company-specific basis of representative prices of the subject merchandise sold by the foreign producer in the export market and either (1) representative prices of comparable products sold by the foreign producer in its home market or (2) credible estimates of the foreign producer's cost of production. The petitioner must supply such company-specific evidence with

respect to at least four foreign producers or, alternatively, foreign producers accounting for a significant portion (for example, at least 40 percent) of subject imports. With respect to evidence of injury and causation, the petitioner must supply documentation of trends in (1) subject import volumes (including market share); (2) prices in the export market; and (3) the domestic industry's sales volumes (including market share), profitability, and employment.

For purposes of the above proposal, "representative" price data means prices of major products that are representative of price levels throughout the period of investigation. "Credible estimates" of production costs should, to the extent possible, be based on the foreign producer's own data or at least data relating to the foreign industry under investigation.

The requirements proposed above would not stop the filing of antidumping petitions for harassment purposes. However, they would at least bring some minimal discipline to the initiation process and thereby afford some additional protection against the harassment of healthy import competition. Such an improvement in antidumping policy would be in keeping with the basic concepts, principles, and objectives of the Antidumping Agreement.

Mandate "Lesser-Duty Rule"

Article 9.1 of the current Antidumping Agreement states that it is "desirable" that antidumping duties "be less than the [dumping] margin if such lesser duty would be adequate to remove the injury to the domestic industry." This express preference for the so-called lesser-duty rule is in keeping with the basic concepts, principles, and objectives of the Antidumping Agreement. After all, the avowed purpose of antidumping remedies is to restore a "level playing field"—in other words, to neutralize artificial competitive advantages created by market-distorting government policies. If a particular duty rate is deemed sufficient to eliminate injury to the domestic industry, there is no justification for imposing a higher rate; a higher rate exceeds the mandate of creating a level playing field and slants the field in favor of the domestic industry.

A number of WTO members—including the European Union—follow the approach recommended in Article 9.1 and apply a lesser-duty rule in their antidumping investigations. The basic approach is to calculate "noninjurious prices"—prices for export sales that would not depress or suppress the prices charged by the domestic industry. The difference between the export price and the noninjurious price is referred to as the "injury margin." If the injury margin is greater than the dumping margin, then the antidumping duty rate is equal to the dumping margin; if, however, the injury margin is lower than the dumping margin, the lesser duty applies and is set at the level of the injury margin.

The lesser-duty rule can result in significant reductions in the antidumping duty rates that would otherwise apply. Consider the following examples of definitive duties imposed by the European Union during 2000. In the investigation of seamless pipes and tubes from Croatia and Ukraine, the authorities found final dumping margins of 40.8 percent and 123.7 percent, respectively; application of the lesser-duty rule, though, brought the actual duty rates down to 23 percent for Croatia and 38.5 percent for Ukraine—reductions of 44 percent and 69 percent, respectively. In the investigation of hot-rolled steel from China, the final dumping margin came to 55.5 percent, but because of the lesser-duty rule the actual duty rate was only 8.1 percent—an 85 percent reduction. And in the investigation of black colorformers (i.e., dyes) from Japan, the dumping margin was 49.8 percent, but the final duty rate was only 18.9 percent—or 62 percent lower—because of the lesser-duty rule.[42]

Because the language in Article 9.1 is not mandatory, WTO members are under no obligation at present to adopt a lesser-duty rule. The U.S. law, for instance, does not have such a rule. Among jurisdictions that do have some kind of lesser-duty rule, there is no consistency and little transparency in the manner in which it is applied. As a result, antidumping duties in excess of those that can be justified by the basic concepts, principles, and objectives of the Antidumping Agreement are being imposed routinely.

To cure this glaring defect in current antidumping practice, we recommend a change in the Antidumping Agreement along the following lines:

> **Reform Proposal 17**: Article 9.1 of the Antidumping Agreement should be revised to require that antidumping duties be less than the dumping margin if the lesser duty is sufficient to remove the injury to the domestic industry. Specifically, antidumping authorities should be required to calculate noninjurious prices for export sales, which would be at levels

that do not depress or suppress the prices charged by the domestic industry. If the difference between the noninjurious prices and the export prices (known as the injury margin) is less than the dumping margin, the antidumping duty should be set at the lesser rate equal to the injury margin.

Raise de Minimis *to 5 Percent in Investigations and Reviews*

The calculation of dumping margins is plagued with methodological difficulties. Most obviously, there are the distortions that tend to skew the analysis in favor of finding dumping: the failure to require evidence of underlying market distortions, the cost test, the inclusion of profit in constructed value, the asymmetric treatment of indirect selling expenses, the use of zeroing in dumping calculations, and so forth.

Even if all those obvious distortions were eliminated, the measurement of dumping margins would still be highly inexact. In the typical investigation, antidumping authorities compare home-market and export prices of physically different goods, in different kinds of packaging, sold at different times, in different and fluctuating currencies, to different customers at different levels of trade, in different quantities, with different freight and other movement costs, different credit terms, and other differences in directly associated selling expenses (for example, commissions, warranties, royalties, and advertising).

Admittedly, antidumping authorities try to adjust for some of those differences, but the adjustments are necessarily crude and imprecise. For example, when the U.S. DOC compares physically different merchandise, it adjusts for differences in materials, direct labor, and variable overhead costs. While this makes a certain amount of sense, in a real-world context it goes without saying that actual price differences may be more or less than the differences in variable manufacturing costs. As we pointed out in relation to second-quality merchandise, sometimes huge differences in commercial value can exist without any measurable differences in manufacturing costs. Similarly, the DOC adjusts for differences in warranty terms on the basis of differences in repair parts and labor costs. While this approach is logical enough, it is still extremely unlikely that the actual real-world price differences between products with different warranties are precisely equal to the differences in warranty costs.

189

And in many cases, antidumping authorities make no adjustment at all. Thus, prices of goods sold in the export market may be compared to prices of goods sold many months earlier or later in the home market, without any adjustment for market fluctuations. And although unit prices typically decline with larger order quantities, the U.S. DOC rarely adjusts for quantity discounts.

Calculations of unit costs of production are similarly rife with more-or-less arbitrary guesswork. Especially vexing is the allocation of shared costs, whether in the special case of coproducts that share raw material costs or the ubiquitous phenomenon of products that share various overhead costs. Some allocation of shared manufacturing costs is necessary for cost-accounting purposes, but the method of allocation may well determine whether a given product shows a profit or a loss.

The fact is that the accounting treatment is and should be irrelevant to proper business decisions. Managers should decide what mix of goods to produce, not on the basis of arbitrary unit costs, but on the basis of maximizing total net revenue. Low-value products that cover variable costs and contribute to fixed costs can be integral to boosting a firm's overall profitability even if, on a unit cost basis, they appear to be perpetual money-losers.

In view of all these methodological challenges, a healthy dose of humility is in order regarding the accuracy of any dumping calculations. Appropriately, such humility informs the current Antidumping Agreement's concept of *de minimis* dumping margins. Dumping margins below a certain threshold are deemed to be *de minimis* and are treated as equal to zero. Given the tension between the trade-restrictive effects of antidumping measures and the overall orientation of the WTO agreement toward market opening, a conservative policy of resolving doubts against the imposition of duties is entirely fitting.

The *de minimis* rule badly needs strengthening, however. Under Article 5.8 of the current agreement, the threshold is set at 2 percent. And because of awkward draftsmanship, this provision is claimed by the United States to apply only to investigations—and not to subsequent administrative reviews that recalculate dumping margins after an antidumping duty order goes into effect. Under U.S. law, the *de minimis* threshold in such reviews continues to be a mere 0.5 percent.

The threshold needs to be raised and applied equally to original investigations and reviews:

> **Reform Proposal 18**: Article 5.8 of the Antidumping Agreement should be revised to provide that any margin of dumping of less than 5 percent should be treated as *de minimis*. The same definition of *de minimis* should apply in both original investigations and administrative reviews.

In view of the irreducible imprecision of dumping calculations, the *de minimis* threshold should be raised even if all of the reform proposals in this paper for addressing methodological distortions are ultimately adopted. If, however, any of the existing distortions are left intact, the case for raising the *de minimis* threshold becomes that much stronger. A relatively high *de minimis* threshold would act as a limited check on unremedied methodological abuses.

Mandate a Public-Interest Test

A number of WTO members—including the EU, Canada, Thailand, and Malaysia—have incorporated a "public-interest test" into their antidumping regulations. The basic idea behind such public-interest provisions is to make the imposition of antidumping measures permissive rather than mandatory. Specifically, a public-interest provision allows authorities to refuse to impose duties, even when dumping and injury have been found, on the ground that antidumping measures in a particular case would be contrary to the broader public interest.

A public-interest test, if properly devised and implemented, can help to reconcile a country's antidumping policy with its larger national interests. After all, even staunch defenders of antidumping remedies must recognize that resorting to such remedies carries costs. Even if a domestic industry is being harmed by allegedly dumped imports, other domestic interests—namely downstream import-using industries and consumers—are benefited by them. Indeed, the fact that the imports are entering the country in sufficient quantities to injure domestic producers shows that many domestic interests prefer those imports to products made at home. Accordingly, antidumping investigations involve more than a dispute between a domestic industry and its foreign rivals; they also involve a conflict of interest between that domestic industry and other domestic industries.

191

An antidumping law with no public-interest provision fails to take account of these conflicting interests. If the requisite showings of dumping and injury are made, trade-restrictive remedies follow automatically—regardless of the consequences for the rest of the country. That is hardly a recipe for rational policymaking: if major affected interests are systematically ignored in the decisionmaking process, it's hardly likely that the resulting policy will reflect an optimal accommodation of all competing interests.

Furthermore, given the tension between the trade-restrictive effects of antidumping measures and the market-opening thrust of the WTO agreements as a whole, due restraint in the application of antidumping measures is in keeping with the basic concepts, principles, and objectives of the Antidumping Agreement. In that regard, Article 9.1 of the current agreement states, "It is desirable that the imposition [of duties] be permissive in the territory of all Members."

The present agreement, however, does not require any kind of public-interest test, much less specify standards for how it should be applied. Consequently, many WTO members—including the United States—have no public-interest provision at all. Meanwhile, there is little consistency or transparency in the public-interest provisions that do exist; by and large they are standardless "black boxes" that occasionally block the imposition of duties for no clearly defined reason. In some countries, such as Canada, the public-interest provision merges with a lesser-duty rule, so that a public-interest determination must be made before the lesser-duty rule is invoked.

Antidumping policy around the world would be greatly improved by mandating the inclusion of a public-interest test and then specifying standards for how it should be applied. On the latter point, the critical challenge is to find some set of criteria that give the public-interest test real teeth without causing it to swallow up all of anti-dumping policy. Thus, if the public interest is defined as "whatever's good for domestic import-competing industries," then a public-interest provision will have no effect at all. On the other hand, if the public interest is defined as pure economic efficiency, then the test would work to block the imposition of duties in virtually all cases.

Accordingly, we suggest that the Antidumping Agreement be amended along the following lines:

Reform Proposal 19: Article 9.1 of the Antidumping Agreement should be revised to require the application of a public-
interest test before antidumping measures are imposed. For
purposes of this test, antidumping measures would be
deemed contrary to the public interest if the harm inflicted
by those measures on downstream import-using interests
is deemed disproportionate to the benefit conferred on the
petitioning domestic industry. "Disproportionate," for these
purposes, should be defined explicitly in reference to specified benchmarks.

Note that we suggest the use of some kind of "disproportionate
impact" standard for purposes of applying the public-interest test.
The existence of a disproportionate impact could be measured in a
number of different ways. For example, the estimated welfare gain
for the petitioning industry could be compared to the estimated
welfare loss for specific downstream industries, or for consumers.
If the loss is some designated multiple of the gain, the impact would
be deemed disproportionate and duties would not be imposed.
Alternatively, the estimated number of jobs saved in the petitioning
industry could be compared to the estimated number of jobs lost in
downstream import-using industries. If the ratio of downstream
jobs lost to petitioning industry jobs saved crosses some designated
threshold, duties would not be imposed on the ground of disproportionate impact. Or authorities could calculate the deadweight loss
to the economy per job saved in the petitioning industry and compare that to average wages in the industry. If the economic cost is
some designated multiple of the average wage, disproportionate
impact would be found and no duties would be imposed.

Any of these cost/benefit comparisons could be made with the
use of fairly basic techniques of quantitative economic analysis.
Relatively easy to administer, such a public-interest test would have
real teeth while still giving wide scope for the use of antidumping
measures. Exactly how sharp the teeth or wide the scope can be
settled by choosing a higher or lower threshold for "disproportionate": the higher the designated multiple of harms to benefits is set,
the more modest the effect of the public-interest test.

Make Termination of Antidumping Duty Orders Automatic

Before the WTO Antidumping Agreement, some jurisdictions—
in particular, the United States—lacked any regularly scheduled

"sunset" process for terminating antidumping duty orders. As a result, the average lifetime of U.S. orders exceeded a decade, and some continued for more than 30 years.

Such a state of affairs was glaringly inconsistent with any theory of antidumping policy as a response to market distortions. If antidumping measures are to be justified on the ground that they offset artificial competitive advantages caused by market distortions, it follows that those measures should be discontinued as soon as the distortions are eliminated or the advantages disappear. But if imports can be subject to antidumping remedies year after year despite the fact that they are no longer injuring a domestic industry, then antidumping has ceased to have anything to do with a level playing field and crossed over to simple protectionism.

To address this issue, the current WTO Antidumping Agreement provides for a so-called sunset review process. Specifically, Article 11.3 of the agreement mandates the automatic termination of antidumping duty orders after five years unless a special review initiated before expiration determines that termination of the order "would be likely to lead to the continuation or recurrence of dumping and injury."

Unfortunately, Article 11.3 has proved less than successful in phasing out old orders. In the United States, for example, there were 354 sunset reviews initiated between July 1998 and August 2002. Of the 263 completed reviews that were contested by petitioners, the DOC made affirmative sunset determinations to continue the order in all but 4 cases, while the ITC voted affirmative 72 percent of the time.[43]

The sunset review process is fundamentally flawed. At the root of the problem is the fact that the review is prospective and counterfactual in its focus and thus inherently speculative. It seeks to determine whether dumping and injury will happen in the future if an order is lifted. It is difficult enough to control antidumping authorities' abuse of discretion when their investigations are tied to a clear evidentiary record; it is next to impossible when the authorities are allowed to gaze into a crystal ball.

Accordingly, to ensure that antidumping measures do not continue after the artificial competitive advantages that are their supposed target have been neutralized, we suggest the following reform:

Reform Proposal 20: Article 11.3 of the Antidumping Agreement should be amended to provide for automatic termination of antidumping duty orders after five years. Domestic industries would be able to file new petitions immediately upon expiration, but they would be required to show evidence of actual injury or threat of injury by reason of dumped imports just as in any normal case. For petitions filed within one year of the expiration of a prior order, special procedures would be required to expedite relief for petitioners. Specifically, the administering authorities would be required to make a preliminary finding as to injury within 45 days of the initiation of the new investigation. If that preliminary determination is affirmative, preliminary antidumping measures would go into effect at the rates that applied at the expiration of the old order.

This proposal strikes a reasonable compromise between two competing interests: on the one hand, ensuring that antidumping measures are not maintained even after the conditions that justified them no longer exist, and, on the other hand, continuing to provide a remedy when those conditions happen to persist. Under the suggested reform, automatic termination ensures that all orders will come to an end; at the same time, though, special provisions for follow-up investigations ensure reasonable continuity of relief if conditions warrant. As to the preliminary injury finding proposed, we envision something along the lines of the U.S. ITC's preliminary injury investigation. An affirmative finding in this preliminary phase would trigger the imposition of preliminary measures at the old rates even before any new finding on dumping margins. Subsequent preliminary and final determinations on dumping in the follow-up investigation would replace the old rates with new ones.

Other than the special provisions for ensuring continuity of relief, follow-up investigations would be just like original investigations in every respect: the same evidentiary requirements for initiation, the same standards for determining dumping and injury. The all-too-often bogus guessing games of the sunset process would be replaced by full-blown dumping and injury analysis in accordance with the normal provisions—and the basic concepts, principles, and objectives—of the Antidumping Agreement.

Other Issues

The 20 reform proposals discussed do not target all of the flaws in current antidumping practice. Indeed, some of the most glaring flaws are not addressed—at least not directly. In crafting our proposals, we chose to focus on problems that are (1) serious and (2) susceptible to reform by changes in the WTO Antidumping Agreement. Unfortunately, some of the worst abuses of antidumping laws cannot be remedied effectively by adding one particular provision or another to WTO rules.

The use of facts available in calculating dumping margins is one of the most important issues that we did not address. Normally, antidumping authorities calculate a foreign producer's dumping margin on the basis of company-specific price and cost data submitted during the course of the investigation. If, however, the foreign producer declines to participate in the investigation, or if the authorities determine that the information submitted is either incomplete or inaccurate, the authorities may use facts available to calculate the company's dumping margin. Those facts available frequently include the alleged dumping margins featured in the domestic industry's antidumping petition.

The use of facts available typically results in extremely high dumping margins. As shown in Table 2.2, our examination of 141 U.S. dumping determinations over a three-year period found that the average dumping margin calculated on the basis of facts available was a whopping 95.58 percent—compared to 27.22 percent[44] when the foreign producer's data were used. In that period, the DOC used facts available just more than 25 percent of the time.

U.S. exporters are frequent victims of facts available determinations. As we discussed in Chapter 4, between 1995 and 2000 five of eight Indian dumping determinations against U.S. products were based on facts available—and the average dumping margin in those five cases was 83 percent. Three of four South African dumping determinations against U.S. products over the same period were based on facts available, with an average dumping margin of 89 percent.

Unfortunately, no clear-cut solution to abuses of facts available is apparent. Since antidumping authorities do not have subpoena power, they have to rely on the voluntary cooperation of investigated companies. If those companies refuse to participate, the authorities cannot simply give up; otherwise, stonewalling would be a perfect defense. And authorities must be able to throw out incomplete data; otherwise, respondent firms could submit fragmentary data that appear to exonerate them and the authorities would again be stymied.

Accordingly, there seems to be no alternative to allowing authorities the discretion to disregard respondents' price and cost data. Given that fact, authorities must also have the discretion to choose the facts available that will substitute for respondents' data in the dumping calculations. And where there is discretion, there is the ever-present possibility of abuse of discretion.

We do not see how WTO rules could define with any clarity either (1) the circumstances under which resort to facts available is justified or (2) the standards for selecting facts available for use in dumping calculations. The propriety or impropriety of antidumping authorities' conduct on either front will inevitably turn on case-specific factual circumstances that cannot be specified in advance. The best that can be done is to lay out broad, general standards for when and how facts available should be used.

The current Antidumping Agreement already establishes such standards. Article 6.8 states that facts available can be used only when a respondent "refuses access to, or otherwise does not provide, necessary information within a reasonable period or significantly impedes the investigation." Annex II, paragraph 5 of the agreement further states that respondents' information should not be disregarded "even though the information provided may not be provided in all respects, . . . provided the interested party has acted to the best of his ability." Also, paragraph 7 of Annex II provides guidance regarding sources of facts available to be used by antidumping authorities.

It is possible that the existing language could be tightened up and improved. Even if that is done, however, little will have changed. Authorities will still have broad discretion to disregard respondents' data, and even wider discretion about what to use in their stead. If antidumping authorities are intent on abusing the law and achieving a protectionist outcome, they will still have wide latitude to do so. On occasion, victimized countries might challenge the use of facts available through WTO dispute settlement and win a reversal. But by and large, the facts available loophole cannot be closed.

Another serious problem with current antidumping practice is the lack of transparency and basic administrative fairness. With its complexity and wide scope for discretion, the antidumping law creates enormous potential for abuse in poorer countries that lack well-established traditions of transparency and the rule of law. Failure to provide respondent companies with the factual and legal

197

bases for determinations, to allow them a fair hearing, to take account of their claims of legal and factual errors in determinations, and to safeguard the privacy of their confidential business data are all procedural irregularities that are in clear violation of current WTO rules, yet they are alleged to be distressingly common in many countries. Consequently, substantive flaws in antidumping rules are all too often compounded by egregious procedural unfairness.

Abuses caused by nontransparency or outright corruption are difficult to remedy through changes in WTO rules. Since current rules are being widely ignored, it is doubtful that new rules will meet a better fate. Indeed, the very essence of nontransparency and corruption is that government officials don't follow the stated rules. The only effective way to reduce the abuses of facts available and nontransparency is to reduce the number of unjustified antidumping investigations that are initiated and conducted in the first place. Because of the glaring flaws in existing antidumping rules, investigations are routinely instituted without any evidence of unfair trade under any plausible definition of that term. The harm caused by those unjustifiable investigations can then be exacerbated by abuses of administrative discretion or outright misconduct. If the number of unjustifiable investigations can be reduced, the number of investigations plagued by facts available or nontransparency can likewise be expected to fall.

The reform proposals set forth in this paper thus constitute an indirect and partial solution to other problems that resist straight-on efforts at reform. All of our reform proposals take the form of specific rules—as opposed to broad, discretionary standards. Such clear-cut rules provide authorities with little discretion about how to implement them and thus are hard to circumvent. If the new rules proposed here are adopted and incorporated into the WTO Antidumping Agreement, dramatic improvements in antidumping practice would almost certainly ensue. With some coherence achieved between the basic concepts, principles, and objectives of the Antidumping Agreement and the specific provisions of that agreement, there would be a significant reduction in unjustifiable antidumping activity—that is, in antidumping investigations and measures that have no rational relation to offsetting artificial competitive advantages created by market-distorting government policies. As a result, there would be fewer opportunities for authorities to misuse facts available or run roughshod over the requirements of procedural fairness.

Conclusion

Antidumping reform faces formidable obstacles. Use of antidumping laws around the world is widespread and growing; and wherever those laws operate, the protectionist status quo enjoys the support of entrenched bureaucracies and import-competing corporate interests. In the United States in particular, energetic and well-organized protectionist lobbies have mobilized nearly overwhelming political support for their position on antidumping issues. As a result, for many years the world's most powerful country and leader of the multilateral trading system has stood as the principal opponent of meaningful changes in antidumping rules.

Of all the obstacles hindering antidumping reform, however, none is greater than ignorance. Failure to understand how antidumping laws actually operate in practice—and how they fail so spectacularly to do what their supporters say they are supposed to do—lies at the root of much of the resistance to antidumping reform. Many supporters of the antidumping status quo honestly believe that these laws in their present form are necessary to combat unfair trading practices and thereby ensure a level playing field. If those supporters fully understood the reality of contemporary antidumping practice—if they understood how frequently trade-restrictive measures are inflicted on normal, healthy competition—their opposition to needed reforms would likely soften.

Of course, protectionist interests support the antidumping status quo so fervently precisely because of its flaws. Their goal is to squelch foreign competition in whatever way they can, and the antidumping law in its current form has proved very handy indeed. And because of ignorance about the law's complex workings, protectionist interests are able to cloak their special pleading in the high-minded rhetoric of fairness and concern for a level playing field. If they were forced to defend the status quo honestly, for the protectionist scam that it is, they would find it much harder to win adherents to their cause.

Accordingly, supporters of antidumping reform need to make education and clarification their top priorities in WTO negotiations.

199

Negotiations that focus exclusively on specific changes to the Antidumping Agreement are doomed to achieve disappointing results. Instead, the first order of business ought to be clarifying what exactly are the basic concepts, principles, and objectives of the Antidumping Agreement. Here we have sought to identify those basic concepts, principles, and objectives by relying on the justifications for antidumping measures offered by U.S. antidumping supporters. We believe that WTO negotiations would ultimately arrive at more or less the same position—namely, that the basic objective of the Antidumping Agreement is to allow member states to offset artificial competitive advantages created by market-distorting government policies.

A consensus along those lines would be of enormous value in guiding negotiations about specific provisions of the Antidumping Agreement. That consensus would provide a benchmark by which to evaluate contemporary antidumping practice—a benchmark in comparison to which much of contemporary practice would be found sadly deficient. This critical evaluation, in turn, would help to define the work program of negotiators—namely, to reduce the huge gap between antidumping's accepted goals and its actual practice. We believe that the specific reform proposals advanced here define, at least in broad outline, the work program that needs to be undertaken.

This work program may prove too ambitious to be accomplished in a single round. But at least the work can be started—and the groundwork for ongoing progress in future rounds can be laid. In the Uruguay Round agreements on agriculture and services, for example, actual reductions of market barriers were modest, but at least a consensus was built for the need to make further progress in the future. As a result, in the current Doha Round, there is no dispute about whether market barriers in agriculture and services should be reduced; the only question is how much.

By contrast, the Uruguay Round achieved no consensus on the proper objectives of antidumping policy. Negotiators succeeded in hammering out the Antidumping Agreement, but all it really did was to codify existing U.S. and EU practice with a few technical modifications around the edges. Without any consensus on why the agreement exists or what purpose it serves, when the time came to launch a new round, supporters of reform had to struggle ferociously just to get antidumping on the negotiating agenda.

200

Antidumping reform shouldn't have to start from scratch every time. Now is the time to build a durable foundation for an ongoing project of reform. Now is the time to change the terms of the debate. If supporters of reform play their cards right, the Doha Round will end the question of whether antidumping abuses should be curtailed. How much will be the only topic for negotiation in future rounds.

Notes

Introduction

1. See, for example, Hyun Ja Shin, "Possible Instances of Predatory Pricing in Recent U.S. Antidumping Cases," in ed. Robert Z. Lawrence, *Brookings Trade Forum 1998* (Washington: Brookings Institution, 1998), pp. 81–97.

Chapter 1

1. The antidumping statute is codified at 19 U.S.C. §§ 1673–1677n. The DOC's antidumping regulations may be found at 19 C.F.R. § 351.

2. In antidumping cases against so-called nonmarket economies, the DOC calculates constructed value, not with the foreign producer's own cost data, but with data from "surrogate" market economies. See Chapter 2 for additional details.

3. In the three-year period between April 1999 and March 2002, the ITC rendered 147 preliminary determinations, of which 116 were affirmative. These figures were compiled from data available at the ITC website (www.usitc.gov).

4. Typically, the DOC attempts to send questionnaires to all known foreign producers. If, however, the number of foreign producers is too large, the DOC will send questionnaires to only the largest foreign producers.

5. There were 125 specific final margins assigned in original investigations during 2001. Of those 125, 117 were higher than *de minimis*—or at least 2 percent. These figures were compiled from public data available in *Federal Register* notices.

6. In the three-year period between April 1999 and March 2002, the ITC rendered 58 final determinations, of which 48 were affirmative. These figures were compiled from data available at the ITC website (www.usitc.gov).

7. These figures were compiled as of August 14, 2002, from data available on the ITC website (www.usitc.gov).

8. Generally, the foreign producer's home market is deemed viable if sales volume in that market of the product under investigation exceeds 5 percent of its sales volume in the United States (although other factors can render a home market not viable). For the sake of simplicity, we generally assume that the home market is the comparison market.

9. Theoretically, there could be hundreds of thousands and even millions of products. The number of possible products, theoretically, equals the product of multiplying the number of options within each characteristic. So, if there are 10 characteristics, each with five alternative values, the number of theoretical products equals $5 \times 5 \times 5 \times 5 \times 5 \times 5 \times 5 \times 5 \times 5 \times 5$, or 9,765,625 products.

10. The definition of an affiliated person, as provided in the DOC's standard antidumping questionnaire, is as follows:

Affiliated persons (affiliates) include (1) members of a family, (2) an officer or director of an organization and that organization, (3) partners, (4) employers and their employees, and (5) any person or organization directly or indirectly owning, controlling, or holding with power to vote, 5 percent or more of the outstanding voting stock or shares of any organization and that organization. In addition, affiliates include (6) any person who controls any other person and that other person, or (7) any two or more persons who directly control, are controlled by, or are under common control with, any person. "Control" exists where one person is legally or operationally in a position to exercise restraint or direction over the other person [section 771(33) of the act].

11. In some cases, there are no sales to unaffiliated customers of products sold to affiliates, so the comparison cannot be made. As long as there is a sufficient basis for comparing prices (normally just one common product), then the arm's-length test is performed. If there are no common products, the affiliated customer generally fails the test.

12. Until November 2002, the DOC rejected sales to affiliates when the ratio fell below 99.5 percent, but accepted sales no matter how high the ratio might be. The World Trade Organization ruled that this asymmetry violated the WTO Antidumping Agreement, and so the DOC switched to the current approach.

13. Average expenses and profit for purposes of CV are normally based on the experience of home-market sales in the ordinary course of trade. However, when there are no such sales because they have all failed the arm's-length and cost tests, this information is estimated from other sources.

14. Actually, the averaging process is even more refined. An average price is calculated for each unique combination of U.S. CONNUM and sales type (EP or CEP).

Chapter 2

1. Greg Mastel, *Antidumping Laws and the U.S. Economy* (Armonk, N.Y.: M. E. Sharpe, 1998), p. 43.

2. Ibid., p. 41.

3. Ibid., p. 40.

4. See Ronald A. Cass and Richard D. Boltuck, "Antidumping and Countervailing-Duty Law: The Mirage of Equitable International Competition," in ed. Jagdish N. Bhagwati and Robert E. Hudec, *Fair Trade and Harmonization: Prerequisites for Free Trade?* (Cambridge, Mass.: MIT Press, 1996), vol. 2, p. 351.

5. "Facts available" were formerly known as "best information available."

6. Biases in antidumping methodologies are reviewed extensively in Richard Boltuck and Robert Litan, eds., *Down in the Dumps: Administration of the Unfair Trade Laws* (Washington: Brookings Institution, 1991). We add our own analysis in Chapter 3.

7. The antidumping statute authorizes the DOC, in making a "facts available" determination because a foreign producer has failed to cooperate, to "use an inference that is adverse to the interests of that party." Section 776(b) of the Tariff Act of 1930, as amended, codified at 19 U.S.C. § 1677e(b).

8. In constructed-value cases the costs used are the foreign producer's own, whereas in NME cases costs are calculated by valuing the foreign producer's "factors of production" according to price data from a surrogate market-economy country.

9. It can be argued that inclusion of an amount for profit is appropriate on the ground that a "normal" profit is part of a company's cost of capital. In other words, a company earning a subnormal return is selling below its full *economic* costs, if above its full *accounting* costs. First of all, it should be noted that antidumping supporters clearly convey the impression that the law targets sales at a loss, not insufficient profitability. More fundamentally, the claim that low profitability is evidence of market distortions is much weaker than is the case with respect to outright losses. Determining exactly what constitutes a normal profit for a given company in a given industry at a given time is significantly more difficult than determining whether or not that company is losing money. Moreover, low profits are generally sustainable over a much longer period than are outright losses. Persistent failure to earn competitive returns can undermine a company's ability to make necessary investments and thereby may lead eventually to outright losses; it may also threaten the employment security of the company's management. Unlike sustained losses, though, low profitability in and of itself does not imperil a company's solvency and future as a going concern. Accordingly, even chronically low profits are much less suggestive of "artificial" market conditions caused by government interventionism than are either acute or chronic losses.

10. DOC investigations are specific to a particular product from a particular country. In a single investigation, though, the DOC may calculate separate dumping margins for numerous different foreign producers.

11. In original antidumping investigations, any dumping margin of less than 2 percent is considered *de minimis* and effectively equal to zero.

12. For 34 of the 36 determinations, the DOC relied entirely on "facts available"; in other words, it made no use whatsoever of information provided by the foreign producers. For 2 of the determinations (Maktas in the investigation of pasta from Turkey and Winbond in the investigation of SRAMs from Taiwan), the DOC relied on a combination of foreign producers' information and facts available. These two determinations were included because in both cases the partial use of facts available was both extensive and punitive (that is, the DOC purposefully selected adverse facts).

13. This figure is a subset of the 37 determinations mentioned above in which the DOC partially or totally rejected home-market or third-country comparison product sales. This smaller figure excludes those determinations in which any third-country sales were used and those in which all comparison-market sales were rejected.

14. See Chapter 3 for a more in-depth treatment of this issue.

15. Interestingly, ISSI is a U.S.-based "fabless producer" that designs chips in the United States but relies on a semiconductor "foundry" in Taiwan for production. In this case, then, the antidumping law was used by one American company (Micron Inc., the petitioner) against another.

16. Specifically, the program was run without the "cost test" element, so that below-cost home-market sales were not excluded from the calculation. The recalculation was performed by ISSI's counsel at the law firm of White & Case. We then reviewed the revised dumping margin calculation program.

17. This total consists of 16 determinations in which the DOC used constructed value because of an absence of viable comparison markets or similar comparison products, and another 4 determinations in which publicly available information makes clear that the DOC rejected all comparison-market sales as below cost and therefore relied exclusively on constructed value.

18. The total consists of the 31 "mixed" cases discussed above, plus an additional 2 determinations in which the DOC rejected at least some third-country sales as below cost and instead relied either on above-cost third-country sales or constructed value. In those 33 determinations, it cannot be determined with certainty from the public record whether the DOC in fact used constructed value in every instance (such use would be unnecessary if there were any above-cost sales of the comparison products), nor can the extent to which constructed value was used be determined.

19. This respondent consists of two companies with common ownership whose operations are partially integrated. They were treated as a single company for purposes of the antidumping investigation.

20. These recalculations were performed by the companies' counsel at the law firm of White & Case. We then reviewed the revised dumping margin calculation programs.

21. Profit rates were derived from the following sources: Chen Hao Taiwan, the DOC disclosure documents for correction of ministerial errors, January 31, 1997; brake drums and rotors from China, DOC final factors memorandum, February 21, 1997; cut-to-length steel plate from China, DOC final factors memorandum, October 24, 1997; PT Multi Raya, DOC disclosure documents for correction of ministerial errors, January 31, 1997; collated roofing nails from China, DOC final dumping margin calculation memorandum, September 23, 1997. These documents were made available by the companies' counsel at the law firm of White & Case. The DOC usually calculates the profit rate as a percentage of cost of production. To express the profit rate as a percentage of sales, the DOC figures were divided by one plus the DOC profit percentage.

22. The products under investigation and their equivalent U.S. industries are as follows: melamine institutional dinnerware, rubber and miscellaneous plastic products; brake drums and rotors, motor vehicles and equipment; cut-to-length steel plate, iron and steel; collated roofing nails, fabricated metal products. Profit rates for U.S. industries were the average rate of pre-tax profits per dollar of sales during the year the investigation was initiated, as reported in Bureau of the Census, "Quarterly Financial Report for Manufacturing, Mining, and Trade Corporations," Fourth Quarter 1997, Table B, available at www.census.gov/prod/www/abs/qfr-mm.html.

23. The practice of "zeroing" is discussed in further detail in chapter 3.

24. This recalculation was performed by Dieng/Surya Jaya's counsel at the law firm of White & Case. We then reviewed the revised dumping margin calculation program.

25. The scope of antidumping investigations and duty orders is defined by a verbal description of the "subject merchandise," not by U.S. Harmonized Tariff System numbers. The HTS numbers selected here were the ones that corresponded most closely with the product description; if multiple HTS numbers corresponded equally well with the product description, the one with the highest imports in the period immediately preceding the initiation of the investigation was selected.

26. Since the U.S. tariff system and foreign systems are not harmonized all the way to the 10-digit level, the foreign tariff items most closely corresponding to the relevant U.S. HTS numbers were selected. Foreign tariff rates are from the relevant country's tariff schedule for the year that the antidumping investigation was initiated, with the following exceptions: steel concrete-reinforcing bars from Turkey (1997), SRAMs from Korea (1996), SRAMs from Taiwan (1995), stainless steel wire rod from Trinidad and Tobago (1998), and stainless steel wire rod from Korea (1996). U.S. tariff rates are as of the year that the relevant antidumping investigation was initiated.

27. The dumping margins included in Table 2.5 exclude determinations calculated on the basis of "facts available," as well as those calculated purely on the basis of constructed value.

28. The two investigations in question are SRAMs from Korea and stainless steel wire rod from Japan. With respect to the former, the 1996 and 1998 NTE reports charge that import licensing and product pre-approvals impede foreign sales of electronics and high-tech products to Korea, but no specific mention of SRAMs is made. As to the latter, all NTE reports reviewed allege anti-competitive practices and restriction of distribution channels in the Japanese steel sector, but the clear focus of those allegations is on carbon steel. The distinctive stainless steel industry is not specifically mentioned.

29. ISSI's profit rate was derived from the DOC's final computer printout, February 19, 1998. This document was made available by ISSI's counsel at the law firm of White & Case. Since the DOC calculates profit as a percentage of cost of production, it was necessary to divide the DOC figure by one plus the DOC profit rate to arrive at profit as a percentage of sales. The profit rate for the U.S. electrical and electronics products industry was taken from Bureau of the Census, "Quarterly Financial Report for Manufacturing, Mining, and Trade Corporations," Fourth Quarter 1997, Table B.

30. ISSI's Taiwan and U.S. sales figures were taken from its August 6, 1997, supplemental response to the DOC's antidumping questionnaire. This document was made available by ISSI's counsel at the law firm of White & Case.

31. Michael Porter, *Competitive Strategy: Techniques for Analyzing Industries and Competitors* (New York: Free Press, 1980), p. 9.

32. The U.S. antidumping law does attempt to match U.S. and comparison-market sales made at the same "level of trade" and make price adjustments when such matching is impossible. The variations in competitive intensity referred to here, however, can occur within the same level of trade as defined by the DOC and thus elude any adjustment.

33. One not-too-recent estimate found that gray-market imports total $10 billion a year. S. Tamer Cavusgil and Ed Sikora, "How Multinationals Can Counter Gray-Market Imports," *Columbia Journal of World Business* 23, no. 294 (Winter 1988): 76.

34. Lawrence M. Friedman, "Business and Legal Strategies for Combating Grey-Market Imports," *International Lawyer* 32, no. 1 (Spring 1998): 28.

35. U.S. Bureau of the Census, *Statistical Abstract of the United States: 1998,* Table 863, p. 544.

36. Financial information taken from companies' 10-K reports.

37. See, for example, Pankaj Ghemawat, "Building Strategy on the Experience Curve," *Harvard Business Review* 85, no. 2 (March–April 1985): 143–49.

38. Michael Porter, *Competitive Advantage: Creating and Sustaining Superior Performance* (New York: Free Press, 1985), pp. 436–37. Emphasis in original.

39. Charles T. Horngren, George Foster, and Srikant M. Datar, *Cost Accounting: A Managerial Emphasis,* 9th ed. (Upper Saddle River, N.J.: Prentice Hall, 1997), p. 555.

40. See, for example, John C. Panzar and Robert D. Willig, "Economies of Scope," *American Economic Review* 71, no. 2 (May 1981): 268. Panzar and Willig coined the term "economies of scope."

41. David Besanko, David Dranove, and Mark Shanley, *The Economics of Strategy* (New York: John Wiley & Sons, 1996), p. 178.

42. Ibid., p. 184.

43. Specifically, profit, selling expenses, general and administrative expenses, and interest expenses were stripped out of the calculation of normal value. What remained was total manufacturing costs—raw materials, direct labor, and factory overhead. This remainder still overstates variable costs, since it includes fixed overhead costs (for these respondents it was not possible to separate out fixed and variable overhead). The recalculations were performed by the companies' counsel at the law firm of White & Case. We then reviewed the revised dumping margin calculation programs.

44. Some antidumping supporters argue that cross-subsidization is itself an unfair trading practice. Thus, Terence Stewart, a prominent attorney who represents complaining U.S. industries in antidumping cases, has argued that the antidumping law is designed to "offset any artificial advantage that flows from closed foreign markets, *cross-subsidization by multi-product firms*, government largesse, or other factors that have nothing to do with comparative advantage." Terence P. Stewart, "Administration of the Antidumping Law: A Different Perspective," in ed. Boltuck and Litan, p. 288 (emphasis added). This position, however, is untenable. Cross-subsidization is endemic among multiproduct firms, both foreign and American; indeed, the potential for cross-subsidization is one of the main reasons that multiproduct firms exist. It makes no sense to condemn cross-subsidization by foreign companies as unfair when identical business practices are routinely pursued by their American rivals.

45. Admittedly, the scope of interventionist policies that the antidumping law claims to address is broader than that covered under the CVD law: first, the CVD law does not apply to NME countries; second, it does not purport to address sanctuary-market situations or broad structural distortions like insufficiently developed commercial law. Nevertheless, for constructed-value cases—which are limited to market economies and (as seen above) generally occur in situations in which sanctuary markets are highly unlikely—there is a significant overlap in the ostensible targets of CVD and antidumping investigations.

46. There are limits on obtaining double relief through simultaneous antidumping and CVD petitions. Specifically, the CVD law distinguishes between export subsidies (subsidies tied to exports) and domestic subsidies (subsidies targeted to specific industries). For export subsidies, the antidumping law provides an offset for any CVD duties paid; for domestic subsidies, though, there is no offset, and therefore it is possible that simultaneous antidumping and CVD actions could double count the market-distorting effects of such subsidies.

47. Those four investigations are pasta from Italy, carbon steel wire rod from Canada, carbon steel wire rod from Trinidad and Tobago, and stainless steel wire rod from Italy. In each of those cases the DOC conducted contemporaneous antidumping and CVD investigations. In addition, another constructed value-based antidumping investigation included in the sample—stainless steel wire rod from Spain—covers a product that is subject to an outstanding CVD order. That CVD case has been inactive, however, since an administrative review determination in 1990 found *de minimis* subsidies. Furthermore, three other CVD investigations overlapped with antidumping investigations included in the sample reviewed in this study: pasta from Turkey, carbon steel wire rod from Germany, and carbon steel wire rod from Venezuela. In those three cases, however, the DOC's determinations were based on "facts available," not constructed value.

48. Indeed, in 1 of those 22 investigations, fresh Atlantic salmon from Chile, the DOC did conduct a CVD investigation but made a negative finding. Yet for three of the five respondents in the antidumping case, the DOC made affirmative determinations on the basis of comparing U.S. sales to constructed value (the other two respondents received negative determinations). It is hard to square an affirmative constructed-value-based dumping finding—which supposedly points to market-distorting government subsidies—and a negative subsidy determination in a corresponding CVD case.

Chapter 3

1. These determinations were made in nine separate original investigations and three separate administrative reviews. In other words, in some cases we were able to obtain determinations for multiple companies in a single investigation or review.

2. The one DOC determination examined in which the cost test did not inflate margins was a nonmarket-economy case. The cost test is not used in nonmarket-economy cases because normal value is based on cost, and home-market sales are never considered.

3. In addition, narrower product definitions heighten the distortions caused by the practice of zeroing discussed below.

4. Appellate Body Report on *European Communities—Anti-Dumping Duties on Imports of Cotton-Type Bed Linen from India*, WT/DS141/AB/R, March 1, 2001.

5. The 88.65 percent figure is based on allowing the full effect of negative dumping margins. In practice, a negative dumping margin is equivalent to a 0 percent margin.

6. Typically, there are hundreds, thousands, or even tens of thousands of individual sales observations in a Section B response.

7. The average net U.S. price is calculated in Appendix 3.9. Note that this calculation is marred by the asymmetric deduction from U.S. prices of indirect selling expenses and CEP profit. If those distortions were corrected, U.S. prices in this example would be even higher relative to home-market prices.

8. Another screening procedure, the arm's-length test, has been omitted from this hypothetical example for the sake of simplicity. In this hypothetical example, all home-market sales are made to unaffiliated customers.

Chapter 4

1. J. Michael Finger, ed., *Antidumping: How It Works and Who Gets Hurt* (Ann Arbor: University of Michigan Press, 1993), p. 16.

2. Ibid., p. 26.

3. See Table 2.2. As shown in the table, the average dumping margin where normal value was based on all home-market prices was 7.36 percent. When some home-market sales were excluded as below cost, the average dumping margin rose to 17.95 percent. When constructed value was used as the basis of normal value, the average dumping margin was 35.70 percent.

4. Finger, Table 1.1, p. 4.

5. Ibid.

6. Article XII of the GATT provided for trade restrictions to safeguard the balance of payments—a loophole that developing countries were allowed to exploit more or less unconditionally. Furthermore, Article XVIII of the GATT further recognized the right of poorer countries to employ trade restrictions in the name of development planning.

7. The term "traditional users" as used herein refers collectively to the United States, Canada, the European Union, Australia, and New Zealand.

8. These figures count the countries of the European Union as a single user.

9. World Trade Organization, "Report (2002) of the Committee on Anti-Dumping Practices," G/L/581, October 29, 2002.

10. The figure of 2,483 investigations initiated during 1990–99 was extracted from United Nations Conference on Trade and Development, "Impact of Anti-Dumping and Countervailing Duty Actions," TD/B/COM.1/EM.14/2, October 24, 2000, p. 26. Cited hereinafter as UNCTAD Report. By contrast, a total of 1,558 investigations were initiated between January 1980 and June 1989. Finger, p. 4.

11. UNCTAD Report, p. 26.

12. The slight reduction in initiations should not be perceived as a move away from the use of antidumping measures. Rather, it reflects strong economic growth (and a corresponding reduction in the likelihood of proving injury to a domestic industry) experienced in many countries, in particular the United States, during this period.

13. UNCTAD Report, p. 26.

14. Statistics cited herein regarding antidumping measures in force are based on our analysis of semiannual reports on antidumping activity filed with the WTO by WTO members. See Appendix 4.1 for an overview of how those data were collected and analyzed.

15. Unless otherwise indicated, definitive antidumping measures include minimum price undertakings and refer only to measures taken by WTO members.

16. Industry groups correspond to the "section" level of the Harmonized Tariff Schedule.

17. Details are provided in Appendix 4.3. Note, however, that in that appendix members of the European Union are broken out separately.

18. UNCTAD Report, p. 22.

19. Note that some countries bring antidumping cases against members of the European Union individually, while others bring cases against the European Union as a whole. To reconcile those differences, we treated measures against the European Union as 15 measures against the 15 EU members. If measures against EU exports are treated as a single measure, total measures against traditional users went up 18 percent between 1995 and 2000, and total measures by new users against traditional users increased 117 percent.

20. Note that these appendices include initiations and measures by China and Taiwan—non-WTO members during the years in question—against U.S. exports.

21. During 1996–2000 an average of 65.6 foreign antidumping measures were in effect against U.S. goods, compared to 46.6 during 1991–95.

22. One of the 28 was the United States, which should be excluded from any ratio of countries bringing measures against the United States.

23. We have not attempted to calculate the effect of antidumping measures on specific U.S. exports. Instead, we have simply reported cases in which U.S. export data show a significant decline in exports after the imposition of antidumping measures. Of course, in many cases the negative effect of antidumping measures on U.S. exports is masked in the export data by the intervention of other factors (for example, the inclusion of nonsubject merchandise in the tariff headings in question). Appendix 4.8 compares exports one year before imposition of an antidumping measure to

exports either one or two years after the imposition of the measure. The export data used were aggregated at the six-digit level of the Harmonized Tariff Schedule.

24. Information on U.S. antidumping initiations was derived from the DOC website. For initiations against U.S. exports, see Appendix 4.6.

25. José Tavares de Araujo Jr., Carla Macario, and Karsten Steinfatt, "Antidumping in the Americas," Organization of American States, Washington, March 2001, p. 3.

26. We examine here only dumping determinations, not injury determinations. Our discussion is based on analysis of official notices of determinations in antidumping investigations. It is difficult enough to glean from official notices what antidumping authorities have actually done when calculating dumping margins; it is virtually impossible to discern from those notices what were the major issues that determined the outcome of the injury analysis. Since it is the determination of dumping that evaluates the alleged "unfairness" of U.S. exporters, those determinations are of primary interest here in any event.

27. Canada, Department of National Revenue, Preformed Fibreglass Pipe Insulation with a Vapour Barrier, Originating in or Exported from the United States of America, Final Determination, October 20, 1993.

28. Canada, Department of National Revenue, Final Determination of Dumping of Certain Concrete Panels, Reinforced with Fibreglass Mesh, Originating in or Exported from the United States of America, May 27, 1997.

29. India, Ministry of Commerce, "Anti Dumping Investigation Concerning Imports of Acrylic Fibres from Thailand, Korea RP and USA—Final Findings," October 14, 1997.

30. India, Ministry of Commerce, "Anti Dumping Investigation of Graphite Electrodes from USA, Austria, France, Germany, Italy, Spain, China PR and Belgium—Final Findings," March 27, 1998.

31. Canada, Department of National Revenue, "Final Determination of Dumping of Refined Sugar from the United States of America, Denmark, the Federal Republic of Germany, the Netherlands, the United Kingdom and the Republic of Korea," October 5, 1995.

32. South Africa, Board on Tariffs and Trade, "Report No. 4088: Investigation into the Alleged Dumping of Meat of Fowls of the Species Gallus Domesticus, Originating in or Imported from the United States of America: Final Determination," 2000.

33. The determinations based on "facts available" included those in the investigations of aniline, bisphenol-A, oxo alcohols, sodium cyanide, and styrene butadiene rubber. The figure of 83 percent was derived from, with one exception, the ad valorem rates stated in the official notices of final determinations. For the rate in the bisphenol-A case, the ad valorem equivalent of the specific rate listed in the final determination was calculated using import prices listed in that determination.

34. The determinations based on facts available included those in the investigations of acetaminophenol, aldicarb, and suspension polyvinyl choloride. The figure of 89 percent was derived from the ad valorem rates stated in the official notices of final determinations.

35. Some WTO members did not file any documents but reported to the authorities that they had taken no actions during the relevant time period. Other WTO members did not file documents for all periods, and still others did not file any documents at any time.

Chapter 5

1. The agreement is available online at www.wto.org.

2. Trade Act of 2002, Public Law 107-210, sec. 2102(b)(14)(A).

3. House Con. Res. 262, 107th Cong., 1st sess., November 7, 2001. Interestingly, at the same time the resolution also instructed the president to "ensure that United States exports are not subject to the abusive use of trade laws, including antidumping and countervailing duty laws, by other countries."

4. "62 Senators Call on President Not to Weaken Trade Remedy Laws," *Inside U.S. Trade,* May 11, 2001.

5. See Gary Horlick, "The Speed Bump at Seattle," *Journal of International Economic Law* 3 (March 2000): 167.

6. World Trade Organization, Ministerial Declaration, November 14, 2001, WT/MIN(01)/DEC/W/1, para. 28. Emphasis added.

7. An earlier U.S. antidumping law with criminal sanctions was enacted in 1916 (and is at this writing still on the books despite a WTO ruling that it is inconsistent with the Antidumping Agreement), but the current law that imposes antidumping duties traces back to 1921.

8. During 1995–2001, the United States initiated 255 antidumping investigations, more than any other country. The second most frequent antidumping user over the same period was India, with 248 initiations; the European Union followed closely with 246 initiations. Argentina was a distant fourth with 170 initiations. For statistics on antidumping initiations worldwide during 1995–2001, see www.wto.org.

9. "Basic Concepts and Principles of the Trade Remedy Rules," Communication from the United States to the WTO Negotiating Group on Rules, TN/RL/W/27, October 22, 2002.

10. Ibid., p. 3.

11. Ibid.

12. On the other hand, a focus on national economic efficiency may very well conflict with concerns about fairness. Even if worldwide economic efficiency is harmed by trade-distorting practices, it may still be in the national economic interest of an importing country to allow "unfair" imports to enter freely and thereby reap the gains of their artificially low prices. In such situations, trade-restrictive antidumping remedies will sacrifice national economic efficiency for the sake of fairness to domestic import-competing industries.

13. "Basic Concepts and Principles of the Trade Remedy Rules," p. 3.

14. Ibid., p. 4.

15. "Observations on the Distinctions between Competition Laws and Antidumping Rules," Submission of the United States to the WTO Working Group on the Interaction of Trade and Competition Policy, Meeting of July 27–28, 1998. Cited hereafter as U.S. WTO 1998 Submission.

16. U.S. 1998 WTO Submission, p. 1.

17. Ibid., p. 2.

18. Ibid.

19. Ibid., p. 9.

20. Ibid., p. 14

21. Ibid., p. 4.

22. Alan Wolff, "Role of the Antidumping Laws," Remarks before the Steel Manufacturers Association, May 3, 1995, p. 2. Emphasis in original.

23. Terence P. Stewart, "Administration of the Antidumping Law: A Different Perspective," in *Down in the Dumps: Administration of the Unfair Trade Laws*, Richard Boltuck and Robert E. Litan, eds. (Washington: Brookings Institution, 1991), p. 288.

24. Greg Mastel, *Antidumping Laws and the U.S. Economy* (Armonk, N.Y.: M. E. Sharpe, 1998), pp. 42–43.

25. Ibid., p. 43.

26. U.S. 1998 WTO Submission, p. 2.

27. Mastel, p. 40.

28. These figures are derived from Table 2.2 and Appendix 2.1.

29. "Basic Concepts and Principles of the Trade Remedy Rules," p. 3.

30. Appellate Body Report on *European Communities—Anti-Dumping Duties on Imports of Cotton-Type Bed Linen from India*, WT/DS141/ AB/R, March 1, 2001.

31. In the *EU-Bed Linen* case, the Appellate Body found that zeroing is inconsistent with Article 2.4.2 of the Antidumping Agreement, which provides that dumping shall be determined on the basis of comparing average normal values to average export prices except under special circumstances. Zeroing, the Appellate Body concluded, departs inappropriately from a true average-to-average comparison and thus runs afoul of WTO rules. Because of the Appellate Body's ruling, the EU has discontinued zeroing in cases in which dumping margins are based on average-to-average comparisons.

However, Article 2.4.2 allows a departure from average-to-average comparisons in cases where "authorities find a pattern of export prices which differ significantly among different purchasers, regions or time periods." In those so-called targeted dumping situations, authorities may calculate dumping by comparing individual export transactions to average normal values. The EU's present position is that, in cases where individual-to-average comparisons are used, zeroing is not inconsistent with the Appellate Body's ruling in *EU-Bed Linen*. Accordingly, the EU will continue to perform zeroing in those kinds of cases. See, for example, "Proposal for a Council Regulation Imposing a Definitive Anti-Dumping Duty and Collecting Definitively the Provisional Duty Imposed on Imports of Recordable Compact Disks Originating in Taiwan," *Official Journal of the European Communities*, 2002/C 227E/362, September 24, 2002, para. 32–33.

32. See discussion in Note 31.

33. At present, the Appellate Body has not ruled on whether zeroing is permissible in targeted dumping situations, or whether individual-to-average comparisons are generally permissible in administrative reviews. It is possible that, if these issues are ever litigated, the Appellate Body could decide to close the loopholes that exist under current WTO rules. Such an outcome, though, cannot be assumed.

34. Note that, under certain circumstances, it may be necessary to use some kind of time lag when determining whether increasing imports and declining operating profits are substantially correlated. Specifically, the effect of increasing imports on a domestic industry's profitability may not be immediate. In such cases, imports during one period would have to be compared to profitability during a somewhat later period.

35. Appellate Body Report on *United States—Anti-Dumping Measures on Certain Hot-Rolled Steel Products from Japan*, WT/DS184/AB/R, July 24, 2001, para. 228.

36. Although these decisions concern the Agreement on Safeguards rather than the Antidumping Agreement, the conceptual issues regarding causation of injury are identical in the two agreements. Accordingly, Appellate Body interpretations of the Safeguards Agreement on this point are very likely to be followed when the same issue arises under the Antidumping Agreement.

37. Appellate Body Report on *United States—Safeguard Measures on Imports of Fresh, Chilled or Frozen Lamb Meat from New Zealand and Australia*, WT/DS177/AB/R, WT/DS178/AB/R, May 1, 2001, para. 168, quoting Appellate Body Report on *United States—Definitive Safeguard Measures on Imports of Wheat Gluten from the European Communities*, WT/DS166/AB/R, December 22, 2000, para. 69.

38. These figures were derived from U.S. International Trade Commission, *Hot-Rolled Steel Products from Argentina, China, India, Indonesia, Kazakhstan, Netherlands, Romania, South Africa, Taiwan, Thailand, and Ukraine*, Investigation nos. 701-TA-404-408 (preliminary) and 731-TA-898-908 (preliminary), USITC Publication no. 3381, January 2001; *Hot-Rolled Steel Products from Argentina and South Africa*, Inv. nos. 701-TA-404 (final) and 731-TA-898 and 905 (final), USITC Publication no. 3446, August 2001. Note that the difference between the merchant market and total domestic consumption lies in the fact that approximately 65 percent of hot-rolled steel produced by the U.S. industry is "captively consumed" by U.S. steel producers in the manufacture of downstream products.

39. See Thomas J. Prusa, "On the Spread and Impact of Antidumping," National Bureau of Economic Research Working Paper 7404, October 1999.

40. The average DOC dumping margin was calculated as the simple average of all the company-specific dumping margins from original investigations during 2001 in which adverse facts available were not used. Since adverse facts available are generally based on figures in the petition, inclusion of these determinations would have created circularity problems when comparing the DOC's findings to petitioners' allegations. For petition dumping margins, we used company-specific allegations if available; otherwise, we used either the simple average of the lowest and highest rates alleged or the countrywide average rate if one was alleged. We then calculated the simple average of all the petition rates thus derived from all original investigation determinations during 2001 in which the DOC calculated a company-specific rate not based on adverse facts available.

41. Panel Report on *Guatemala—Definitive Anti-Dumping Measures on Grey Portland Cement from Mexico*, WT/DS156/R, October 24, 2000.

42. See Commission of the European Communities, "Nineteenth Annual Report from the Commission to the European Parliament on the Community's Anti-Dumping and Anti-Subsidy Activities (2000)," October 12, 2001.

43. These figures were compiled as of August 14, 2002, from data available on the ITC website, www.usitc.gov.

44. This figure is the weighted average of all the average dumping rates shown in Table 2.2 other than the average rate when facts available were used.

Index

Page references followed by a *t* denote references to tables.

Accounting, joint products, 40, 190
Antidumping Code of 1967, Kennedy Round and, 148
Antidumping duty orders, automatic termination of, 193–95
Antidumping laws, vii–xii, 103–4, 199
  backdoor protectionism and, 103–11
  enforcement, 122
  foreign protectionism and U.S. companies, 112, 114–16t, 118–22
  history, 148
  ignorance of, 199
  "leveling the playing field," vii, 80–82, 150, 152–60
  primary justification for, 18
  proliferation and effect on U.S. exports, xii, 122–24
  success/failure of, 54, 160
  targeting "unfair trade," xii, 81–82, 147
  threat to U.S. interests, xii, 122–24
  U.S. exports/exporters and, 103, 111–18, 139t, 140t, 141–43t
Antidumping remedies, xi, xii, 152–63
  See also Aligning antidumping theory and practice
Antidumping users, 106–7, 108t, 111, 138t, 152
  nontraditional users, 105–6
  targets of WTO users, 1995–2000, 127–29t
Argentina, 105, 106, 122, 183
Arm's-length test, 12, 13
Artificial price, 53, 156–57, 167
Australia, 104, 148
Austria, 31, 32t, 33
Average home-market direct selling expenses. *See* HMDSEL
Average home-market indirect selling expenses. *See* HMISEL
Average U.S. price. *See* USPR

"Basic Concepts and Principles of the Trade Remedy Rules," 152–54, 159, 168
Below-cost dumping, 157, 159
Below-cost sales, vii, 17–18, 55–59, 104, 153–54
  acute or chronic loss regarding, 41–42
  eliminating the cost test and, 164–66
  market distortions and, 27, 28, 37–43
  methods of calculating dumping and, 19–30
  requiring evidence of, 161–63
Brazil, 105, 106, 112, 122
Bush administration, 146
  "Basic Concepts and Principles of the Trade Remedy Rules," 152–54, 159, 168
Byrd amendment, x

Calculating dumping. *See* Procedures for calculating dumping
Canada
  antidumping laws, 103, 148
  antidumping use, 106, 107
  investigation of / measures against U.S. exports, 111–120
  number of investigations, 103
  targeting U.S. exports, 117, 118
CEP offset, 11
CEP offset cap, 68–70, 174–76
CEP profit, 70, 81
  calculations, 77, 95–97t
  price adjustment, 11
  See also CEPPROFIT
CEP sales, 77
  indirect selling expenses and, 68–70, 81
CEPPROFIT
  definition, 83t
  in hypothetical case study, 78
China, 111, 112, 183, 188
Clinton administration, 146
  1998 submission to WTO Working Group on the Interaction of Trade

215

About the Authors

Brink Lindsey is a senior fellow at the Cato Institute in Washington, D.C. Formerly an international trade attorney, Lindsey founded and serves as director of Cato's Center for Trade Policy Studies, a leading voice for free trade and open markets in the Washington trade policy debate. He is a contributing editor of *Reason* magazine and author of *Against the Dead Hand: The Uncertain Struggle for Global Capitalism*.

Daniel Ikenson is a trade policy analyst at the Cato Institute's Center for Trade Policy Studies. He has written extensively about antidumping policy and other trade issues. Ikenson has served as a consultant in numerous antidumping proceedings.

Cato Institute

Founded in 1977, the Cato Institute is a public policy research foundation dedicated to broadening the parameters of policy debate to allow consideration of more options that are consistent with the traditional American principles of limited government, individual liberty, and peace. To that end, the Institute strives to achieve greater involvement of the intelligent, concerned lay public in questions of policy and the proper role of government.

The Institute is named for *Cato's Letters*, libertarian pamphlets that were widely read in the American Colonies in the early 18th century and played a major role in laying the philosophical foundation for the American Revolution.

Despite the achievement of the nation's Founders, today virtually no aspect of life is free from government encroachment. A pervasive intolerance for individual rights is shown by government's arbitrary intrusions into private economic transactions and its disregard for civil liberties.

To counter that trend, the Cato Institute undertakes an extensive publications program that addresses the complete spectrum of policy issues. Books, monographs, and shorter studies are commissioned to examine federal budget, Social Security, regulation, military spending, international trade, and myriad other issues. Major policy conferences are held throughout the year, from which papers are published thrice yearly in the *Cato Journal*. The Institute also publishes the quarterly magazine *Regulation*.

In order to maintain its independence, the Cato Institute accepts no government funding. Contributions are received from foundations, corporations, and individuals, and other revenue is generated from the sale of publications. The Institute is a nonprofit, tax-exempt, educational foundation under Section 501(c)3 of the Internal Revenue Code.

CATO INSTITUTE
1000 Massachusetts Ave., N.W.
Washington, D.C. 20001
www.cato.org